FLOWERS FROM
A PURITAN'S GARDEN

FLOWERS FROM
A PURITAN'S GARDEN

Illustrations and Meditations

C. H. Spurgeon

THE BANNER OF TRUTH TRUST

THE BANNER OF TRUTH TRUST
3 Murrayfield Road, Edinburgh EH12 6EL, UK
PO Box 621, Carlisle, PA 17013, USA

*

First published by Passmore & Alabaster, London, 1883

*

ISBN
Print: 978 1 84871 776 3
EPUB: 978 1 84871 777 0
Kindle: 978 1 84871 778 7

*

Typeset in 11/14 pt Adobe Garamond Pro
at The Banner of Truth Trust, Edinburgh.

Printed in the USA by
Versa Press, Inc.,
East Peoria, IL.

PREFACE

WHILE commenting upon the One Hundred and Nineteenth Psalm, I was brought into most intimate communion with Thomas Manton, who has discoursed upon that marvellous portion of Scripture with great fulness and power. I have come to know him so well that I could choose him out from among a thousand divines if he were again to put on his portly form, and display among modern men that countenance wherein was a 'great mixture of majesty and meekness'. His works occupy twenty-two volumes in the modern reprint: a mighty mountain of sound theology. They mostly consist of sermons; but what sermons! They are not so sparkling as those of Henry Smith, nor so profound as those of Owen, nor so rhetorical as those of Howe, nor so pithy as those of Watson, nor so fascinating as those of Brooks; and yet they are second to none of these. For solid, sensible instruction forcibly delivered, they cannot be surpassed. Manton is not brilliant, but he is always clear; he is not oratorical, but he is powerful; he is not striking, but he is deep. There is not a poor discourse in the whole collection: he is evenly good, constantly excellent. Ministers who do not know Manton need not wonder if they are themselves unknown.

Inasmuch as Manton used but a few figures and illustrations, it came into my head to mark them all, for I felt sure that they would be very natural and forcible: I will give you the reasoning of which this volume is the result. I thought that here we should find a set of workable illustrations. It never occurred to this good man to introduce a metaphor by way of ornament; he was too intent upon telling his message to think about how his sentences might be adorned, and hence it fell out that if he did use a simile, it was because one was absolutely needful, or, at least, because it was the preferable mode of making himself understood. Here, then, is a man whose figures will be sure to be usable by the earnest preacher who has forsworn the baubles of rhetoric, and aims at nothing but the benefit of his hearers. I thought it worth while to go through volume after volume, and mark the metaphors; and then I resolved to complete the task by culling all the best figures out of the whole of Manton's works. Thus my communing with the great Puritan ends in my clearing his house of all his pictures, and hanging them up in new frames of my own. As I leave his right to them unquestioned and unconcealed, I do not rob him, but I bless him by giving him another opportunity of speaking.

One kind of work leads on to another, and labour is lightened by being diversified: had it not been for *The Treasury of David* I had not been found among the metaphors of Manton.

I see it is thirteen years ago since I issued a volume of illustrations; I may surely take the liberty to put forth another. The former was entitled, *Feathers for Arrows*; it has met with a large sale, and it may be presumed to be useful, seeing it has been appropriated, almost every scrap of it, by the compilers of Cyclopaedias of Illustrations.

To make this little book more generally acceptable, I have thrown it into a somewhat devotional form, using Manton's figures as texts for brief meditations: this I humbly hope may be found profitable for reading in the chamber of private worship. The latter half of the work was composed in the gardens and olive-groves of Mentone, where I found it a pleasure to muse, and compose. How I wish that I could have flooded my sentences with the sunlight of that charming region! As it is, I have done my best to avoid dulness, and to aim at edification. If a single practical truth is the more clearly seen through my endeavours, I shall be grateful; and doubly so if others are helped to make their teaching more striking.

It is my design to bring out a third volume, consisting of illustrations which I have long been collecting at home and abroad, and patiently jotting down in pocket-books till leisure should be found for their proper shaping and arranging. Time is short, and it behooves each one to be working for his Lord, that when he is called home he may leave behind him something for the generations following. Highly shall we be favoured if the gracious Master shall accept our service now, and grant us the consciousness of that acceptance; happier still if we may hope to hear him say, 'Well done.'

That all my readers may meet with so great a blessing is the earnest prayer of

Their grateful Servant,

C. H. Spurgeon

Westwood, January 1883

FLOWERS FROM
A PURITAN'S GARDEN

BIRD TIED BY A STRING

*A bird that is tied by a string seems to have more liberty than a bird
in a cage; it flutters up and down, and yet it is held fast.*

When a man thinks that he has escaped from the bondage
of sin in general, and yet evidently remains under the power
of some one favoured lust, he is woefully mistaken in his judgment as to his spiritual freedom. He may boast that he is out
of the cage, but assuredly the string is on his leg. He who has
his fetters knocked off, all but one chain, is a prisoner still. 'Let
not any iniquity have dominion over me' is a good and wise
prayer; for one pampered sin will slay the soul as surely as one
dose of poison will kill the body. There is no need for a traveller
to be bitten by a score of deadly vipers, the tooth of one cobra
is quite sufficient to insure his destruction. One sin, like one
match, can kindle the fires of hell within the soul.

The practical application of this truth should be made by
the professor who is a slave to drink, or to covetousness, or to
passion. How can you be free if any one of these chains still
holds you fast? We have met with professors who are haughty,
and despise others; how can these be the Lord's free men while

I

pride surrounds them? In will and intent we must break every bond of sin; and we must perfect holiness in the fear of the Lord, or we cannot hope that the Son has made us free. O thou who art the free Spirit, break every bond of sin, I beseech thee.

FADING FLOWERS

The flowers which grow in earth's garden wither in our hands while we smell at them.

They are as frail as they are fair. They grow out of the dust, and to the dust must they return. As Herbert says,

> Their root is ever in their grave,
> And they must die.

How speedy is their withering, they are gathered by the hand, and laid before us, and they wilt and become sickly, fainting, decaying objects. At the very longest, their lives smile through a day or two, and all is over. Which of earth's joys is better than her flowers? Health flies, wealth takes to itself wings, honour is a puff of air, and pleasure is a bubble. Only from heaven can we expect 'pleasure forever more', and 'everlasting joy'. The Rose of Sharon blooms through all the ages, and the Lily of the Valley, which is Jesus himself, out-lasts all time,—yea, this is the only Everlasting Flower, for he only hath immortality. Why, then, should we seek for the living among the dead, or search for substance in the land of shadows? Henceforth, my soul, gather thy Hearts-ease in the garden of the Lord, pluck thy Forget-me-nots from beds which Christ has planted, and look for thy Crown-Imperial only in the Paradise above.

The flowers of the field are children's adornments. See how the little ones garland themselves, and fashion chaplets with the buttercups and daisies. Earth's loveliest joys are good child's play; but, my soul, thou hast to act a nobler part: seek thou the bliss which fadeth not away. Turn thou to God, thine exceeding joy, and then if thy years be multiplied upon earth thou shalt have a life-long possession, or if thou be caught away suddenly thou shalt carry with thee in thy bosom the rosebud of a life which will open to perfection in the land where fading and withering are things unknown.

DEAD FISH

They are dead fish which are carried down the stream.

Living fish may go with the stream at times, but dead fish must always do so. There are plenty of such in all waters: dead souls, so far as the truest life is concerned, and these are always drifting, drifting, drifting as the current takes them. Their first inquiry is—what is customary? God's law is of small account to them, but the unwritten rules of society have a power over them which they never think of resisting. Like the Vicar of Bray, they can twist round and round if the stream is running in an eddy; or, like the sluggard, they can remain at their ease if the waters are stagnant. They stand in awe of a fool's banter, and ask of their neighbour leave to breathe.

Is this a right state to be in? Each one of us must give an account for himself before God: should not each one act for himself? If we follow a multitude to do evil, the multitude will not excuse the evil nor diminish the punishment. Good men have generally been called upon to walk by themselves. We can sin abundantly by passively yielding to the course of this world; but to be holy and gracious needs many a struggle, many a tear.

Where, then, am I? Am I sailing in that great fleet which

bears the black flag, under Rear-Admiral Apollyon, who commands the ship Fashion? If so, when all these barks come to destruction I shall be destroyed with them. Better part company, hoist another flag, and serve another sovereign. Come, my heart, canst thou go against stream? It is the way of life. The opposing waters will but wash and cleanse thee, and thou shalt ascend to the eternal river- head, and be near and like thy God. O thou who art Lord of the strait and narrow way, aid me to force a passage to glory and immortality.

THE BRIGHT COUNTERFEIT

A counterfeit coin may look better and brighter than the true piece of money, and yet be almost or altogether worthless.

And in the same manner a base professor may for a while seem to be brighter than a true Christian. He is not downcast, for he has none of those inward strivings which cause sincere believers so much anguish of soul. He is not sad, for he has no penitence of heart at the remembrance of those shortcomings which humble the living child of God. Doubts and fears he has none, for these are the moss which grows upon faith, and of this grace he is quite destitute. Failures in holiness, loss of communion, non-success in prayer, smitings of conscience, all of which happen to the elect of God, come not near to him, for he is a stranger to the inward, sensitive principle of which these are the tokens.

Sad sons of God, be not utterly dispirited by these men's equable tempers and quiet assurances, for they will be troubled indeed when the testing hour shall come. As for you, your gracious disquietudes and holy anxieties are a proof of the reality of your spiritual life, and evidences of grace which ought to afford you comfort. Dead men do not suffer from changes of weather; and mere imitations of life, such as paintings and statues, know nothing of the aches and pains of living men. Pity those who are never in soul trouble, and bless the Lord that he has not left you to their vainglorious peace. Better be dim gold than shining brass. Do you not think so?

SULPHUR IN THE INCENSE

How often do we mingle sulphur with our incense!

A strong expression, but most sadly true. When we offer prayer, is there not at times a sorrowful mixture of self-will, petulance, and impatience? Does not unbelief, which is quite as obnoxious as brimstone, too often spoil the sweet odour of our supplications? When we offer praise, is it all pure spices after the art of the heavenly apothecary? Do not self-laudation and pride frequently spoil the holy frankincense and myrrh? Alas, we fear that the charge must lie against us, and force us to a sorrowful confession.

As the priests of God, our whole life should be the presentation of holy incense unto God, and yet it is not so. The earthly ambitions and carnal lustings of our nature deteriorate and adulterate the spices of our lives, and Satan, with the sulphur of pride, ruins the delicate perfume of perfect consecration.

What grace the Lord displays in accepting our poor, imperfect offerings! What rich merit abides in our Lord Jesus! What sweet savour beyond expression dwells in him, to drown and destroy our ill-savours, and to make us accepted in the Beloved! Glory be unto our glorious High Priest, whose perfect life and sin- atoning death is so sweet before the Divine Majesty that the Lord is well pleased for his righteousness' sake, and accepts us in him with our sweet savour.

THE SHIP WHICH IS ALWAYS SAILING ON

The ship holds on her course, and makes for the desired port, whether they on board sit, lie or walk, eat or sleep.

Thus time is at all times bearing us onward to the land where time shall be no more. There is never a pause in our progress toward eternity, whether we trifle or are in earnest. Even while we read these lines the great ship is still speeding onward at the same rapid and unvarying rate. We shall soon see the shore of eternity; far sooner than we think! It becomes us to be ready for the landing, and for the weighty business which will then engage us, namely, judgment at the hands of Christ.

If we could lie becalmed a while and make no movement toward eternity we could afford to sport; but if we look over the ship's stern we may see by her shining wake how she is cutting through the waves. Past time urges us to diligence, for it has reported us in heaven; and future time calls us to earnestness, for it must be short, and may end this very day. And then!

MAN'S TAILORING

Men make laws as tailors make garments—to fit the crooked bodies they serve for, to suit the humours of the people who are to be governed by those laws.

This is man's poor tailoring, and it betrays the sinfulness both of those who frame laws and of those for whom they are made: the Judge of all the earth acts on other principles. God has ordained his law according to the rule of perfect equity, and he will not adapt it to our prejudices and deformities. Some men treat the law and testimony of the Lord as if it were like plaster of Paris, to be poured over their features to take the cast of their own boasted loveliness. Religion is to them a matter of opinion and not of fact; they talk about their 'views' and their ideas, as if Christians were no longer believers but inventors, and no more disciples but masters. This cometh of evil, and leadeth on to worse consequences. Our sentiments are like a tree, which must be trained to the wall of Scripture; but too many go about to bow the wall to their tree, and cut and trim texts to shape them to their mind. Let us never be guilty of this. Reverence for the perfect word should prevent our altering even a syllable of it. 'The law of the Lord is perfect, converting the soul'; let it convert *us*, but never let us try to pervert *it*. Our ideas must take the mould of Scripture—this is wisdom: to endeavour to mould Scripture to our ideas would be presumption.

THE TRAVELLER AND THE MERCHANT

A traveller and a merchant differ; thus: a traveller goes from place to place that he may see; but a merchant goes from port to port that he may take in his lading, and grow rich by traffic.

Thus there are travelling hearers who merely observe and criticise, and go their way very little the better for what they have heard; and there are also merchant-hearers who listen to profit and make a gain to their souls out of every sermon. O Lord, put me among the wise merchantmen, and in my trading may I find the one pearl of great price, even Jesus, thy Son.

EACH BIRD FROM ITS OWN EGG

It would be monstrous for the eggs of one creature to bring forth a brood of another kind, for a crow or a kite to come from the egg of a hen. It is as unnatural a production for a new creature to sin.

Each creature brings forth after its own kind: the old nature being radically evil continues to produce and to send forth swarms of sins; it is not reconciled to God, neither indeed can be, and therefore its thoughts and acts are those of rebellion and hatred toward God. On the other hand the new nature 'cannot sin because it is born of God'; it must have its fruit unto holiness, for it is holiness itself. Out of a dove's nest we expect only doves to fly. The heavenly life breeds birds of paradise, such as holy thoughts, desires, and acts; and it cannot bring forth such unclean birds as lust, and envy, and malice. The life of God infused in regeneration is as pure as the Lord by whom it was begotten, and can never be otherwise. Blessed is the man who has this heavenly principle within, for it must appear in his life, and cause him to abound in holiness, to the glory of God. Reader, have you this divine seed within you, or do you remain under the dominion of corrupt nature? This question deserves a present and thoughtful reply.

THE CRACKED POT

The unsoundness of a vessel is not seen when it is empty, but when it is filled with water, then we shall see whether it will leak or no.

It is in our prosperity that we are tested. Men are not fully discovered to themselves till they are tried by fulness of success. Praise finds out the crack of pride, wealth reveals the flaw of selfishness, and learning discovers the leak of unbelief. David's besetting sin was little seen in the tracks of the wild goats, but it became conspicuous upon the terraces of his palace. Success is the crucible of character. Hence the prosperity which some welcome as an unmixed favour may far more rightly be regarded as an intense form of test. O Lord, preserve us when we are full as much as when we are empty.

THE BEST OF WAYS TO THE BEST OF POSSESSIONS

If a man should offer a lordship or a farm to another, and he should say, The way is dirty and dangerous, and the weather very troublesome, I will not look after it; would you not accuse the man of folly who thus loved his ease and pleasure? But, now, if this man were assured of a pleasant path and a good way if he would but take a little pains to go over and see it, it were gross folly indeed to refuse it.

Such is the folly of those who refuse the great inheritance of God. It were worthwhile to spend a lifetime in prison if thereby we could obtain the kingdom of God; but we are not called to such suffering, the way to eternal life by Christ Jesus is made plain and easy by the Holy Spirit who bids us believe and live. To believe that which is most surely true cannot be unpleasant to a sincere mind; to trust in one who cannot lie cannot be a hardship to an honest heart. In fact, the way of true religion is the path of wisdom, and we know that her ways are ways of pleasantness, and all her paths are peace. Who would not go to heaven when Christ is the way?—the dearest, holiest, and happiest way that can be conceived. Since the way to heaven is heavenly, and the road to bliss is bliss, who will not become a pilgrim? My soul, be thou in love with the way as well as with the end, since thy Lord is the one as well as the other.

IVY IN THE WALL

Man's corrupt nature has been compared to a wild fig-tree, or to ivy growing upon a wall, of which you may cut off the body, boughs, sprigs, and branches, yet still there will be something that will be sprouting out again until the wall be digged down.

When we think that we have fairly done with sin it suddenly sprouts again and seems as vigorous as ever. As it is said of a tree, 'at the scent of water it will bud', so is it true of our corrupt nature, at the first opportunity it will shoot forth. Vainglorious professors have talked of their being free from all likelihood of sinning, but experienced believers in the depth of their hearts are made to feel the evil of their nature and therefore they walk humbly with God and cry to him to keep them from evil. Often does it happen that the boaster is tripped up by the enemy whom he thought to be dead and buried, while the watchful, careful Christian is preserved in the midst of the fiercest temptations and enabled to maintain his integrity.

We may well believe in the vitality of evil when we see how it survives the efforts of grace; and yet the Lord Jesus can and will destroy it, root and branch, and we shall forever adore him when this marvellous work is accomplished. Divine Master, uproot in me the root of bitterness, and tear away the follies which twine about my soul.

UNJUST BALANCES

In a pair of scales, though the weights be equal, yet if the scales be not equal there may be wrong done: so, though the arguments used be powerful, yet, if the heart be biassed by unhallowed affections, the scale will not be turned according to truth and righteousness.

Many instances of this false weighing may be quoted. Eternal realities appear to be mere trifles when the heart is hot after some engrossing pleasure. The most fallacious estimates are made under the influence of corrupt desires. Like a judge that has been bribed, the understanding gives a false verdict. In one scale lies eternity with endless joy or bliss, and in the other lies a passing gain of gold or honour. The comparison needs no studying, it is as a ton to an ounce, and yet the balances are so false that the ounce is declared to have greater weight than the ton. God hateth unjust balances, and we may wisely do the same when we see how souls are ruined by the insane trickery with which a man cheats himself out of his own soul.

O Lord of truth, teach my conscience the law of truth, for Jesus' sake. Hold my hand while I hold the scales, and let me weigh all things in the balances of the sanctuary.

TREASON IN COINING FARTHINGS

There is as much felony in coining pence, as shillings and pounds.

The principle is the same, whatever the value of the coin may be: the prerogative of the Crown is trenched upon by the counterfeiter, even if he only imitates and utters the smallest coin of the realm. He has set the royal sign to his base metal, and the small money-value of his coinage is no excuse for his offence.

Any one sin wilfully indulged and persevered in is quite sufficient to prove a man to be a traitor to his God. Though he may neither commit murder nor adultery—which would be like counterfeiting the larger coins—he may be as surely a felon in the sight of heaven if he deliberately utters falsehood or indulges pride—which some think as lightly of as if they were but the counterfeits of pence. The spirit of rebellion is the same whatever be the manner of displaying it. A giant may look out through a very small window, and so may great obstinacy of rebellion manifest itself in a little act of wilfulness.

How careful should this consideration make us! How earnestly should we watch against what are thought to be minor offences. The egg of mischief is smaller than that of a midge; a world of evil lurks in a drop of rebellion. Lord, keep us from pence transgressions and then we shall not commit the pound offences.

A CHILD'S FAILING

A father out of indulgence may pass by a failing when his son waits upon him; for instance, suppose he should spill the wine and break the glass; but surely he will not allow him to throw it down carelessly or wilfully.

Everyone can see that there is a grave distinction between sins of infirmity and wilful transgressions. A man may splash us very badly with the wheel of his carriage, as he passes by, and we may feel vexed, but the feeling would have been very much more keen if he had thrown mud into our face with deliberate intent. By the grace of God, we do not sin wilfully. Our wrongdoing comes of ignorance or of carelessness, and causes us many a pang of conscience, for we would fain be blameless before our God. Wilfully to offend is not according to our mind. In this the children of God are manifest, and the children of the devil. Deliberation and delight in sin are sure marks of the heirs of wrath. Sin in believers is a terrible evil, but there is this mitigation of it, that they do not love it, and cannot rest in it. The true son does not wish to do damage to his father's goods; on the contrary, he loves to please his father, and he is himself grieved when he causes grief to one whom he so highly honours. O my Lord, I pray thee let me not sin carelessly, lest I come to sin presumptuously. Make me to be watchful against my infirmities, that I may not fall by little and little.

ESTHER GOING IN UNTO THE KING

Queen Esther would go into the king's presence, even though there might be no golden sceptre held forth; so, believer, venture into God's presence when you have no smile and no light from the countenance of your God. Trust in a withdrawing God.

A good child will believe in his father's love even when his father is angry. We believe in the sun when he is under a cloud, and shall we not believe in God when he hideth himself? When the door of mercy is shut, then is the time for knocking. When the blessing appears to be lost, then is the season for seeking; and when favours seem to be denied, then is the hour for importunate asking. When we have had many denials we should be the more earnest in prayer, that the hindrance may be removed. Esther succeeded in her suit though she went without a call, and much more shall we if we boldly come unto the King of kings, from whom no sincere petitioner ever was dismissed unheard. If we knew the worst time for prayer had come, we ought still to pray. Come, my soul, get thee to thy chamber and seek the King's face, for thou hast great need.

MEADOWS AND MARSHES

Meadows may be occasionally flooded, but the marshes are drowned by the tide at every return thereof.

There is all this difference between the sins of the righteous and those of the ungodly. Surprised by temptation, true saints are flooded with a passing outburst of sin; but the wicked delight in transgression and live in it as in their element. The saint in his errors is a star under a cloud, but the sinner is darkness itself. The gracious may fall into iniquity, but the graceless run into it, wallow in it, and again and again return to it.

Lord, grant that we may be uplifted by thy grace, so that the great water-floods of temptation may not come near us; and if through the prevalence of our inward corruption the enemy should come in like a flood, O Lord, deliver thy servants by thy great power.

THE NEEDLE AND ITS POLE

The needle that hath been touched with the loadstone may be shaken and agitated, but it never rests until it turns toward the pole.

Thus our heart's affections when once magnetized by the love of Christ find no rest except they turn to him. The cares and labours of the day may carry the thoughts to other objects, even as a finger may turn the needle to the east or west, but no sooner is the pressure removed than the thoughts fly to the Well-beloved just as the needle moves to its place. We are unable to rest anywhere but in Jesus. The new birth has disqualified us for contentment with the world, and hence we have no choice but to find our all in Christ. Blessed necessity! Driven to Jesus by an unrest which finds no remedy elsewhere! Drawn to Jesus by an impulse which we have no desire to resist! It is our life's business and our heart's delight to point to him so plainly that if any would see Jesus they have only to look in the direction in which our whole being is always pointing. We are subject to many deflections and disturbances, but thou knowest, O Lord, that our inmost soul seeks after thyself.

IMPLICIT OBEDIENCE

John Cassian makes mention of one who willingly fetched water near two miles every day for a whole year together, to pour it upon a dead, dry stick, at the command of his superior, when no reason else could be given for it. And of another it is recorded, that he

professed that if he were enjoined by his superior to put to sea in a
ship which had neither mast, tackling, nor any other furniture, he
would do it; and when he was asked how he could do this without
hazard of his discretion, he answered, The wisdom must be in him
that hath power to command, not in him that hath power to obey.

These are instances of implicit obedience to a poor fallible human authority, and are by no means to be imitated. But when it is God who gives the command, we cannot carry a blind obedience too far, since there can be no room for questioning the wisdom and goodness of any of his precepts. At Christ's command it is wise to let down the net at the very spot where we have toiled in vain all the night. If God bids us, we can sweeten water with salt, and destroy poison with meat, yea, we may walk the waves of the sea, or the flames of a furnace. Well said the Blessed Virgin, 'Whatsoever he saith unto you, do it.' My heart, I charge thee follow thy Lord's command without a moment's question, though he bid thee go forward into the Red Sea, or onward into a howling wilderness.

SUN-DIAL WITHOUT THE SUN

A sun-dial may be well and accurately set, and yet, if the sun shines
not, we cannot tell the time of day.

Our evidences of grace are in much the same condition: they are good signs, but we cannot see them unless the grace of God shines upon them, and then we can almost do without them, even as an observant person can tell the time of day without a sun-dial, by looking to the sun itself. Present faith in a present Saviour is better than all the marks and evidences in the world. Yet let no man be content if the marks of a child of God are absent from his life, for they ought to be there, and must be there. The presence of sensible evidences must not be too much relied on; but the absence of them should cause great searching of heart. Our main concern should be to look daily and hourly unto Jesus, trusting in *him*, and not in evidences; judging the progress of our soul's day, rather by our view of the Sun of righteousness than by our own sun-dial. If Jesus be gone, all is gone: without his love we are darkness itself. What a sun-dial is without the sun, that is the fairest character, the choicest past experience, and the maturest knowledge without Jesus' fellowship. Rise, O Sun of my soul; end my doubts, if I have any; prevent them, if I have none.

WINDING UP THE CLOCK

The conscience of a sinner is like a clock, dull, calm, and at rest, when the weights are down; but when wound up, it is full of motion.

Sometimes God winds up conscience in this life, and then it works vigorously, and strikes the time of day in the sinner's ears. Shame attends his sin, and he trembles in secret. A dreadful sound is in his ears, and like the troubled sea he cannot rest. This is far better than a dead calm. Alas, in many cases the clock runs down, conscience is again still, and the man returns to his false peace. Of all states this is most dangerous.

In the world to come the ceaseless activity of conscience will be the torture of hell. Rendered sensitive by the removal of hardening influences, the lost soul will find memory accusing, and conscience condemning forever, and no advocate at hand to suggest a defence. A man had better be shut up with a bear robbed of her whelps, than live with an accusing conscience. No racks or fires can equal the misery of being consciously guilty, and seeing no way of escape from sin. May the Lord make our conscience to be an alarm to us here that it be not a torment to us hereafter.

EMPTY THE BUCKET

Empty the bucket before you go to the fountain.

Wise advice. If the pail be full of the best and cleanest water it is idle to carry it to the well, for its fulness disqualifies it for being a receiver. Those who think themselves full of grace are not likely to pray aright, for prayer is a beggar's trade, and supposes the existence of need. What does a full bucket want with the well? Let it stay where it is. Fitness for mercy is not found in self-sufficiency, but in emptiness and want. He can and will receive most of the Lord who has least of his own.

If the bucket is full of foul water, it is wise to throw it away as we go to the crystal spring. We must not come to the Lord with our minds full of vanity, lust, covetousness, and pride. 'If I regard iniquity in my heart, the Lord will not hear me.' He will not make his grace the medium of floating our unclean desires. Grace will cleanse out sin, but it will not mix with it, neither may we desire such a dishonourable compromising of the holy name of the Lord our God. Let the bucket of the heart be turned upside down and drained of the love of sin, and then prayer will be heard, and Jesus will come in and fill it.

Lord, empty me of self, of pride, of worldliness, of unbelief, and then fill me with all the fulness of God.

THE HYPOCRITE'S TRICKS

A hypocrite has been likened to one who should go into a shop to buy a pennyworth, and should steal a pound's worth; or to one who is punctual in paying a small debt, that he may get deeper into our books and cheat us of a greater sum.

Hypocrites make much ado about small things that they may be more easy in their consciences while living in great sins. They pay the tithe of mint to a fraction, but rob God of his glory by their self-righteousness. Punctilious to the utmost about ritual and rubric, they set up their own righteousness in the place of Christ, and rob him of his crown, while all the while they pretend to be serving him. They honour him with their church adornments, in the way of pictures and images, and thereby insult him with idolatry. In the mass they pretend to great devotion for the Lord Jesus, and yet the sum of it is that they put a piece of bread into the throne of his eternal Godhead. In a word, they give God the shells, and steal the kernels for their own pride and self-will. Christ may have their names, and they will be his disciples if they can turn a penny thereby, either for their purse or their pride, but all the while they are robbing him of his glory. O Lord, whatever I may be, let me not be a hypocrite. Suffer me to be the least among thy true children, rather than the chief among pretenders.

THE WEAK STRONG, AND THE STRONG WEAK

It is related of Laurence Saunders the martyr, that one day in the country, meeting his friend Dr Pendleton, an earnest preacher in King Edward's reign, they debated upon what they had best do in the dangerous time that Mary's accession had brought upon them. Saunders confessed that his spirit was ready, but he felt the flesh was at present too weak for much suffering. But Pendleton admonished him, and appeared all courage and forwardness to face every peril. They both came, under the control of circumstances, to London, and there, when danger arose, Pendleton shrunk from the cross, and Saunders resolutely took it up.

The reader has probably met with this story before, but it will not harm him to learn its lesson again. We are certainly stronger when we feel our weakness than when we glory in our strength. Our pastoral observation over a very large church has led us to expect to see terrible failures among those who carry their heads high among their brethren. Poor timid souls who are afraid to put one foot before another, for fear they should go an inch astray, go on from year to year in lovely, bashful holiness, and at the same time the very professors who condemned them, and distressed them by their confident pretensions, fall like Lucifer, never to hope again. The fault which has happened to others may be yet seen in me, unless the Lord shall guard me from it. It is no time for boasting while we are still in the enemy's country.

THE SUN IN WINTER

A summer's sun, even when beclouded, yields more comfort and warmth to the earth than a winter's sun that shines brightest.

The comforts of the Spirit at their lowest, are far superior to the joys of the world at their highest pitch. When saints are mourning, their inward peace is still superior to that of worldlings, when their mirth and revelry overflow all bounds. Lord, I had rather take the worst from thee than the best from thine enemy. Only do thou graciously shine within me, and let mine outward condition be as dull as thou pleasest.

THE NURSE AND THE FALLING CHILD

The nurse lets the child get a knock sometimes, in order to make it more cautious.

Thus does the Lord in providence allow his children to suffer by their sins, that they may be more thoughtful in future. He has no hand in their sin; but, since the sin is in them, he allows circumstances to occur by which the evil is made manifest in open acts, which cause them sorrow. When a physician sees a person suffering from an inward complaint, he may think it wise so to deal with his patient that the disease is brought to the surface; and thus also God may permit the sins of his people to come to an open sore, that they may be aware of them, and seek for healing. The nurse does not make the child careless or cause it to tumble, but she withdraws her interposing care for the best of reasons, namely, that the little one may learn to avoid danger by a measure of suffering on account of it. It would be blasphemous to attribute sin to God; but it is a matter of fact that, by smarting for one fault, gracious men learn to avoid others.

GRACE FOR USE, AND NOT TO BE PLAYED WITH

Grace is not only donum, *but* talentum.[1] *Grace is not given, as a piece of money, to a child to play withal, but as we give money to factors, to trade withal for us.*

Everything is practical in the great gifts of God. He plants his trees that they may bear fruit, and sows his seed that a harvest may come of it. We may trifle and speculate; God never does so. When a man imagines that grace is given merely to make him comfortable, to give him a superiority over his fellows, or to enable him to avoid deserved censure, he knows not the design of the Lord in the bestowal of grace, and, indeed, he is a stranger to the grand secret. God works in us that we may work, he saves us that we may serve him, and enriches us with grace that the riches of his glory may be displayed. Are we putting out our

---

[1] Latin: *donum*: gift; *talentum*: talent

talents to proper interest? Do we use the grace bestowed upon us? 'He giveth more grace', but not to those who neglect what they have. Men do not long trust ill-stewards. Lord, help us so to act that we may render our account with joy and not with grief.

STUDY MUST BE FOLLOWED UP BY MEDITATION

The end of study is information, the end of meditation is practice, or a work upon the affections. Study is like a winter's sun that shineth but warmeth not; but meditation is like blowing up the fire, where we do not mind the blaze, but the heat.

Meditation being thus the more practical of the two, should not be placed second to study, but should even take precedence of it.

In study we are rather like vintners, who take in wine to store for sale; in meditation, like those who buy wine for their own use and comfort. A vintner's cellar may be better stored than a nobleman's. The student may have more of notion and knowledge, but the practical Christian hath more of taste and refreshment.

The student, therefore, is in a sad case if he go no further, for his soul may starve, notwithstanding his stores, if he does not use them. How miserable to die of cold while your cellar is full of coals! To perish with hunger when your granary is full of corn! This is a species of suicide which many commit. For want of due examination and meditation the precious truth of God is of no avail; but the blame lieth at the man's own door because he would not consider and turn unto the Lord. My soul, see to it that thy knowledge is well used for thy sustenance and growth. Retire more than thou hast done and chew the cud by meditation. Thou hast had too little of this. Be zealous, therefore, and mend thy ways in this respect.

CLEAN VESSELS FOR CHOICE LIQUORS

As precious liquors are best kept in clean vessels, so is the mystery of faith in a pure conscience.

Who, indeed, would knowingly pour a choice wine into a tainted cask? It would be no instance of his wisdom if he did so. When we hear of men living in sin and yet claiming to be the ministers of God, we are disgusted with their pretences, but we are not deceived by their professions. In the same manner, we care little for those who are orthodox Christians in creed if it is clear that they are heterodox in life. He who believes the truth should himself be true. How can we expect others to receive our religion if it leaves us foul, false, malicious, and selfish? We sicken at the sight of a dirty dish, and refuse even good meat when it is placed thereon. So pure and holy is the doctrine of the cross that he who hears it aright will have his ear cleansed, he who believes it will have his heart purged, and he who preaches it should have his tongue purified. Woe unto that man who brings reproach upon the gospel by an unhallowed walk and conversation.

Lord, evermore make us vessels fit for thine own use, and then fill us with the pure blood of the grapes of sound doctrine and wholesome instruction. Suffer us not to be such foul cups as to be only fit for the wine of Sodom.

THE RHODIANS

Plutarch tells us that the Rhodians appealed to the Romans for help, and one suggested that they should plead the good turns which they had done for Rome. This was a plea difficult to make strong enough, very liable to be disputed, and not at all likely to influence so great a people as the Romans, who would not readily consider themselves to be debtors to so puny a state as that of Rhodes. The Rhodians were, however, wiser than their counsellor, and took up another line of argument, which was abundantly successful: they pleaded the favours which in former times the Romans had bestowed upon them, and urged these as a reason why the great nation should not cast off a needy people for whom they had already done so much.

Herein is wisdom. How idle it would be for us to plead our good works with the great God! What we have done for him is too faulty and too questionable to be pleaded; but what he has done for us is grand argument, great in itself and potent with an immutable benefactor. Legal pleading soon meets a rebuff; yea, it trembles even before it leaves the pleader's mouth, and makes him ashamed while he is yet at his argument. Far otherwise fares it with the humble gratitude which gathers strength as it recalls each deed of love, and comforts itself with a growing assurance that he who has done so much will not lose his labour, but will do even more, till he has perfected that which concerneth us. Sinners run fearful risks when they appeal to justice: their wisdom is to cast themselves upon free grace. Our past conduct is a logical reason for our condemnation; it is in God's past mercy to us that we have accumulated argument for hope. The Latin sentence hath great truth in it, *Deus donando debet.* God by giving one mercy pledges himself to give another; he is not indebted to our merit, his only obligation is that which arises out of his own covenant promise, of which his gifts are pledges and bonds. Let us remember this when next we urge our suit with him.

CHOKING THE WEEDS

The way to destroy ill weeds is to plant good herbs that are contrary.

We have all heard of weeds choking the wheat; if we were wise we should learn from our enemy, and endeavour to choke the weeds by the wheat. Preoccupation of mind is a great safeguard from temptation. Fill a bushel with corn, and you will keep out the chaff: have the heart stored with holy things, and the vanities of the world will not so readily obtain a lodging-place.

Herein is wisdom in the training of children. Plant the mind early with the truths of God's word, and error and folly will, in a measure, be forestalled. The false will soon spring up if we do not early occupy the mind with the true. He who said that he did not wish to prejudice his boy's mind by teaching him to pray, soon discovered that the devil was not so scrupulous, for his boy soon learned to swear. It is well to prejudice a field in favour of wheat at the first opportunity.

In the matter of amusements for the young, it is much better to provide than to prohibit. If we find the lads and lasses interesting employments they will not be so hungry after the gayeties and ensnarements of this wicked world. If we are afraid that the children will eat unwholesome food abroad, let us as much as possible take the edge from their appetites by keeping a good table at home.

BROKEN BONES COMPLAINING

Old bruises may trouble us long after, upon every change of weather, and new afflictions revive the sense of old sins.

We know one who broke his arm in his youth, and though it was well set, and soundly healed, yet before a rough season the bones cry out bitterly; and even so, though early vice may be forsaken, and heartily repented of, and the mind may be savingly renewed, yet the old habits will be a lifelong trouble and injury. The sins of our youth will give us many a twist fifty years after they have been forgiven. How happy, then, are those who are preserved from the ways of ungodliness, and brought to Jesus in the days of their youth, for they thus escape a thousand regrets. It is well to have a broken bone skilfully set, but far better never to have had it broken. The fall of Adam has battered and bruised us all most sadly; it is a superfluity of naughtiness that we should incur further damage by our own personal falls. The aches and pains of age are more than sufficient when every limb is sound, and recklessly to add the anguish of fractures and dislocations would be folly indeed. Young man, do not run up bills which your riper years will find it hard to pay; do not eat today forbidden morsels, which may breed you sorrow long after their sweetness has been forgotten.

THE CHARIOT OF THE SPIRIT

The Spirit of God rides most triumphantly in his own chariot.

That is to say, he is best pleased to convey conviction and comfort by means of his own word. God's word, not man's comment on God's word, is the most usual means of conversion. This is done to put honour upon the divine revelation, and to make us prize it with all our hearts. Our Lord said not only, 'Sanctify them', but, 'sanctify them through thy truth'; and then he added, 'thy word is truth.' Our author does well to liken the Scriptures to a chariot, because they are the ordinary means by which the Holy Ghost comes to us, but they are only the chariot, and without the quickening Spirit they bring us no good. The Scriptures do not make our hearts burn till the Spirit kindles them into flames, and then we say, 'Did not our hearts burn within us while he talked with us by the way, and while he opened to us the Scriptures.' Let us reverence Holy Scripture because the Holy Ghost is its author, expositor, preserver, and applier. We cannot too often use the weapon which the Spirit himself calls his sword.

COVETOUSNESS AS A SERVANT

Covetousness may be entertained as a servant, where it is not entertained as a master—entertained as a servant to provide oil and fuel to make other sins burn.

Where avarice is the absolute master, the man is a miser; but even he is not more truly miserable than the man whose gainings only furnish opportunity for indulging in vice. Such persons are greedy that they may become guilty. Their money buys them the means of their own destruction, and they are eager after it. Winning and saving with them are but means for profligacy, and therefore they think themselves fine liberal fellows, and despise the penurious habits of the miser. Yet in what respects are they better than he? Their example is certainly far more injurious to the commonwealth, and their motive is not one whit better. Selfishness is the mainspring of action in each case; the difference lies in the means selected and not in the end proposed. Both seek their own gratification, the one by damming up the river, and the other by drowning the country with its floods. Let the profligate judge for himself, whether he is one grain better than the greediest skinflint whom he so much ridicules.

Lord, help us to live for thee and not for self, and both in giving and in spending may thy glory be our only aim.

UNDISTURBED DEVOTION

It is a strange constancy of fixedness that is attributed to the priests at Jerusalem, who, when Faustus, Cornelius, Furius, and Fabius broke into the city with their troops, and rushed into the temple ready to kill them, yet they went on with the rites of the temple, as if there had been no assault. And strange is that other instance of the Spartan youth, that held the censer to Alexander while he offered sacrifice. A coal lighting upon his arm, he suffered it to burn there rather than that any crying out of his should disturb the worship.

These instances are a shame to Christians, that we do not more intensely fix our hearts when we are in the service of God; instead of which, many may be seen looking hither and thither, and turning their heads to the door to observe every new comer. Even in our private devotions, how soon we are distracted and carried away from the point in hand. Our minds flit and fly like birds on the hedges, which have scarcely time to settle, for as one passenger moves along the road and then another, they are ready for flight at once. At the sound of every footstep the bird is on the wing, and thus some hearts are the prey of every trifling circumstance. Saints have been undisturbed amid a crowd, while others find their prayers crowded out when they are alone.

O Lord, assist me in my communion with thee, that my whole soul may be set upon it, and not a single thought may wander from thee. Let not even pain and care prevent my whole heart from adoring thee.

RARE EXOTICS NEED CARE

The more supernatural things are, the more we need diligence to preserve them. A strange plant [an exotic] requires more care than a native of the soil. Worldly desires, like nettles, breed of their own accord; but spiritual desires need a great deal of cultivating.

The more spiritual the duty, the sooner the soul wearies of it. An illustration of this is seen in the case of Moses, whose hands grew weary in prayer, while we never read that Joshua's hands hung down in fight. Spirituality is a tender plant, and without great care it soon flags, while sin needs neither hoeing nor watering, but will spring up in the dark, and flourish even amid the wintry frosts of trouble. The fair flower of grace, is, however, so precious that God himself has promised to tend it. What must be the value of that plant of which the Lord hath said, 'I will water it every moment; lest any hurt it, I will keep it night and day'? Let us watch and pray, and never dream that things will go well with us if we neglect these necessary duties. No spiritual grace will thrive if we neglect it. We ought to be very diligent in our spiritual husbandry; nor should our labour be grudged, for the fruit will well reward our pains.

THE MARTYR AND THE CHAIN

When Hooper, the blessed martyr, was at the stake, and the officers came to fasten him to it, he cried, 'Let me alone; God that hath called me hither will keep me from stirring; and yet', said he, upon second thought, 'because I am but flesh and blood, I am willing. Bind me fast, lest I stir.'

Some plead that they have no need of the holdfasts of an outward profession, and the solemn pledges of the two great ordinances, for the Holy Spirit will keep them faithful; yet surely, like this man of God, they may well accept those cords of love wherewith heavenly wisdom would bind us to the horns of the altar. Our infirmities need all the helps which divine love has devised, and we may not be so self-sufficient as to refuse them.

Pledges, covenants, and vows of human devising should be used with great caution; but where the Lord ordains we may proceed without question, our only fear being lest by neglecting them we should despise the command of the Lord, or by relying upon them we should wrest the precept from its proper intent. Whatever will prove a check to us when tempted, or an incentive when commanded, must be of use to us, however strong we may conceive ourselves to be. 'Bind the sacrifice with cords, even with cords to the horns of the altar.'

Lord, cast a fresh band about me every day. Let the constraining love of Jesus hold me faster and faster.

> Oh, to grace how great a debtor,
>   Daily I'm constrained to be!
> Let that grace, Lord, like a fetter,
>   Bind my wandering heart to Thee.

BEGGING OF THE RICH

Beggars in the streets, if they see a poor man, meanly clad, they let him alone; but when they see a man of quality and fashion they rouse up themselves, and besiege him with importunate entreaties and clamours, and will not let him go until he hath left something with them.

Thus should we do in our spiritual begging. Vain is the help of man, and therefore we should ask little of him: he is as poor as we are, and it will be a waste of time to wait upon such a pauper. As for the Lord Jesus, he is so rich that if all the beggars in the universe would call at his door, he would not refuse one of them, but would set open the doors of his granaries and the hatches of his butteries, and feast the world. He is the heir of all things. There is no bottom to his treasuries. He is the true Solomon, and his daily provision is not only enough for all his household, but for all those who lie starving on the highways and in the hedges. The wealth of nations is nothing to the wealth of Jesus. Come, then, my heart, beg largely of thy Lord, and when he hears thee, beg again. His quality and fashion invite thee to follow him with importunity whithersoever he goeth.

SOUR GRAPES

Ungodly men are too impatient to wait for solid and eternal pleasures, but snatch at the pleasures of sin, which are but for a season. These resemble children who cannot tarry till the grapes are ripe, and therefore eat them sour and green.

Pleasure lies mainly in hope, and yet some men will not give space for hope to grow in: it must be now or never; all today, and tomorrow may starve. In business, men put out their money, foregoing its use themselves, that it may, after a while, return to them with increase; but carnal men are all for keeping the bird in the hand, and cannot wait for joys to come.

Yet these hasty delights are not satisfying. Man was not made to find his heaven upon earth, nor can he do so, even though he labours after it. The grapes plucked in this untimely season cause ere-long a griping of the heart, and a gnawing within the soul. We are not ready for fulness of joy, nor is the joy ready for us. Our wisdom is to be preparing for eternal bliss by present holiness, believing that he who is making us ready for heaven is making heaven ready for us. This is the surest way to present satisfaction, which must always be found in careful obedience to the divine will from day to day, and in a believing expectation of glory to be revealed.

O thou who art 'the God of hope', grant that, by thy hope which thou hast wrought in us, we may be daily purified, and set free from the defilement of this present evil world.

THE SINGLE MILLSTONE

The Egyptians, in their hieroglyphics, expressed the unprofitableness of a solitary man by a single millstone, which, being alone, grindeth no meal, though with its fellow it would be exceedingly profitable for that purpose.

Let this serve as a symbol to those unsociable Christians who endeavour to walk alone, and refuse to enter into the fellowship of the saints. They are comparatively useless. The Lord has made us dependent upon each other for usefulness. Our attainments are not put to their right use till they supply the deficiencies of others: this is one side of our necessity for fellowship—we need to associate with the weak, that we may find a sphere in which to trade with our talents, by helping them. On the other hand, our infirmities and deficiencies are meant to draw us into association with stronger brethren, from whom we may receive help and direction. Whether we be of the stronger or the feebler sort, we have an equal reason for seeking Christian communion. It is of the nature of the Lord's people to assemble themselves together, and live in companies: wild beasts may roam the woods alone, but sheep go in flocks. David said, 'I am a companion of all them that fear thee', and he showed his piety not only by being select in his company, but in loving such fellowship when he found it.

O thou who didst call thy disciples 'friends', give me ever the friendly spirit, and make me to love all those whom thou lovest.

RAIMENT, THE BODY, THE SOUL

A man who is wounded, and cut through his clothes and skin and all, will be more anxious to have the wound closed up in his body than to have the rent in his garment mended.

His body is much more himself than the garment with which he covers it, and, therefore, he gives it his first attention. Now, on the same principle, we should take more care of the soul than of the body, for the soul is more truly the man than the mere flesh and blood which he inhabits. As a man may get a new coat, so shall he obtain a new body at the resurrection; but his spirit, which is his real self, abides the same as to identity, and should, therefore, be carefully guarded. Yet what fools the most of men are; they spend a lifetime in providing for a body which will soon be worms' meat, and their immortal soul is left uncared for, to go before God, naked, and poor, and miserable. If there were as much as a pennyworth of wisdom to be found among ten thousand sinners they would no longer neglect their own souls.

O Lord, heal thou my soul; and as for the rents in my garments, they shall give me small concern.

THE IMAGE NOT THE MAN

As Michal laid a statue in David's bed, and, covering it with David's apparel, made Saul's messengers believe it was David himself sick in bed; so, many persons cover themselves with certain external actions belonging to religion, and the world believeth them truly sanctified and spiritual, whereas, indeed, they are but statues and apparitions of devotion to God.

Formalism is a vain show, and will, in the end, be discovered, and the cheat will cease to impose upon anyone. Of all matters, religion is the very worst to play with. It may be easy to mimic it, but the price to be paid for such fooling will be terrible. If men must act a borrowed part, let them ape the princes of this world, but let them not put such an affront upon the princes of the blood royal of heaven. Let them go to their theatres if they would wear a mask; to do so in the house of God is an insult which the Lord will not brook. The best imitation of religion will make its possessor wail forever when the hand of eternal truth shall lay bare its falsehood.

O thou who art 'the truth', deliver me from all seeming, and let me be in truth that which I profess to be.

RUNAWAY KNOCKS

Watch in prayer to see what cometh. Foolish boys, that knock at a door in wantonness, will not stay till somebody cometh to open to them; but a man that hath business will knock, and knock again, till he gets his answer.

To pray and not to look for an answer argues either a mere formality in prayer, and that makes the prayer to be dead; or else unbelief as to the truth of God, and that makes the prayer to be corrupt. He who presents a cheque at the banker's looks to have money for it; if not, he is not a business man, but a mere trifler. So in our pleadings of the divine promise we expect a fulfilment, or otherwise we do but play with God.

How many runaway knocks we give at mercy's gate! Let us put away such childish things, and treat prayer as a reality: then shall we be answered of a truth. 'I will direct my prayer unto thee, and will look up.'

He who writes these lines bears witness that he has never knocked in vain at the Lord's door, and he begs the reader to make trial of that which he has found so effectual. 'Knock, and it shall be opened unto you.'

THE RUSSET COAT

Man is a proud creature, and would fain establish his own righteous-ness, and have somewhat wherein to glory in himself (Rom. 10:3). Our proud heart takes up the old proverb and thinketh—A russet coat of our own is better than a silken garment that is borrowed of another.

Man would sooner wear his own rags than Christ's fine white linen. Pride, however, is too expensive a luxury when a man must give up all hope of heaven in order to indulge it. Such is the case. There can be no feasting with the King unless we wear the wedding-garment which he supplies. Our own silk and satin would not suit his courts, much less our russet and our corduroy. We must accept the righteousness of God, or be unrighteous forever. Surely we shall be worse than madmen if we insist upon going naked rather than put on the royal apparel of free grace.

Lord, I cannot longer err in this fashion, for I perceive my righteousnesses to be filthy rags, and I am heartily glad to be rid of them. Clothe me, I pray thee, with the righteousness divine.

FIRE SPREADING

A good man is always seeking to make others good, as fire turneth all things about it into fire.

You cannot make fire stay where it is, it will spread as opportunity serves it. It will subdue all its surroundings to itself. Carlyle says that 'man is emphatically a proselytizing creature', and assuredly the new creature is such. Life grows, and so invades the regions of death, and spiritual life is most of all intense in its growing and spreading. Liberty to hold our opinions but not to spread them is no liberty, for one of our main opinions is that we should bring all around us to Jesus, and to obedience to the truth.

Lord, help us ever to be doing this, subduing the earth for thee by spreading on all sides the name of Jesus. Let our life burn till the whole world is on a blaze.

NO OLD AGE IN GRACE

We have our infancy at our first conversion, when liable to childish ignorance and many infirmities; we have our youth and growing age, when making progress in the way of grace toward perfection; and lastly, we have our perfect manly age when we are come to our full pitch, when grace is fully perfected in glory. In Scripture there is nothing said of a fading and declining time of old age in grace.

The fact being that, unlike the natural life, the spiritual life does not conclude in declining strength and inevitable decrepitude, but continues its progress even beyond the grave. We go from strength to strength, not from strength to weakness. The old age of grace is maturity, not decay; advancement, not decline; perfection, not imbecility. In the advanced years of nature we lose many of our faculties, but in advanced grace our spiritual senses are more quick and discerning than ever. The aged man feels the grasshopper to be a burden, and the clouds return after the rain; but to the advanced believer the greatest loads are light and the rain is over and gone. Old age goes down to death, but ripe grace ascends to everlasting life.

Lord, let me grow ripe but not rotten, maturing but not decaying, for thy glory's sake.

INFANTS AND SICK FOLK

Though we cannot love their weaknesses, yet we must love the weak, and bear with their infirmities, not breaking the bruised reed. Infants must not be turned out of the family because they cry, and are unquiet and troublesome; though they be peevish and froward, yet we must bear it with gentleness and patience, as we do the frowardness of the sick; if they revile we must not revile again, but must seek gently to restore them, notwithstanding all their censures.

This patience is far too rare. We do not make allowances enough for our fellows, but sweepingly condemn those whom we ought to cheer with our sympathy. If we are out of temper ourselves we plead the weather, or a headache, or our natural temperament, or aggravating circumstances; we are never at a loss for an excuse for ourselves, why should not the same ingenuity be used by our charity in inventing apologies and extenuations for others? It is a pity to carry on the trade of apology-making entirely for home consumption; let us supply others. True, they are very provoking, but if we suffered half as much as some of our irritable friends have to endure we should be even more aggravating. Think in many cases of their ignorance, their unfortunate bringing up, their poverty, their depression of spirit, and their home surroundings, and pity will come to the help of patience. We are tender to a man who has a gouty toe, cannot we extend the feeling to those who have an irritable soul?

Our Lord will be angry with us if we are harsh to his little ones whom he loves; nor will he be pleased if we are unkind to his poor afflicted children with whom he would have us be doubly tender. We ourselves need from him ten times more consideration than we show to our brethren. For his sake we ought to be vastly more forbearing than we are. Think how patient *he* has been to *us*, and let our hard-heartedness be confessed as no light sin.

PILLS

We should not expect to see a reason for everything which we believe, for many doctrines are mysteries, and we must receive them as we do pills. We do not chew pills, but swallow them; and so we must take these truths into our souls upon the credit of the revealer.

This indeed is true faith—this taking truth upon trust because of the divine authority of the revelation which contains it. We are persuaded that the Lord cannot lie, and so we believe, for this sole reason, that 'thus saith the Lord'. Why should we chew the pill by wishing to know more than is revealed? Must our Father explain everything to us on pain of not being believed if he reserves any point in his proceedings? Would not such a demand savour more of a proud, rebellious spirit than of humble, childlike love? Has a man any faith in God if he will believe no more than his reason proves?

Many a truth when taken into the soul as a whole has proved to be very sweet to the heart. We could not understand it; but no sooner had we believed it than we were conscious of its delightful influence upon the inner nature. Who can understand the twofold nature of our Lord's person, or the doctrine of the Trinity in unity, or the predestination which does not violate free agency? And yet what a delight these truths create in minds which cheerfully accept them.

My soul, thou canst not know or understand all things, else wert thou omniscient, and that is the prerogative of God alone. Be it thine, therefore, to believe the testimony of thy God, and then his omniscience will be all at thy disposal. He will teach thee what else thou couldst never learn, if thou art but willing to sit at his feet and receive of his word. We sometimes speak of a scholarly man; in the best sense every Christian should be *scholarly*, that is, willing to be a scholar.

HARD BEGINNINGS

Some beginners are discouraged in their first attempts at a godly life, and so give over through despondency. They should remember that the bullock is most unruly at the first yoking, and that the fire at first kindling casts forth most smoke.

They forget this, and therefore are tempted to give over religion and its graces as hopeless. When a man is new to the ways of God those duties are difficult which afterward become easy. Use in common life is called 'second nature', and in gracious matters it helps our second nature. Gracious habit gives impetus to gracious action. Self-denials, which seem hard at first, become delights in due season, so that we even wonder that we thought them denials. Some things there are which are most easy in our first days of grace, but other things will be found to improve as we proceed upon the way: let not the young beginner be discouraged, but fully believe that 'it is better on before'. We have heard persons talk of the days of childhood as the happiest in mortal life, but we do not agree with them: the sorrows of childhood take a very intense possession of the little ones, and in their grief everything seems lost, whereas the full-grown mind is divided in sorrow, and other considerations come in to temper the wind of trouble. Even so, childhood in grace is by no means our best time; for its trials, though less in themselves, are greater to our weakness and rawness of mind. The yoke will be easier soon, and the fire will yet burn with a clearer blaze.

Lord, help thy babe. Nurse me into vigour by thy good Spirit.

LEAD

Lead is lead still, whatever stamp it beareth.

A change of form is a very different thing from a change of substance. You may cast lead into the shape of a shilling, but you cannot make silver of it. Now, the only change which can save us is a thorough transformation of nature, and this is as clearly beyond human power as the turning of lead into silver. When we see a great moral improvement in any man we ought to be glad, and to admire the power of conscience; but if the man's heart remains the same, the alteration is only casting a lump of lead into a pretty form. When the man's nature and disposition are radically altered, we may then exclaim, 'This is the finger of God'—this is transmuting lead into silver. 'Ye must be born again': nothing less will suffice.

Lord, grant that I may truly know this change. If I am mistaken and have never been regenerated, be pleased to exercise thy gracious power upon me now, for Jesus' sake.

WHY A CANDLE IS LIT

God seldom lighteth a candle, but he hath some lost groat[1] to seek.

This is assuredly true, and its practical bearings are worthy of our attention. If God raises up a preacher or any other useful worker, we may conclude that he has a people to be sought out and won for his kingdom. All capacities and abilities in the church are intended for this great purpose—the finding of the lost treasure. The same is true of the doctrines of the gospel, the ordinances, and the promises: these are all lights kindled with the view of finding lost souls. The whole Scripture has an eye in this direction. By one text one man is found, and by

[1] A coin.

another passage another is discovered. Each Scripture has its own ray and by its means its own lost piece is perceived. Some texts are great candles, and have found out many; but probably there is not one tiny taper of Holy Writ which has not shed its saving beams on some one or other of the Lord's precious ones. Certainly every light which the Lord has given has a gracious design, and will be used for a saving purpose.

Lord, use me also, though I be but a poor rushlight, and find out some poor lost sinner by my means.

THE KING'S EXAMPLE

Alexander, when his army grew sluggish because laden with the spoils of their enemies, to free them from this incumbrance, commanded all his own baggage to be set on fire, that when they saw the king himself devote his rich treasures to the flames they might not murmur if their mite and pittance were consumed also. So, if Christ had taught us contempt of the world, and had not given us an instance of it in his own person, his doctrine had been less powerful and effectual.

But what an example we now find in him, seeing he had not where to lay his head in life, nor a rag to cover him in death, nor anything but a borrowed grave in burial. What manner of persons ought we to be in all unselfishness when we have such a Lord! He hath not said to us in matters of self-denial, 'Take up thy cross and go', but 'Come, take up thy cross, and follow me.' Fired by the heroic self-sacrifice of our King, the sternest abnegation of self and the severest renunciation of the world should become an easy matter. Well may the soldiers endure hardness when the King himself roughs it among us, and suffers more than the meanest private in our ranks.

My soul, I charge thee, endure hardness, and look not for ease where Jesus found death.

THE BEST WEATHER FOR ME

The same weather does not fit every soil; that drought which burneth up the hotter grounds comforteth those that are more chill and cold. If one man had another's blessings he would soon run wild, as another would grow desperate if he had our crosses. Therefore the infinite wisdom of the great Governor of the world allots every one his portion.

It may be, my soul, that thou art a dry and thirsty plot which will never yield a harvest at all unless thou art continually under the watery sign. For thee the clouds must return after the rain, and rough weather last long and come again. Thou hast had little sunshine, but thy long glooms are wisely appointed thee, for perhaps a stretch of summer weather would have made thee as a parched land and a barren wilderness. Thy Lord knows best, and he has the clouds and the sun at his disposal. Let me therefore bless him for such weather as he sends to me from day to day, for foul is fair to me if the Lord appoints it in love.

Let me not envy those whom the sun shines on. Maybe they need it all to make them fruitful. Why should they not have it? There is all the more sunshine for me when it shines for others. Lord, I bless thee for other men's joys, and I will not repine if I am denied an equal share with them. I have thee; and what more can I ask?

THE PAPER-STAINER AND THE ARTIST

A paper-stainer will think a painter too curious, because his own work is but a little daubing. The broad way pleaseth the world best, but the narrow way leadeth to life.

Our author means that the maker of wall-papers gets over a great deal of ground as compared with the artist who is producing a masterly painting. Of rough daubing there is plenty to be had, and there is a great market for it; and yet, though thoroughly fine art is scarce, it is infinitely more precious than daubing. That religion which needs no care, and takes no trouble, is in great demand in the world; it is produced by the acre, and may be seen spread over the surface everywhere. Not so the religion of grace; it costs many a tear, and a world of anxious thought, and solemn heart-searching, and it is but slow work at the best; but then it is of great price, and is not only acceptable with God, but even men perceive that there is a something about it to which the common religious daubers never attain. If we let the boat drift with the stream, and leave our religion to random influences, without care or thought, what can we look for but slovenliness and worthlessness? If we would please God we must watch every stroke and touch upon the canvas of our lives, and we may not think that we can lay it on with a trowel and yet succeed. We ought to live as miniature-painters work, for they watch every line and tint. O for more careful work, more heart work! Otherwise we shall lose that which we have wrought.

SAVE THE JEWELS

As men in a great fire and general conflagration will hazard their lumber to preserve their treasure, their money, or their jewels, so should we take care, if we must lose one or the other, that the better part be out of hazard. Whatever we lose by the way, let us make sure that we come well to the end of our journey.

Herein is wisdom. See how men throw overboard the lading of the ship when it becomes a question of saving their lives.

Reason teaches them that the less precious must go first: they do not throw over first their gold and then their corn, neither do they lose their lives to save their ingots. So let us, above all things, care for our souls and their eternal interests. He whose house was burned to ashes kneeled down and thanked the Lord because his child was safe; and he who loses the whole world but obtains eternal salvation has so much to rejoice in that he would waste his tears if he shed them over his losses. Suppose it were said that Virgil died worth half a million of money, it is so long ago that it would be stale intelligence, and if the same were said of a man who died yesterday there would really be no more in it; yet if the soul of Virgil's slave was saved, though he never owned a single gold coin, heaven has not ceased to ring with joy concerning his salvation. The soul should be our main care. It is our all, for it is ourself. Lord, teach men this wisdom; teach me this wisdom.

THE CARVER FOR HIMSELF

He that will be his own carver seldom carveth out a good portion to himself. Wilful spirits who would fain be their own providence intrench upon God's prerogative, and take the work out of his hands; and, therefore, no wonder if their wisdom be turned into folly.

It is God's business to regulate providence, and when we attempt it we cause confusion and trouble. Not only does the carver for himself get a poor portion, but he frequently cuts his fingers, and spoils his clothes by spilling the contents of the dish. Israel went into Canaan well enough when the Lord led the way; but when the people before the set time presumed to go up of their own head, they brought defeat upon themselves. It is never well either to run before the cloud, or to stay behind it: in either case we may expect to fall under clouds of another sort, which will darken our way and becloud our peace. Cannot we trust the Lord with his own business? Can we supplement infallible wisdom, or improve upon infinite goodness? Have we not enough to do if we earnestly endeavour to obey our Lord? Do we want to be rulers? Are we tired of being disciples and followers? Why do we strain after things too high for us, intruding into spheres which belong to God alone?

My soul, stand thou still, and see the salvation of God! He is at the helm, and is well able to pilot the vessel. Keep thy hand off the tiller. Down with thee, unbelief, what hast thou to do while God himself provides for his people?

THE GHOST

Guilt raked out of its grave is more frightful than a ghost, or one risen from the dead.

Nor is the terror which sin excites in the awakened conscience at all an idle one. There is in evil a horror greater than can be found in hobgoblin, sprite, or apparition. Great is the mystery of iniquity, and he who comes under its spell will have no joy of his life till the ghost is laid in the Red Sea of Jesus' precious blood. Blessed be God, our Lord has done this for us; and we are not afraid of being haunted by sins which are buried in his grave.

NO DAY WITHOUT THE SUN

When the sun is gone all the candles in the world cannot make it day.

Vain would be the attempt, though we should kindle a mountain of wax. So when the Lord denies comfort to a man, neither wealth, nor honour, nor power can enlighten the darkness of his mind. We can procure our own sorrow, but we cannot produce our own comfort. A secret curse eats out the heart of earthly joys when God does not smile upon them. Without God the world is, says Manton, '*a deaf nut, which we crack, but find nothing in it but dust*'. Vanity of vanities, all is vanity, till the Lord becomes our all in all. Reader, do you know this by personal experience?

ARE THEY HAPPY?

Do you account him a happy man who is condemned to die, because he hath a plentiful allowance till his execution? Or him a happy man that makes a fair show abroad and puts a good face upon his ruinous and breaking condition, while at home he is pinched with want and misery, which is ready to come upon him like an armed man; one who revels in all manner of pleasure today, but is to die at night? Then those who remain in the guilt of their sins may be happy.

If we view unpardoned sinners aright we shall heartily pity them. Let their condition be what it may, at this present the wrath of God abideth on them, and they are 'condemned already'; and as for the future, it is black with certain doom. Alas for the unhappy man against whom God sets his face! What misery can be greater than to be reserved against the great day of the wrath of God? We wonder at the mirth of men condemned to hell, their infatuation is terrible to behold.

Hence we cannot join with them in their carnal mirth. Sinners may dance, but it will not be to our piping. They may revel and riot, but we dare not countenance them in their jollity, for we know that their day is coming. Let no desire to share their base delights lurk in your mind if you be indeed a child of God. Be not envious at the transgressors. Who would envy a criminal about to be executed his last draught of wine? Let not their frivolities attract you. Every sensible man pities the wretch who can dance under the gallows. Sinners on the road to hell sporting and jesting are worse than mad, or their singing would turn to sighing.

THE SUN ECLIPSED

To put out a candle is no great matter; but to have the sun eclipsed, which is the fountain of light, that sets the world a-wondering! For poor creatures to lose their comforts is no great wonder, who, though they live in God, are so many degrees distant from him; but for Christ, who was God-man in one person, to be forsaken of God, that is a difficulty to our thoughts and a wonder indeed, for by this means he was so far deprived of some part of himself.

Yes, indeed, this is the wonder of wonders, the miracle of miracles, at which my mind would forever stand amazed. That the thrice Holy One should take the sinner's place, and, coming under the sinner's doom, should be smitten of God, is a mystery past finding out! Hell is horribly amazing, but the death of Jesus is far more astounding, and especially that in death he should cry, 'My God, my God, why hast thou forsaken me?' Only the Son of God could endure this great grief; yet is it a mystery of mysteries, that so divine a person should be capable of enduring it. The marvel is thought to be that a man should be able to suffer so much; but the real marvel is that, being God, he should suffer at all that which was the very essence of his grief—the being forsaken by the Father.

My soul, adore and love; understand thou canst not. Behold the eclipse of thy soul's Sun, and know that, had not this been, thou wouldst have been in the dark forever.

THE ASS WISER THAN THE SINNER

You cannot drive a dull ass into the fire that is kindled before his eyes.

The ungodly are far more brutish, for they choose the way of destruction, and rush with eagerness into the flames of hell. 'Surely in vain is the net spread in the sight of any bird', and yet men see the net, and hasten into it. Sinners take more pains to go to hell than the saints to go to heaven. They are more bold to destroy themselves than saints are in their salvation. What greater proof can we have of the madness of their hearts, and what plainer evidence that salvation is not by the will of man, but by grace alone?

Lord, save me and mine from that obstinate love of sin which makes men more brutish than the ox and the ass.

SURFACE MELTING

Some are frightened into a little religiousness in their straits and deep necessities, but it is poor work and superficial work. They are like ice in thawing weather, soft at top and hard at bottom.

They melt, but to no very great extent. It is upon the surface only that they yield to heavenly influences. This is a sorry state of things, for it generally ends in a harder frost than before, and the bonds of cold indifference bind the very soul. Let those in whom there are any meltings of holy feeling take heed, for their danger lies in being content with partial subjection to gracious influences. Grace will be all or nothing: the ice must all melt, and the soul must flow like a river. Jesus did not come to create temporary and partial religious feeling, but to make new creatures of us. He will have nothing to do with those Ephraimites who are as half-done cakes, which are black on one side with too much baking, but have never been turned so as to feel the fire on the other side. The centre of the heart must feel the warmth of divine love, or nothing is done.

Lord, shine on my soul till I am wholly melted, and all my ice has vanished. Thou alone canst break up nature's frost, but thou canst do it. Shine on me, most patient Lord.

THE DRUNKEN SERVANT STILL A SERVANT

A drunken servant is a servant, and bound to do his work; his master loseth not his right by his man's default.

It is a mere assumption, though some state it with much confidence, that inability removes responsibility. As our author shows, a servant may be too drunk to do his master's bidding, but his service is still his master's due. If responsibility began and ended with ability, a man would be out of debt as soon as he was unable to pay; and if a man felt that he could not keep his temper he would not be blamable for being angry. A man may be bound to do what he cannot do: the habitual liar is bound to speak the truth, though his habit of falsehood renders him incapable of it. Every sin renders the sinner less able to do right, but the standard of his duty is not lowered in proportion to the lowering of his capacity to come up to it, or it would follow that the more a man is depraved by sin the less guilty his actions become, which is absurd.

Every Christian will confess that it is his duty to be perfect, and yet he mourns over his inability to be so. It never enters into the Christian's head to excuse his failings by pleading the incapacity of his nature; nay, this is another cause for lamentation.

The standard of responsibility is the command of God. The law cannot be lowered to our fallen state. It is sin to neglect or break a divine command. All the theology which is based upon the idea that responsibility is to be measured by moral ability or inability has the taint of error about it.

Lord, make me to know my obligation, that I may be humbled, and help me to adore thy grace, by which alone holiness can be wrought in me.

CYPRESS TREES

Some talk, but do nothing; like cypress trees, tall and beautiful, but unfruitful; or, like the carbuncle, afar off seeming all on fire, but the touch discovers it to be key-cold: their zeal is more in their tongues than their actions.

These are a numerous race, and never more so than at this time. Persecution is an unhealthy season for false professors, who prefer to flourish in the piping times of peace, when godliness is gain, and it pays to get Christ today and sell him tomorrow. The cypress tree is an excellent emblem of the more prominent specimens of this class. They are conspicuous, and aim to be so: rising above their fellows, they invite attention; but when you turn your eyes toward them you cannot discover even a tiny apple upon them, or any other useful fruit. Certainly they are shapely and stately, and when you have said *that*, you have said all. They look most at home near the grave, and a melancholy air surrounds them, but still they are not half as valuable as the more lowly fruit-bearers which flourish unobserved with a cheerful verdure. Certain professors whom we know are prim, stiff, orderly, and melancholy, but we are not fond of their neighbourhood; for they yield no refreshing shade or nourishing fruit, and make us feel doleful to the last degree.

Lord, let me be as low and unnoticed as thou pleasest, but do enable me to bear fruit, to the honour of thy name and to the comfort of thy people.

THE EMPTY BRAG

A Roman bragged 'that he had never been reconciled with his mother',
implying that he had never disagreed with her. So, some say they
were never comforted, they never needed it; they lay nothing to
heart.

Of this company are those who were born free, and were never in bondage to any man, and yet, by their boastings, set the fetters of their pride a-clanking. Those who were never wounded, and therefore have never been healed, may glory in their state, but the time will come when they will wish it were otherwise with them, and envy the very least of those broken-hearted ones whom Jesus has bound up. A day shall dawn when the self-righteous, who are now at ease in Zion, would gladly exchange places with those whom they now despise as morbid and melancholy.

Lord, let me be among those who confess that they were once thine enemies, and have been reconciled to thee by the death of thy Son. Let me be numbered among those who were the servants of sin, but have, through thy grace, obeyed from the heart the doctrine of thy word. Let me ever vividly perceive that I have undergone a radical change, which I greatly needed, and without which I should have been an heir of wrath, even as others.

THE HEDGE OF THORNS

Wicked men are preserved in reference to the godly; they are but as
a defence of thorns about a garden of roses. Now, when the roses
are cropped off, what will become of the thorns?

This is a solemn question, and should arouse the care-less. Ungodly men are a sort of scaffold to God's house, and when the house is finished they must be pulled down. The husk is needful to the wheat at a certain time, but when the corn is ripe the husk is useless chaff, and must be separated from it. An ungodly mother is to a pious son as the chaff to the wheat, and ere-long the chaff must be driven away. What think ye of this, ye unsaved parents of godly children? What think ye of this, ye unregenerate brothers and friends, by whom the godly are succoured, while you yourselves remain unsaved?

When good men die the wicked should reflect that there is so much the less salt left to preserve society. There is one pleader less for the preservation of the barren tree. Every saint taken home brings the world so much nearer its end. Much as they may despise the godly, the deaths of righteous men ought to be solemn warnings to the thoughtless world, as they reflect upon what must happen to the world when those who are its light and its salt are taken away.

THE UNUSED KEY

A key rusteth that is seldom turned in the lock.

It becomes hard work to stir it, for it becomes rusted into its place. Neglect of prayer makes prayer become hard work, whereas it should be a privilege and a delight. We cannot restrain prayer, and yet enjoy prayer. Frequency in this matter helps fervour, and constancy in it brings out the comfort of it.

Am I becoming slack in devotion? O Lord, forgive me, and save me from this grave neglect before it begins to eat into my soul and corrode my heart!

THE SERPENT'S EGG

It is easier to crush the egg than to kill the serpent.

It is prudent to break up all the eggs we can find before the reptiles are hatched. Far greater wisdom will be shown in early dealing with an error or a temptation than in allowing it time to make headway. In our own cases, it will be best to correct ourselves betimes, and unhesitatingly to stamp out the first sparks of ill desire, before passion rises to a flame. A serpent's egg a child can break, but who is to contend with the venomous creature which may be hatched from it, if it be left unbroken? So is it with that vice which stingeth like a viper. The first glass can readily be refused; it is quite another matter to stop when the wine has entered the brain. The first impropriety we may readily avoid; but when unclean desires are fully aroused, who shall bridle them?

O Lord, of thy grace, teach me to crush sin betimes, lest it should gather strength and crush me.

INVISIBLE INK

Things written with the juice of a lemon, when they are brought to the fire are plain and legible; so when wicked men draw near to the fires of hell, their secret sins stand out before them, and they cry out upon their beds.

The prospect of eternity discovers those secret beliefs and inward fears which they laboured so hard to deny and conceal. Few men can keep up a deceit when they approach their end. The skeleton hand readily tears off the mask. A deathbed is not always free from hypocrisy; but, assuredly, it is hard for the dying sinner to keep up his deceit. The fire of his approaching doom brings out the secret writing upon his soul, which even he himself had not before cared to read, and then he who thought himself a firmly rooted sceptic finds out that he had after all an inward conviction which he could not stifle, and a fear in his heart which he could not smother. O that men would seek to know themselves, for it might turn out that the defiant blasphemy of their tongues is not, by any means, a sure index that their heart is at rest in unbelief.

What must be that man's condition whose very infidelity is feigned? It is a terrible thing to be a sham Christian, but what must be the worthlessness of a hypocritical infidel? When the genuine metal is worthless, what shall we say of its counterfeit? Yet we doubt not that thousands of sceptics, in their inmost hearts, believe what they blusteringly deny, and the day will come when, like him whose children they are, they will believe and tremble.

Lord, help me to read my own heart. Let me know my true state, and let that state be such as thou wilt approve.

ONE RAINY DAY

All the tediousness of the present life is but like one rainy day to an everlasting sunshine.

How readily, then, should we bear these short-lived troubles! They are but for a moment; just a passing shower, and then the sun will shine out forever. Time is nothing when compared with eternity. To a believer, this sorrowful life is like one drop of grief lost in a sea of glory, one speck of rain in a year of fair weather. These light and momentary afflictions are not worthy to be compared with the eternal bliss which awaits us.

THE TRUMPET AND THE PIPE

There is a time for the trumpet as well as the pipe.

We must sometimes sound an alarm; we should be traitors to men's souls and to our Master if we always piped to dulcet music. He who is always comforting his people will find no comfort when he is called to answer for it before his God another day. Many souls need Boanerges more than Barnabas, thunder more than dew. By many who think themselves great judges the trumpet discourse is judged to be too harsh, and the piper is commended for his pleasant strains; and yet the Lord may distribute the praise and the blame very differently.

My heart, be not thou always craving for soft music. Be willing to be startled and stimulated. Life is a conflict, and thou needest battle music to keep thee up to fighting pitch. Let those who dance with the world pay the pipers who play to them; as for thee, give thine ear to the King's trumpeters.

POISONED MEAT

If a man had poison mixed with his meat, although the excellence of his digestion or the strength of his constitution might bear him through, yet he would run great hazard.

Thus a soul may survive grave doctrinal error; it is possible for it to struggle out of the power of a strong dose of Popery, or Socinianism, or 'Modern Thought'; but it runs great risks, of a character so violent that no one should lightly venture upon them. Our safest course is to take heed what we hear, and partake of nothing which comes from doubtful quarters.

O my Lord, do thou feed me with the bread of life. Suffer me not to taste of Satan's dainties. I have no strength to spare. Forbid that I should test it by imbibing the deadly teachings of those who err from thy truth.

TASTE

Love maketh faith more operative; there is a knowledge by sight, and a knowledge by taste. A man may guess at the goodness of wine by the colour, but more by the taste; that is a more refreshing apprehension. Augustine prayeth, 'Lord, make me taste by love what I perceive by knowledge.' Surely, we are never sound in Christianity till all the light that we receive be turned into love.

It is so. Love comes to close dealings with truth, and gets a truer knowledge of it than any other grace. A hot iron, even though blunt, will penetrate further into a board than a cold tool, though it be sharp; and so love enters further into truth than mere thought or study can do. David would have us 'taste and see'; for the palate sees more into the essence of things than the eye can do; love discovers more than reason can ever know. That which love learns is also more useful than the cold notions of the brain, for it sets men working for Jesus, and leads them to follow him, and makes them willing to suffer for him. We have heard of some who could not dispute for their Lord, and yet they died for him, and were not such among the best of his followers? He who only knows truth in the light of it, is not worthy to be compared with the believer who receives truth in the love of it.

O Lord, let me never use thy gospel as a pillow for my head, but as a medicine for my heart. Do not suffer me to be content with mere knowing; cause me always to be deeply in love with thy word.

FAR OFF LOOKS SMALL

Look, as the stars, those vast globes of light, by reason of the distance between us and them, do seem but as so many spangles; so we have but a weak sight of things which are set at a great distance, and their operation on us is usually but small.

Hence the need of faith, by which things are brought near to us, and made to stand out in their reality. A far-off hell is the dread of no man, and a far-off heaven is scarce desired by anyone. God himself, while thought of as far away, is not feared or reverenced as he should be. If we did but use our thoughts upon the matter we should soon see that a mere span of time divides us from the eternal world, while the Lord our God is nearer to us than our souls are to our bodies. Strange that the brief time which intervenes between us and eternity should appear to the most of men to be so important, while eternity itself they regard as a trifling matter. They use the microscope to magnify the small concerns of time; O that they would use the telescope upon the vast matters of eternity! How differently would they order their lives with judgment felt to be at their doors! How would they seek to escape from infinite wrath, if they felt it to be nigh!

Lord, arouse me, and all around me, to a due estimate of eternal matters. Enable me to project my soul into the infinite. Break me free of this narrow present, and launch my soul upon the wide and open sea of the ages to come. Thou art in eternity, and let my soul even now dwell there with thee.

PLEADING THE HANDWRITING

We have a strong tie upon God, because he giveth us the promise, which is our ground of hope. Surely we may put his bonds in suit, and say, 'Thy handwriting is placed before thee, O Lord.'

We say among men—we have it in black and white, and there is no getting over it: a man's handwriting binds him. Now, we may be sure that the Lord will never deny his own writing, nor run back from a bond given under his own hand

and seal. Every promise of Scripture is a writing of God, which may be pleaded before him with this reasonable request, 'Do as thou hast said.' The Creator will not cheat his creature who depends upon his truth; and, far more, the heavenly Father will not break his word to his own child. 'Remember the word unto thy servant, on which thou hast caused me to hope', is most prevalent pleading. It is a double argument: it is thy *word*, wilt thou not keep it? Why hast thou spoken it if thou wilt not make it good? Thou hast caused me to hope in it, wilt thou disappoint the hope which thou hast thyself begotten in me?

How sure are thy promises, O my God. Forgive me that I ever doubt them, and give me more faith, that I may treat them as the blessings which they guarantee, even as men pass cheques and notes from hand to hand as if they were the gold they stand for.

KEEPING OUT THE COLD

A man that would keep out the cold in winter shutteth all his doors and windows, yet the wind will creep in, though he doth not leave any open hole for it.

We must leave no inlet for sin, but stop up every hole and cranny by which it can enter. There is need of great care in doing this, for when our very best is done, sin will find an entrance. During the bitter cold weather we list[1] the doors, put sandbags on the windows, draw curtains, and arrange screens, and yet we are made to feel that we live in a northern climate: in the same way must we be diligent to shut out sin, and we shall find abundant need to guard every point, for after we have done all, we shall, in one way or another, be made to feel that we live in a sinful world.

---

[1] To put a draught-excluding border around the edge of a door.

Well, what must we do? We must follow the measures which common prudence teaches us in earthly matters. We must drive out the cold by keeping up a good fire within. The presence of the Lord Jesus in the soul can so warm the heart that worldliness and sin will be expelled, and we shall be both holy and happy. The Lord grant it, for Jesus' sake.

THE TRAITOR WITHIN

A garrison is not free from danger while it hath an enemy lodged within.

You may bolt all your doors, and fasten all your windows, but if the thieves have placed even a little child within doors, who can draw the bolts for them, the house is still unprotected. All the sea outside a ship cannot do it damage till the water enters within and fills the hold. Hence, it is clear, our greatest danger is from within. All the devils in hell and tempters on earth could do us no injury if there were no corruption in our nature. The sparks will fall harmlessly if there is no tinder. Alas, our heart is our greatest enemy: this is the little home-born thief.

Lord, save me from that evil man, myself.

FIRE FROM HEAVEN

The heathens counted that the fire which was enkindled by a sunbeam was more fit and pure for their altars than a coal taken from a common hearth.

Herein they blindly stumbled upon the image of a great spiritual truth. The right fire for a preacher of the gospel is fire from God himself. All else defiles the sacrifice, and is sure, sooner or later, to die out. When we speak *for* God it is a blessed thing to speak *through* God. Excitement arising from animal spirits is a poor substitute for the Holy Ghost. Far worse is the stimulus of wine or strong drink, which is an absolute profanation of holy things and a presumptuous provocation of God. To attempt to serve God under the influence of the 'mocker' is to mock the Most Holy One.

To preach under the stimulus of anger is horrible, and to do so from motives of ambition is equally so. Nadab and Abihu died before the Lord for offering strange fire, and this should be a perpetual warning to all who bear the vessels of the Lord.

O fire of God, touch our lips, yea, burn in our hearts. Let no strange fire come near us: neither from the furnace of anger, nor from the flames of ambitious desire, nor from the flash of carnal excitement may we ever borrow our fires, when we wait at thine altar, O Lord.

PETER MARTYR'S ILLUSTRATION

Celius Secundus Curio hath a notable passage in the *Life of Galiacius Caracciolas*, as to the occasion of his conversion. One John Francis Casarta, who was enlightened with the knowledge of the gospel, was very urgent with this nobleman, his cousin, to come and hear Peter Martyr, who then preached at Naples. One day, by much entreaty, he was drawn to hear him, not so much with a desire to learn and profit as out of curiosity.

Peter Martyr was then opening the First Epistle to the Corinthians, and showing how much the judgment of the natural understanding is mistaken in things spiritual. Among other things, he used this similitude:

If a man, riding in an open country, should, afar off, see men and women dancing together, and should not hear their music, according to which they dance and tread out their measures, he would think them to be a company of fairies or madmen, appearing in such various motions and antic postures; but if he came nearer, and heard the musical notes, according to which they exactly danced, he would find that to be art which before he thought madness. The same happeneth to him who at first sees a change of life, company, and fashions in his former companions; he thinketh they are brain-sick and foolish; but when he cometh more intimately to weigh the thing, and what an exact harmony there is between such a life and conversation and the motions of God's Holy Spirit and the directions of his word, he findeth that to be the highest reason which before he judged madness and folly.

This similitude stuck in the mind of the noble marquis (as he was wont to relate it to his familiar friends), that ever afterward he wholly applied his mind to the search of the truth and the practice of holiness, and left all his honours and vast possessions for a poor life, in the profession of the gospel, at Geneva.

This needs not a word from us. If ungodly men could only hear the music to which we dance, they would dance too.

THE INWARD REGISTRAR

If conscience speaketh not, it writeth; for it is not only a witness, but a register, and a book of record: 'The sin of Judah is written with a pen of iron, and the point of a diamond' (Jer. 17:1). We know not what conscience writeth, being occupied and taken up with carnal vanities, but we shall know hereafter, when the books are opened (Rev. 20:12). Conscience keepeth a diary, and sets down everything. This book, though it be in the sinner's keeping, cannot be razed and blotted out. Well, then, a sleepy conscience will not always sleep; if we suffer it not to awaken here, it will awaken

in hell; for the present it sleepeth in many, in regard of motion,
check, or smiting, but not in regard of notice and observation.

Let those who forget their sins take note of this. There is a chiel[1] within you taking notes, and he will publish all where all will hear it. Never say, 'Nobody will see me', for you will see yourself, and your conscience will turn king's evidence against you.

What a volume Mr Recorder Conscience has written already! How many blotted pages he has in store, to be produced upon my trial. O thou who alone canst erase this dreadful handwriting, look on me in mercy, as I now look on thee by faith.

STUDY PROPORTIONS

A drop of honey is not enough to sweeten a hogshead of vinegar.

Under great troubles we need great grace to console us. We must seek the special aid of the Holy Spirit, and be more diligent and fervent in prayer, for the eternal consolation of the covenant. A proportion must be maintained: as he who sets out upon a long journey takes all the more money with him, so, in prospect of a great trial, we should seek extraordinary grace. The heavier the wagon, the more horses the farmer puts into the team; and so, the more difficult our service, the more grace must we bring to bear upon it.

Lord, when we have much sorrow, let us taste more of thy love, and the vinegar will become sweet wine. If now thou dost try us severely, be pleased also to comfort us richly.

[1] Scots: a child; a young man.

THE HEN WHICH DOES NOT SIT ON HER EGGS

A sudden glance at truth without meditation upon it bringeth nothing to perfection; as a hen that soon leaveth her nest never hatcheth her chicks.

How can she? Patience is needed, and the quiet self-denial by which she renders up the warmth of her heart, otherwise her eggs will lie as dead as stones. The value of truth will never be known by those who look at it and hurry on: they must brood over it, and cover it with their heart's love, or it will never become living truth to their souls. We must apply ourselves to a doctrine, giving our whole soul and heart to it, or we shall miss the blessing. Herein is wisdom.

Lord, when I hear a sermon, or read in a good book, let me not be as the partridge which sitteth on eggs and hatcheth them not; but make me to see life and power in thy word, and to rejoice over it as one that findeth great spoil.

THE THIEF AND THE CANDLE

A thief is always desirous to have the candles put out.

His trade is best carried on in the dark. This is the reason why Satan is so dead set against faithful preachers and teachers: he can rob the church, and plunder souls so much better when the light of the gospel is withdrawn. How much better could the Pope pick our purses with his purgatory, indulgences, and relics, if the gospel light were quenched among us! The old-fashioned doctrines of grace are the candles of the Lord, and we must keep these well alight among the people, or we shall soon find the Romish thieves busy among us.

This is one reason why creeds and catechisms are so much detested by men of the modern school: these candles are not to their mind, for they prevent their robbing us of the treasures of divine truth.

Lord, I bless thee for the light, and I pray that I may not quench even the tiniest taper by which thou dost enlighten me.

AUGUSTINE'S STORY

Take heed of giving way to sin. The heart that was easily troubled before, when once it is inured to sin, loseth all its sensitiveness and tenderness, and what seemed intolerable at first grows into a delight. Alypius, St Augustine's friend, first abhorred the bloody spectacles of the gladiators, but gave himself leave, through the importunity of friends, to be present for once. He would not so much as open his eyes at first; but at length, when the people shouted, he gave himself liberty to see, and then not only beheld the spectacles with delight, but drew others; to behold what himself once loathed.

The story has had its counterpart in thousands of instances. Men who shuddered at the sight of a dead bird have, by familiarity with cruelty, come to commit murder without compunction. Those who sipped half a glass of wine have come to drink by the gallon. Stanch Protestants have given way to some little form and ceremony, and become more Popish than the Romanists themselves. There is no safety if we venture an inch over the boundary line; indeed, little allowances are more dangerous than greater compliances, since conscience does not receive a wound, and yet the man is undone, and falls by little and little.

Come, my soul, leave sin altogether. Do not give Sodom so much as a look, nor take from it so much as a thread. Do not set a foot within her doors, for God abhors the abode of sin, and would have his people refrain their foot from it.

SLEEPING BY WATERFALLS

Things to which we are used do not work upon us; we are not much moved with them. Custom maketh men sleep quietly by the falls of great waters, where much noise is; and some parts of the body grow callous, brawny, dry, and dead, as the labourer's hand and the traveller's heel, by much use.

So doth the conscience gradually lose its force. At first, like a cataract, its great roar astounds the soul, and effectually prevents its slumbers of carnal security; but by and by its noise is scarcely heard, and men are even lulled to sleep by its sound. Now, this is to be dreaded exceedingly, for it is the forerunner of doom. No more warnings are heard, because sentence has gone forth, and the man's destruction is sealed.

Even on a smaller scale, it is a serious thing to have conscience lose its tenderness. Christian men, by association with the world, and by a want of thorough consideration, may come to do with impunity things which would shock them if their consciences were in a healthy state. It is dangerous for a steam-engine when the tell-tale[1] does not act; and no one knows what mischief may come through the failure of the soul's indicator. We wish to know what is evil that we may avoid it; and it is a serious calamity when the warning faculty has become dulled and silent through continuance in sin. Better far to live in perpetual anxiety to be right, than to remain at ease while doing wrong.

Lord, make my conscience tender as the apple of my eye. Awaken it, and keep it awake.

---

[1] An indicator or recording device used to monitor an engine.

THE DECOY

As a fowler catches many birds by one decoy, a bird of the same feather, so God bringeth us to himself by men of the same nature, and subject to the same temptations and the same commands. He attracts us to himself by men with whom we may have ordinary and visible commerce, and not by angels, that might affright us. He calls us by our fellow-creatures, who are concerned in the message as much as we are; men that know the heart of a man by experience, and know our prejudices and temptations.

In this choice of means, wisdom and condescension are equally manifest, for which we are bound to render grateful adoration. Blessed be God that he calls men by men, adopting thus the kindest and most effectual mode of dealing with us. We should also learn wisdom, and receive practical guidance from this act of God: when we would win our fellow-men for Jesus let us show ourselves to be near of kin to them. If, by a lofty and distant bearing, we act as if we belonged to another race, we shall be poor decoy-birds. The poor bird fascinates its like by being of their kith and kin, and we must capture hearts for Jesus by showing that we are of like passions with them, and love them much. Love men to Jesus—that is the art of soul-winning.

Blessed Lord Jesus, thou didst thus win my heart, for I had never loved thee and trusted thee if I had not perceived thee to be touched with a feeling of my infirmity. Thy sympathetic manhood draws my manhood to thee, and I am won to thy Father by thy brotherly love.

A DISLOCATED BONE

When a bone is out of joint, the longer the setting is forborne the greater will the pain of the patient be; yea, it may be so long neglected that no skill nor art can set it right again. So it is in the cure of a wounded spirit and a bleeding conscience.

Fly, then, O wounded one, to the Lord thy Saviour, at once. When delays are dangerous as well as painful, who would linger? For the most part, injured persons are anxious to be carried to the surgeon at once: they dread the inflammatory action which may be set up in the injured parts. In spiritual wounds the fever of fear soon heats into despair, unless the divine Healer is fetched in. When Jesus comes he suffers no delay; speedily he healeth the broken in heart, and bindeth up their wounds. Unbelief pulls off the bandages, and presumption declares that the limb is as sound as ever; but humble faith waits only upon the Lord, and cries to him to make haste for her deliverance.

O Lord, heal me speedily, I beseech thee.

DRINKING TO DROWN CARE

He is a mountebank who strives to make men forget their spiritual sorrows instead of leading them to the true cure. This is like a man in debt who drinks to drown his thoughts; but this neither pays the debt nor postpones the reckoning.

When conscience is uneasy, it is foolish as well as wicked to attempt to smother its cries with worldly merriment. Nay, let us hear it patiently. If we be in debt let us know it, and set about meeting our liabilities like honest men; but to burn the ledger and discharge the clerk is a madman's way of going to work. O soul, be true to thyself. Face thine own case, however bad it may be; for refusing to know and consider the sure facts will not alter or improve them. He is a cruel doctor who tells the afflicted patient that he ails nothing, and thus sets him for the time at his ease, at the terrible cost of future disease, rendered incurable by delay.

Lord, bring me to the bar of my conscience now, lest I stand condemned at thy bar of judgment hereafter.

THE HEN AND HER EGGS

To be careless of the degree of our grace makes way for the loss of the whole. Christians are like a hen when many eggs are taken out of the nest; as long as one or two remaineth, she taketh no notice of it, and forsaketh not the nest. Be not thus foolish, but consider whether there be not abatement of some degree of your grace, though a little may remain with you still. Content not yourselves that all is not lost because something remains; but seek to have grace in as great a proportion as formerly.

A miser would not be content to miss a part of his gold because a pile still remained; the woman in the parable was not easy because she had many pieces of money left; neither should we be comfortable if a grain of grace is lost by us, even though we may be well assured that a saving portion still remains. Why should we lose any measure of grace? We shall need it all. At our strongest we are weak enough. We have never one whit of love to spare; what a pity that we should lose a fragment of it

No man is more sure of being poor than he who loses his estate insensibly. You may stop a leak if you perceive it, but what can save a ship which sinks imperceptibly? We may heal a wound, but when life oozes away in secret who can save us?

Lord, help us to perceive, to lament, and to recover the least loss in gracious matters.

THE LITTLE WISP

Little sticks set the great ones on fire, and a little wisp is often used to enkindle a great block of wood.

Thus have we known persons of small talent and position influence their superiors by their zeal. Though themselves able to do but little, they have been full of fervour, and so have ventured further than the more solid and prudent felt at first inclined to do. Some of us have had to thank God for our weaker brethren who have been more eager and venturesome than we were: these wisps and bunches of firewood, though they could not keep up the fire, came in very opportunely to give the flames a start. Even rash suggestions have their value. Fools who are all alive may do good service to wise men, when they are sluggish and slow. It is right to get good out of all good men. When we meet with persons of little substance but of considerable kindling power, let us put them together like matches and splinters of wood, for the commencement of an enterprise, and when we find others to be like heavy old logs, let us put them to use when the flame has taken good hold, for if they once get thoroughly alight they will sustain the fire long after the straw and the shavings have passed away.

Reader, which are you, a wisp or a log? In either case there is a place for you, and be it your ambition, in some way or other, to be consumed for your Lord's service.

MATTOCKS[1] OF GOLD

To prefer our own ease, quiet, profit, before the glory of God, is madness. Would it not be insanity to dig for iron with mattocks of gold?

Our author means that it must always be unreasonable to make the means greater than the end. When man lives for the glory of God he spends his strength for something far beyond

---

[1] An agricultural tool shaped like a pickaxe, with an arched blade and a chisel edge as the ends of the head.

himself in value, and thus he acts as reasonably as when men dig for gold with mattocks of iron; but when an immortal mind spends itself upon decaying objects, such as transient gain and pleasure, it is occupied beneath itself, and is like a mattock of gold used in searching for base metal. It is a misapplication of forces for the nobler to spend itself upon the meaner. Men do not usually care to spend a pound in the hope of getting back a groat and no more, and yet, when the soul is given up for the sake of worldly gain, the loss is greater still, and not even the groat remains.

Lord, arouse me from the folly of grovelling among earthly things. Make my soul reasonable, that it may devote itself to worthy pursuits; and what can be so worthy of me as thyself! Thou art above all, and infinitely better than all; to thee I devote my whole being. O help me to live alone for thy glory. Thy grace I need; let thy grace come to me with power.

TREES MARKED FOR THE AXE

To fix our confidence upon a dying world is folly. It is as if we were building our nests when the tree is being cut down, or decorating our cabin when the ship is likely to be dashed in pieces or is already sinking.

Is it a time to drive a trade for ourselves when we are just leaving earth, and hope soon to be in heaven? Yet too many among professors are doing this. Their hearts are set upon their money, they build their nest in the golden grove; or they are wrapt up in their children, and, as it were, nestle down among those who spring up as willows by the watercourses. The axe is laid at the root of all earthly comforts, and, therefore, those who are taught of God soar aloft, and make their eyries[1] on the Rock of Ages.

[1] A large nest (of an eagle or other bird of prey), built high in a tree or on a cliff.

What is our friend doing whose eyes are now scanning this page? Where is your heart? What is its dear delight and joy? Is it of earth? Then be sure that to earth it will return. Is your joy a thing of heaven? Then alone is it stable and sure.

My soul, the world is passing away, set not thy love upon it. The ship is sinking, care little about the little luxuries of the berth which thou hast for a while occupied in it. Up and away! This is not thy rest. See, before thine eyes the fashion of this world passeth away; look to eternity and to thy God, for there alone is solid bliss.

THE SPIRE

The best of God's people have abhorred themselves. Like the spire of a steeple, minimus in summo, *we are least at the highest. David, a king, was yet like a weaned child.*

Manton is not very clear about the steeple, but he means that the higher a spire rises toward heaven the smaller it becomes, and thus the more elevated are our spirits the less shall we be in our own esteem. Great thoughts of self and great grace never go together. Self-consciousness is a sure sign that there is not much depth of grace. He who overvalues himself undervalues his Saviour. He who abounds in piety is sure to be filled with humility. Light things, such as straws and feathers, are borne aloft; valuable goods keep their places, and remain below, not because they are chained or riveted there, but by virtue of their own weight. When we begin to talk of our perfection, our imperfection is getting the upper hand. The more full we become of the presence of the Lord the more shall we sink in our own esteem, even as laden vessels sink down to their water-mark, while empty ships float aloft.

Lord, make and keep me humble. Lift me nearer and nearer to heaven, and then I shall grow less and less in my own esteem.

CHAFF AND WHEAT CONTRASTED

Light chaff is blown up and down by every wind, when solid grain hitcheth in, and resteth on the floor where it is winnowed.

Constancy is one of the evidences of worth. Those who change their religion generally need to be changed by their religion before they will have any religion worth the having. Fickle professors are ready to be the prey of every new teacher; his breath is enough to blow them according to his pleasure. They are everything by turns, and nothing long. Depend upon it, he knows nothing of the preciousness of truth, who is ready to stand and deliver to every footpad[1] of heresy who challenges him: he who has about him doctrines which he esteems to be a treasure will fight for them, and send the robber to the rightabouts.[2]

We know one of whom we usually ask, whenever we see him, *'What are you now?'* Yet are there some good points about him, and he has a mind open to conviction, too open a great deal to be a fit casket for the jewels of truth. We have seen a child in a field of flowers, filling its little hand eagerly, and then dropping its posy, not for better but for other flowers. Many professors are such children.

A heart which is fickle in its love is not likely to make a marriage with the truth. Lord, fix my heart in thy truth, and never let it be removed.

---

[1] A highwayman operating on foot rather than riding a horse.
[2] The opposite facing direction.

THE DEATH-BLOW OF POPERY

When Dr Day discoursed with Stephen Gardiner concerning free justification by Christ, saith he, 'O, Mr Doctor, open that gap to the people, and we are undone!' The more gospel there is discovered, the more Antichrist is discovered. Free grace puts the foundation of Popery out of course.

The doubtful doctrine of many Protestants is a greater encouragement to Romanism than all her own finery can bring to her. Rome has gained more by Oxford than by all her cardinals. The glorious doctrines of grace are the great guns with which the Papal galleys may be blown out of the water. Grace is a word which is as obnoxious to Popery as the name of Jesus to the devil. Reptiles cannot bear salt, nor can Jesuits and priests endure sovereign grace. Their trade is gone when salvation is free. Their honour is gone when Christ is all. When people think much of Jesus and his redemption, they are sure to think little of priests and their fiddle-faddle. It was not Luther's arguments, but Luther's plain teaching of justification by faith, which shook the corner-stone of the Vatican. If men are saved by believing, they are not likely to waste money on purgatory pick-purse, nor on any other of the papal schemes for enriching the Church. Let us then keep gospel truth always to the front, for in our own hearts the best preservative against error is a hearty acceptance of the living Christ and his own sure gospel.

PEARLS AND SWINE

Pearls do not lose their worth though swine trample upon them.

Scriptural truth is none the less worthy to be held and proclaimed because foolish and depraved men pervert it to their own destruction. A knife is a very useful article; and, though some have committed suicide by its means, it is no reason why knives should be discarded. The doctrines of grace are pearls even after Antinomians have turned them over. Justification by faith is the crown-jewel of the gospel, though hypocrites abuse it. Every truth is perverted by polluted minds, but this is no reason for our renouncing what God has revealed; rather is it a strong argument for adorning the doctrine of our Saviour in all things.

My heart, see thou to it that the doctrines of grace are honoured at thy hands. Since so many pour contempt upon them, do thou hold them in high esteem, and by thy life make them to be esteemed by others.

PERSONAL WITNESS

A report of a report is a cold thing and of small value; but a report of what we have witnessed and experienced ourselves comes warmly upon men's hearts.

So a mere formal description of faith and its blessings falls flat on the ear; but when a sincere believer tells of his own experience of the Lord's faithfulness, it has a great charm about it. We like to hear the narrative of a journey from the traveller himself. In a court of law they will have no hearsay evidence. Tell us, says the judge, not what your neighbour said, but what you saw yourself. Personal evidence of the power of grace has a wonderfully convincing force upon the conscience. 'I sought the Lord, and he heard me', is better argument than all the Butler's *Analogies* that will ever be written, good as they are in their place.

Lord, make me ever prompt to bear my personal witness for thee, and eager to magnify thy grace, of which I have been made a partaker. Never permit me to be ashamed of thy salvation, but make me openly to proclaim thy matchless grace to me.

FREE, YET NOT WITHOUT LABOUR

There is a difference between merit and means; a schoolmaster may teach a child gratis, and yet the boy must himself take pains to get his learning. There is, moreover, a difference between cause and effect, and the mere order of coming. Mercy is never obtained but in the use of means: wisdom's dole is dispensed at wisdom's gate (Prov. 8:34).

This is a very important remark, and tends to screen from the charge of legality those who earnestly exhort men to gospel duties. There is no merit in seeking the Lord; but we may not hope to find him without it. Prayer does not deserve an answer, and yet we are to pray without ceasing, neither may we hope to have if we refuse to ask. The cup must be held under the flowing fountain or it will not be filled, yet the cup does not create the water or purchase it. All the exertion which a man makes in running the heavenly race will not merit the prize of eternal life; but it would not therefore be right for him to lie in bed and hope to win it. The Father freely gives the bread of heaven without money and without price, and yet Jesus bade men labour for it.

Lord, thou hast taught me to see a great distinction between the idea of meriting thy favour and the truth that earnest effort is necessary to salvation. Help me to work as if my salvation depended on my working, and then keep me trusting in thee alone, as if I worked not at all. Thou givest me all things, the end and the means to that end. That measure of holy labour which I put forth is first wrought in me, and therefore would I be doubly diligent. I would work because thou workest in me, and strive for victory because thou givest me both the strength and the crown.

BEATEN SPICES

Spices are most fragrant when burnt and bruised, so have saving graces their chiefest fragrancy in hard times. The pillar that conducted the Israelites appeared as a cloud by day, but as fire by night. The excellency of faith is beclouded till it be put upon a thorough trial.

Herein lies one of the benefits of affliction, it fetches out latent sweetness and light. Certain herbs yield no smell till they are trodden on, and certain characters do not reveal their excellence till they are tried. The developing power of tribulation is very great: faith, patience, resignation, endurance, and steadfastness are by far the best seen when put to the test by adversity, pain, and temptation. God has created nothing in vain in the new creation any more than in the old, hence one of the sweet necessities of trial is to bring forth and use those precious graces which else had been unemployed. God is not glorified by unused graces, for these lie hidden and bring him no honour; may we not, therefore, rejoice in tribulation, because it fetches out our secret powers, and enables us to give glory to the Lord whom we love? Yes, blessed be the pestle which bruises us, and the mortar in which we lie to be beaten into fragrance. Blessed be the burning coals which liberate our sweet odours and raise them up to heaven like pillars of smoke. Can we not say this? Then it is time we could, and perhaps our present affliction has been sent for that very end—that we may learn the way of complete consecration, and be made perfect through suffering.

STARS AND THEIR STRANGE NAMES

As the astronomers call the glorious stars bulls, snakes, dragons, and other strange things, so do ungodly men miscall the most shining and glorious graces. Zeal is fury; strictness, nicety; and patience, folly!

So far as the astronomers are concerned, the names which they give to the constellations are no dishonour to the lamps of heaven; it were well if the other misnomers were equally indifferent. Ill names are, however, a kind of persecution, a part of the 'cruel mockings' which are employed by the graceless. Evil comes of it, too, over and above the grieving of pious men, for weak minds avoid zeal when it is stigmatized as fanaticism, and many despise patience when it is maligned as meanness of spirit. Since the weak-minded are so many, this is a great evil which every man who loves his fellows should endeavour to correct. There is a great deal in a name after all. A great falsehood may be wrapped up in a short word, and a current misnomer may produce widespread evil. Let us call things by their right names, and stand up for all that is lovely and of good repute. Why should men bear false witness against the virtues, and vilify the fruits of the Spirit? If they will do so, let us not be so cowardly as to be silent; let us speak out boldly, and avow our hearty appreciation of that which the world despises. We will call the stars stars, and let the world call them bears, and crabs, and scorpions, if they will.

THE CHILD WANTING A KNIFE

God knoweth what is best for us. Like foolish children, we desire a knife; but, like a wise father, he giveth us bread.

It would be a most unfatherly thing for a man to give his son that which would cause his death. The largest generosity must refuse some requests when it is a higher kindness to withhold than to bestow. The limit which is set to prayer—namely, that if we ask anything *in accordance with God's will* he heareth us, is just such a limit as love on God's part *must* fix, and as prudence on our part must approve. Would we have the Lord act according to our ignorance or according to his own wisdom? Shall our uninstructed self become the arbiter of God's providence? Assuredly no Christian in his senses would propose such an arrangement. If it could be proposed and carried out it would place us in daily jeopardy, and work, at its very best, most sadly to our loss.

If we could have our own will absolutely it would be wise not to have it, but to divest ourselves of the horrible privilege. How much more restful are our minds, now that we know that our Father arranges all things, than could possibly be the case if the responsibility of management rested with ourselves. Like Phaethon, who sought to drive the chariot of the sun, we should soon perish by our own folly if the reins of providence were placed in our feeble hands. It is better far that the rule should be, 'not as I will, but as thou wilt.'

Lord, give me not what I ask, but what I should ask, yea, what thou seest to be most for thy glory.

THE STRIPPED STALK

'All flesh is as grass, and all the glory of man as the flower of grass.'
Many times the flower is gone when the stalk remaineth; so man
ofttimes seeth all that he hath been gathering a long time soon
dissipated by the breath of providence, and he, like a withered,
rotten stalk, liveth scorned and neglected.

Alas, for such an one! What is the daffodil without its golden crown, or the crocus without its cup of sunshine? Such is man without the object of his life. What is the thorn without its rose, or the tree without its leaves, or the wood without the birds of song? Such is man without the comforts and joys of his being. It is ill to exist when life is dead, to eat and drink when the taste has departed, to move among men when the heart is broken: yet are there thousands in this condition: a blight is on them, their flower and glory are withered, and they are as those who go down into the pit. So have we seen a tree smitten by lightning standing still among its fellows, but no longer adding to the verdure of the forest. It has been, and this is all that we can say of it, for its continuance is but in semblance. Who has not seen men in a like condition? Alas! for those who have no hereafter when this present faileth them, for they fall indeed, and wither with a vengeance.

Blessed is the man who lives in God, for no such withering shall happen to him. God is his crown and glory, the flower of his true being, and God cannot fail him. He shall be as a tree planted by the rivers of water, and not so much as his leaf shall wither.

Lord, make me to live on thy word, which abideth forever, and then when flesh, like grass, shall fade, I shall find eternal joy in thee.

THE SWORD IN A CHILD'S HAND

Sometimes truth is like a keen weapon in a child's hand, it maketh little impression because it is weakly wielded.

Do not therefore blame the truth, but the weak hand. In many cases of controversy the apparent victory of error has been due to the unfitness of the warrior who championed truth. It may for some men be their truest service to the good cause to leave it in stronger hands. We do not send women and children to our battle-fields, nor do we march our recruits to war before they have been trained; neither should we expect raw youths and timid maidens to put on armour at once and face the adversaries of the gospel. It has happened times without number that a blustering infidel has posed a new convert with his sophistical arguments, and then he has shouted as if he had gained a triumph over the truth; whereas his boasting only proved the weakness of his cause, or the childishness of his own mind. He who could crow so loudly over so slender a success must be conscious of inherent feebleness, and therefore he is astonished and elated at the semblance of victory.

Let us all pray to be strengthened, that our inner life, growing day by day, may reach a fulness of stature and a firmness of strength worthy of the heavenly weapon which the Lord has put into our hand. O sacred Spirit, make us strong in the Lord and in the power of his might!

CAESAR KILLED WITH BODKINS

Not only do great sins ruin the soul, but lesser faults will do the same. Dallying with temptation leads to sad consequences. Caesar was killed with bodkins.[1]

A dagger aimed at the heart will give as deadly a wound as a huge two-handed sword, and a little sin unrepented of will be as fatal as a gross transgression. Brutus and Cassius and the rest of the conspirators could not have more surely ended Caesar's life with spears than they did with daggers. Death can hide in a drop, and ride in a breath of air. Our greatest dangers lie hidden in little things. Milton represents thousands of evil spirits as crowded into one hall; and truly the least sin may be

[1] Daggers.

a very Pandemonium, in which a host of evils may be concealed—a populous hive of mischiefs, each one storing death.

Believer, though thou be a little Caesar in thine own sphere, beware of the bodkins of thine enemies. Watch and pray, lest thou fall by little and little. Lord, save me from sins which call themselves little.

A STITCH IN TIME

He who keeps a house in constant repair prevents all fear of its falling to ruin; by stopping each hole and chink as he finds it he keeps off greater mischief.

We shall do well to use the same economy with our spiritual nature. No great decays of spirit will occur if we look to each of our graces, and lament the first sign of declension in any one of them. A loose stone here, and a fallen tile there, and a rotting timber in a third place, will soon bring on a total ruin to a tenement, but the hand of diligence maintains the fabric. Thus must we watch our spiritual house, lest we fall by little and little. Are there no repairs wanted at this time? Does not my soul show a number of flaws and decays? Come, my heart, look about thee, and pray the Lord to restore that which has fallen.

BUCKETS IN A WELL

The life of sin and the life of a sinner are like two buckets in a well—if the one goeth up, the other must come down. If sin liveth, the sinner must die.

It is only when sin dies that a man begins truly to live. Yet we cannot persuade our neighbours that it is so, for their hearts are bound up in their sins, and they think themselves most alive when they can give fullest liberty to their desires. They raise up their sins, and so sink themselves. If they could be persuaded of the truth, they would send the bucket of sin to the very bottom that their better selves might rise into eternal salvation.

Lord, make my fellow-men wise, that they may do this, and teach me the same lesson. I would fain sink every evil and selfish desire that my heart may rise to holiness, to heaven, to thee.

THE UPRIGHT COLUMN

A straight pillar, the more you lay upon it, the straighter it is, and the more stable; but that which is crooked boweth under the superincumbent weight: so the more God loadeth the godly the more doth he hold fast his integrity, while, on the other hand, the more the Lord casteth in upon carnal men, the more is their spirit perverted.

A little leaning from the right line is a serious thing: uprightness alone is safety. As our author well says, an upright column will bear anything; it would be hard with any known force to crush an erect pillar. So, when a man is upright before God, neither the weight of good or of ill can overthrow him: he stands in his integrity alike under prosperity and adversity, under fawnings or frownings. When the foundations of the earth are removed, he bears up the pillars thereof. He is like Mount Zion, which can never be moved, but abideth forever. 'Let uprightness and integrity preserve me': these are a sure preservative in the day of trial.

The man who gives way to leanings or inclinations out of the straight line is never safe. It is only necessary to supply sufficient pressure and he falls. Whether he be loaded with wealth or pressed with poverty, he will come to the ground with equal certainty in due time. He is out of the perpendicular, and he must fall sooner or later.

O Lord, give me to stand before thee in perfect uprightness of heart! Take from me any inclination to the right hand or to the left, and establish me upon the eternal basis of thy grace, for Jesus' sake. Upright Lord, thou alone canst set me upright, and keep me so; hearken to my prayer, I beseech thee.

THE MISER'S BAG OF MONEY

Affection is a great friend to memory; men remember what they care for: an old man will not forget where he laid his bag of gold. Delight and love are always renewing and reviving their object upon our thoughts. David often asserteth his delight in the law, and because of this delight it was always in his thoughts (Psa. 119:97). 'O how love I thy law! It is my meditation all the day.'

By this, then, we may judge ourselves whether we have a true and lively love to God and his kingdom. If from day to day we have no thought of him or of his ways, we may be sure that our affection to him, if it be sincere, is assuredly by no means fervent. A man hath little love to his espoused if he thinks of others more than of her. Where the thoughts fly, there doth the heart lie. Not that we can be always thinking of divine things, for we could not perform the duties of our calling if we gave no thought to them, and especially in certain pursuits of life the mind must for the time be concentrated upon the work in hand; but still our mind must be ready to fly to Jesus as soon as the pressure is removed. Love will break over all laws, and rules, and engrossments to have a word with its beloved, and so will the soul do when Jesus is truly its delight. It will fly to revel in his charms as the miser hastens to count his money.

Come, my heart, take thyself to task! Is it not true that if thou wert warmer thy memory would be more retentive? Be penitent, then, because thou art convicted of coolness to thy Well-beloved. Thy frequent forgetfulness of him proves the slackness of thy love.

STORY OF THE KNIGHT

Thuanus reporteth of Ludovicus Marsacus, a knight of France, when he was led, with other martyrs that were bound with cords, to execution, and he for his dignity was not bound, he cried, 'Give me my chains, too; let me be a knight of the same order.'

Certainly, it is an honour to be made vile for God; David purposed to abound in such vileness (2 Sam. 6: 22). Shame for Christ's sake is an honour no more to be declined than the highest dignity a mortal man can wear. Among the early Christians the relatives of martyrs were a sort of aristocracy, and the martyrs themselves were regarded as the nobility of the church. We need a spice of the same spirit at this day. A true believer should tremble when the world commends him, but he should feel complimented when it utterly despises him.

What do we suffer, after all? The most of us are but feather-bed soldiers. Our ways are strewn with roses compared with those who endured hardness in the olden time. We are poor and mean successors of noble ancestors—ennobled by their supreme sufferings. If we cannot reach their superior dignity, nor hope to wear the ruby crown of martyrdom, at least let us not shun such glory as may be obtainable, but accept with cheerful patience whatever of opprobrium this worthless world may honour us with.

BERNARD'S CHARITY

When Bernard chanced to espy a poor man meanly apparelled, he would say to himself, 'Truly, Bernard, this man hath more patience beneath his cross than thou hast'; but if he saw a rich man delicately clothed, then he would say, 'It may be that this man, under his delicate clothing, hath a better soul than thou hast under thy religious habit!'

This showed an excellent charity! Oh, that we could learn it! It is easy to think evil of all men, for there is sure to be some fault about each one which the least discerning may readily discover; but it is far more worthy of a Christian, and shows much more nobility of soul, to spy out the good in each fellow-believer. This needs a larger mind as well as a better heart, and hence it should be a point of honour to practise ourselves in it till we obtain an aptitude for it. Any simpleton might be set to sniff out offensive odours; but it would require a scientific man to bring to us all the fragrant essences and rare perfumes which lie hid in field and garden. Oh, to learn the science of Christian charity! It is an art far more to be esteemed than the most lucrative of human labours. This choice art of love is the true alchemy. Charity toward others, abundantly practised, would be the death of envy and the life of fellowship, the overthrow of self and the enthronement of grace.

Charity, be thou my classics, my poetry, my science, my music, for thou art more to be desired than all these. Thou art a Godlike thing, and I would be filled with thee.

A SWORD NOT TO BE JUDGED BY THE BELT

We do not judge a sword to be good merely because it hangs by a golden belt, or because it is set in a jewelled hilt.

Neither is a doctrine to be valued because a fine orator delivers it in gorgeous speech with glittering words. A lie is none the better for being bespangled with poetic phrases and high-sounding periods. Yet half our people forget this, and glittering oratory fascinates them. Alas, poor simpletons!

The same blunders are made about men, who should ever be esteemed according to their native worth, and not according to their position and office. What mistakes we should make if we considered all the hangers-on of great men to be themselves great, or all the followers of good men to be themselves necessarily good. Alas! the Lord himself had his Judas, and to this day swords of brittle metal hang at the golden girdle of his church. A man is not a saint because he occupies a saintly office, or repeats saintly words.

No; the test of a sword's goodness is to be found in battle. Will its edge turn in the fray, or will it cut through a coat of mail? Will our faith bear affliction? Will it stand us in good stead when we are hand to hand with the enemy? Will it avail us in the dying hour? If not, we may suspend it on the glittering belt of great knowledge, and hold it by the jewelled hilt of a high profession; but woe unto us!

Lord, give me the true Jerusalem blade of childlike faith in thee, and may I never rest content with a mere imitation thereof.

THE MOON ECLIPSED ONLY AT THE FULL

The moon is never eclipsed but when it is at the full. Certainly God's people are then in most danger.

When all goes well with them in house and field, in basket and in store, then should they look lest they be full and forget the Lord, and so become eclipsed. For the world to come between us and our Lord is very easy but very terrible. When all is apparently prosperous as to soul matters, and neither doubt, nor fear, nor temptation comes in, then also should the heart look well to its bearings lest at this very moment some evil should interpose between God and the soul, and darkness should be the fearful result.

Remember this, dear reader: eclipses happen at the full moon. Look to thyself, then, in thy moments of greatest happiness and peace, for then is the time of peril.

> Whene'er becalmed I lie,
>   And storms forbear to toss;
> Be Thou, dear Lord, still nigh.
>   Lest I should suffer loss.
> Far more the treacherous calm I dread,
> Than tempests thundering overhead.

EAGLES AND FLIES

Walk worthy of God, who hath called you unto his kingdom (1 Thess. 2:12). Live as kings, commanding your spirits, judging your souls to be above ordinary pursuits. It is not for eagles to catch flies. As of old it was said, 'Cogita te Caesarem esse?'—'Remember that thou art Caesar', so say we to each believer, 'Remember that thou shalt one day be a king with God in glory, and therefore walk becomingly.'

This is important teaching, and much needed in these days. Many who declare themselves to be eagles spend the most of their lives in hawking for flies: we even hear of professing Christians frequenting the theatre. Instead of acting like kings, many who claim to be the sons of God act as meanly as if they were scullions in the kitchen of Mammon. They do not judge themselves to be Caesars, but they demean themselves as if they were Caesar's slaves, living upon his smile, and asking his leave to move. What separation from the world, what brave holiness, what self-denial, what heavenly walking with God ought to be seen in those who are chosen to be a peculiar people, the representatives of God on earth, and courtiers of the new Jerusalem above! As the world waxes worse and worse, it becomes men of God to become better and better. If sinners stoop lower, saints must rise higher, and show them that a regenerate life cannot share in the general corruption.

O Lord, I know that in Christ Jesus thou hast made me a king; help me, then, to live a right royal life. Lay home to my conscience that question—What manner of persons ought we to be? and may I so answer it that I may live worthy of my high calling.

BRIDLES FOR OLD HORSES

Not only colts, but horses already broken, need a bridle.

Indeed they do, and so also do we who are advanced in years and full of experience. Old men are not always wise men. Passions which should have been by this time quite subdued still need bit and bridle, or they may hurry us into fatal errors. Flesh does not improve by keeping, nor do corruptions sweeten by the lapse of years. New converts need to watch in the morning of their days, but old saints must be equally on their guard, for the hours become no safer as they draw toward evening. We are all within gunshot of the enemy as long as we are this side of Jordan.

'Without me ye can do nothing', is as true of strong men as of babes in grace. Temptation, like fire, will burn where the wood is green, and certainly it hath no less power where the fuel is old and sere.[1] We shall need to be kept by grace till we are actually in glory. Those who think themselves at heaven's gate may yet sin their souls into the deepest hell, unless the unchanging love and power of God shall uphold them even to the end.

---

[1] Dry or withered.

Lord, bit and bridle me, I pray thee, and never let me break loose from thy divine control. Conduct me every mile of the road till I reach my everlasting home.

THE COMPASSES

As in a pair of compasses, one part is fixed in the centre, whilst the other foot wandereth about in the circumference, so whatever subjects we may think upon, the soul must stay on Christ, and be fixed on him.

While we search after evidences and additional comforts we must not leave our simple trust in Jesus. Whatever sweep our knowledge may take as we advance in years, we must retain most fixedly the one and only centre which is worthy of a regenerated soul, namely, our Lord Jesus. If the circle of our energies should encompass all the world, still must the heart stay with delightful continuance with the Well-Beloved. Immovable and steadfast must we be, our willing soul unswervingly loyal to its sole object of trust and love, the one and only Lord of our whole being, the chief among ten thousand, the altogether lovely.

To whom else can we go? Where else is there rest for us? Let us then abide in Christ Jesus. Fix the centre with the whole force of a resolute heart, nay, more, with the whole power of divine grace. Never tolerate the idea of novelty in this matter. Here there can be no advance; we are in him rooted and grounded. Only so can we strike out the true circle of life: without a fixed centre the sphere can never be true.

O thou who art the same yesterday, today, and forever, hold me fast forever, and bid me sing, 'O God, my heart is fixed, my heart is fixed!'

THE LARK AND THE FOWLER

Men of abstracted conceits and sublime speculations are but wise
fools; like the lark, that soareth high, peering and peering, but yet
falleth into the net of the fowler. Knowledge without wisdom may
be soon discerned; it is usually curious and censorious.

This is abundantly seen in many who pretend to interpret
seals and vials, and yet neglect family devotion and the plain
precepts of the word. Such are found occupying their time in
hair-splitting over difficult points, but they do not labour to
maintain the unity of the body of Christ. They are very acute
upon speculative topics of no consequence whatever, but they
divide on the slightest pretext from the rest of the brotherhood.
We have enough to do with watching over our own hearts
and endeavouring to bring sinners to Christ without becoming more nice than wise upon matters of theological subtlety
and word-spinning. The wide difference between wisdom and
knowledge is forgotten by many: they hoard up knowledge of
a peculiar sort like collectors of coins, and yet they use it not
as merchants use money, but keep it for show, a rarity to be
looked at, labelled, put away in a glass case and exhibited to
those who are admirers of curios and rarities.

Lord! help me to soar like the lark, but keep me clear of the
net. Make me practical, and let not my head swim with airy
notions till I rush upon my own destruction.

SATAN CASTING OUT SATAN

Lusts are contrary one to another, and therefore jostle for the throne,
and usually take it by turns. As our ancestors sent for the Saxons to
drive out the Picts, so do carnal men drive out one lust by another,
and, like the lunatic in the Gospel (Matt. 17) fall sometimes into
the water, and sometimes into the fire.

Of what use then can reforms be which are wrought by an evil agency? If sobriety be the fruit of pride, it grows upon a pernicious root, and though the body be no longer intoxicated, the mind will be drunken. If revenge be forsworn from considerations of avarice, the meanness of the miserly is a small gain upon the fury of the passionate. If outward irreligion be abandoned out of a desire to gain human applause, the Pharisee will be a very slender improvement upon the prodigal. Satan's casting out of Satan is deceitful work: his intent no doubt is to establish his empire by pretending to overthrow it.

No, there must be another power at work, or little is accomplished. Any fancied good which one devil may bring another is sure to take away, and the last end of the man whom Satan mends is always worse than the first. A stronger than he must enter in by force of grace, and hurl him out by divine force, and take full possession, or the man may be another man but not a new man.

Lord Jesus, cast out all the devils from my soul at once, and never permit one of them to return.

THE DOG

Satan is like a dog that standeth wagging his tail and looking to receive somewhat from those that sit at table; but if nothing be thrown out, he goeth his way. So doth Satan watch for our consent, as Benhadad's servants did for the word 'brother'. He looketh for a passionate speech, an unclean glance, gestures of wrath, or words of discontent, and if he findeth none of these, he is discouraged.

It would be a great shame to please the dog of hell. Nay, let him look and long, but let him have never a look, or a word, from us to stir his wicked heart. O for grace! to starve him out, and to bid him begone to his own den. 'Neither give place to the devil', says the apostle. We are not ignorant of his devices. To tempt him to tempt us is indeed a superfluity of naughtiness. Let this serpent eat his own meat, which is the dust; by no means let us turn servitors to wait upon our enemy.

We have need to watch and pray in the presence of this crafty one. When he came to our Lord, he found nothing in him, but in us he sees much which favours him. O Lord, bid him get behind thee once again! Deliver us from the evil one, and bid him depart from us. This we humbly entreat of thee.

GIBEONITES

Make your sorrows to draw water for the sanctuary. Our natural affections, like the Gibeonites, must not be exterminated, but kept for temple service.

The Stoic slays his emotions, the Christian sanctifies them to noblest ends. It is like a brute not to feel, it is like a man to feel tenderly, and it is like a Christian to feel in a chastened manner. We may weep, and we may rejoice, and when our weeping is in sympathy with the afflicted, and our rejoicing is in brotherly fellowship with the joyful, the Gibeonites are indeed made hewers of wood and drawers of water for the sanctuary.

Business, marriage, travelling, recreation, literature, music, art, should all be placed in the same subordinate condition. They are not distinctly spiritual, and as mere human matters they may be either right or wrong; but it is ours to lay the yoke upon them, and make them serve our spiritual designs. They will make admirable servants; we can never allow them to be our masters. The Gibeonites might not be killed, but they were to be placed under the yoke, and made to be useful, and the same must be done with the matters which we have mentioned.

It would be foolish to endeavour to put these things down, for they are incidental to human existence; it is wise therefore to subdue them to do servile work for the Lord.

O Lord, give me ever so to use worldly things as never to be worldly myself: rather may I sanctify them by the word of God and prayer!

EXPENSIVE ECONOMY

The inhabitants of Constantinople would afford no money to the Emperor Constantinus Palaeologus, when he begged from door to door for a supply for his soldiers; but what was the issue? The barbarous enemy won the city and got all. The like story there is of Musteatzem, the covetous caliph of Babylon, who was such an idolater of his wealth and treasures that he would not spend anything for the necessary defence of his city, whereupon it was taken, and the caliph famished to death, and his mouth by Haalon, the Tartarian conqueror, was filled with melted gold.

Such economy is evidently most extravagant. May not the like be said of those who give grudgingly to the cause of God, and of those who ruin their souls in order to increase their pelf?[1] They refuse to be losers for Christ, and so lose their souls. Religion might cost them a loss in business, by leading them to close the shop on the Sabbath, or to act with strict uprightness: this they cannot afford, and so they throw away their souls in order to keep their coppers. Verily, the race of fools has not yet died out. Thousands still think it profitable to gain the world and lose their own souls.

O Lord, teach me true wisdom! Make me willing to lose wealth, and health, and home, yea, and my life also, in order that I may follow Jesus and possess his salvation.

---

[1] Money, especially when gained in a dishonest or dishonourable way.

SAMSON'S LOCKS

Single prayers are like the single hairs of Samson; but the prayers of the congregation are like the whole of his bushy locks, wherein his strength lay. Therefore you should, in Tertullian's phrase, quasi manu facta,[1] with a holy conspiracy, besiege heaven, and force out a blessing for your pastors.'

This is a fine metaphor wherewith to set forth united prayer. One prayer is a hair of Samson, but our united supplications are as the seven locks of that hero's head. May God grant that the church may never be shorn of the locks of prayer, wherein her great strength lieth, and her great beauty also.

The cumulative power of prayer is well worthy of notice. Abraham alone could not by intercession save a single city of the plain, though his pleas were very weighty. Lot's poor prayer was to Abraham's as an ounce to a ton, and yet that last ounce turned the scale, and Zoar was preserved from the burning. The agreement of two saints is a grand force against which very few obstacles can stand; and when it comes to a praying band, all the smiths in Jerusalem cannot make bolts for the doors, or chains for the wrists, sufficiently strong to hold Peter in prison. Come, then, to the meetings for prayer, for there is the strength of the church, and there are her Samson's locks.

IMPERIAL REVENUES, AND SMALL CHARGES

It is folly to think that an emperor's revenue will not pay a beggar's debt. Christ hath undertaken to satisfy for the sinner's debt, and he hath money enough to pay.

Delightful thought! Great as is my debt before the justice of God, it can assuredly be met by the riches in glory which

[1] Latin: As a band of soldiers.

belong to the Lord Jesus. It is an overwhelming debt to me, but now that my Redeemer has shed his blood, it will be as nothing to him. A Caesar's revenue would discharge a poor man's liabilities and would scarcely suffer diminution; far more will the infinite merits of Jesus discharge my sins, and remain infinitely full. Where, then, can unbelief find an excuse for its existence? There can be no real ground for fear. Come, my heart, look not so much at thy present and urgent need as at thy Lord's supplies which are boundless, and all thine own.

WHY MEN ATE ACORNS

The main reason why men dote upon the world is because they are not acquainted with a higher glory. Men ate acorns till they were acquainted with the use of corn; a candle is much ere the sun riseth.

Now it has happened unto us to eat the bread of angels, and to see the Sun of righteousness, and never again can we find content in baser things. All the joys of the world are now but beggarly elements to us, compared with our delight in Christ Jesus our Lord. Carnal wisdom has become folly in our esteem; the mirth of fools is a weariness; and the pomp and glory of earth are mere baby toys, scarce worthy of a glance. What grace is this which has revealed such precious things to us! Worldly-wise men think us fanatics and fools, but we know what they are, and where the folly really lies. Oh that their eyes were opened to join with us in the joys which they ridicule! If they will persist in their blindness it shall not be for want of plain testimony on our part, for we are bold to declare in all companies that there is more satisfaction in Christ's worst things than in sin's best things, and that a half-hour of his presence is better than all the feasting of royal courts for a lifetime. Oh that they would believe us so far as to try for themselves! Alas, they munch their acorns, and scorn the bread of life!

NEW LEAVES PUSHING OFF THE OLD

Old leaves, if they remain upon the trees through the autumn and the winter, fall off in the spring.

We have seen a hedge all thick with dry leaves throughout the winter, and neither frost nor wind has removed the withered foliage, but the spring has soon made a clearance. The new life dislodges the old, pushing it away as unsuitable to it. So our old corruptions are best removed by the growth of new graces. 'Old things are passed away; behold all things are become new.' It is as the new life buds and opens that the old worn-out things of our former state are compelled to quit their hold of us. Our wisdom lies in living near to God, that by the power of his Holy Spirit all our graces may be vigorous, and may exercise a sin-expelling power over our lives: the new leaves of grace pushing off our old sere[1] affections and habits of sin.

With converts from the world it is often better not to lay down stringent rules as to worldly amusements, but leave the new life and its holier joys to push off the old pleasures. Thus it will be done more naturally and more effectively.

Lord, let thy life in me push off the relics of my former death, that I may put on the new man, and manifest the energy of thy grace.

THE KING AND HIS ATTENDANTS

Those who entertain a king, reckon upon receiving his train.

It is not fit that he should come alone. So those who receive Jesus by faith into their hearts, receive also his church, his

[1] Dry or withered.

ministers, his word, and his cause. They take the Saviour and all his belongings. As the old proverb hath it, 'Love me, love my dog', so they love all who belong to Jesus for their Lord's sake. Where Jesus comes with pardon, he brings all the graces with him, and we are right glad to entertain them all: not only faith, but love, hope, patience, courage, zeal, and the whole band of virtues. It would be idle to say, 'Christ is in me', if none of the graces of his Spirit lodged within our souls.

Come in, great Lord, and dwell in my heart, and bring all thy disciples with thee, and all thy belongings, yea, and thy cross itself.

AN IMAGINARY CARPENTER

Peter Martyr sets forth the holiness of God, by this comparison: 'Take a carpenter when he hath chalked and drawn his line, then he goes and chops the timber. Sometimes he chops right, and sometimes amiss. Why? Because he hath an outward rule, a line outside of himself according to which he cuts the timber. But if you could suppose a carpenter that could never chop amiss, but his hand should be his line and rule; if he had such an equal poise and touch of his hand, that his very stroke is a rule to itself, then he could not err.' By this plain and homely comparison he did set forth the holiness of God and the creature. The holiness of the creature is a rule without us, therefore sometimes we chop amiss; but God's holiness is his inward rule, it is his nature, he can do nothing amiss.

This is an instructive simile, and may be carried further. Sanctification is a renewal of the heart, which creates such a rule within us. The Holy Spirit works in us, according to our measure, a law of our nature, so that it cannot sin because it is born of God; for, after all, it is the nature of the man which determines the nature of his deeds. The fruit is according to the tree. The evil of our life arises from the living evil within. If we could *be* perfect, we should act perfectly. Hence the man himself is first to be looked to.

Lord, purge us, yea, make us new creatures in Christ Jesus, that out of us good may come because thou hast made us good.

RECORDS OF LIFE

The story of our lives is all engraven upon the heart, and when God awakeneth the conscience, it tells of past sin. God will open the sinner's eyes in the next world, not by a holy illumination, but by a forced conviction. We are told in Rev. 20:12, 'The books were opened', and one of these books is conscience, and though it be in the sinner's keeping, and therefore may become blurred and defaced, yet our story will be legible enough, and forgotten sins will stare us in the face: 'Be sure your sin will find you out' (Num. 32:23). We forget it now, and think we shall never hear of it more; but God can make all occur to memory as fresh as if newly committed, and in an instant represent the story of an ill-spent life, and show us all the thoughts, words, and actions that ever we have been guilty of. The paper goeth white into the printing-house; but within one instant it is marked within and without, and cometh forth stamped with words, and lines, and sentences, which were in no way legible there before; even so will it be with the soul when conscience is aroused at the last.

Our lives today are like the picture upon the photographer's plate before he develops it; God hath but to put the soul into a bath prepared according to his divine art, and all the sins of his whole existence will stand out clear before the sinner's astonished gaze. Nothing can be forgotten: all the past must live again. Let the unconverted tremble as they think of this, and let the saved ones bless the Lord Jesus who has so blotted out their sins that no power or process can ever bring them again to remembrance.

THE APPLES DISPLAY THE SAP

The apples appear when the sap is not seen. It is the operative and lively graces that will discover themselves. A man may think well, or speak well; but it is that grace which governeth his actions which most showeth itself.

There could be no apples if there were no sap, but the sap itself has no manifestation except in the leaves and fruit. If we have inward grace it is well for ourselves; but others cannot see it or profit by it till it works itself into our daily life. This it is bound to do, and we may not think lightly of such a result, for as it would be a token that something ailed the sap of the tree if it brought forth no fruit in its season, so it would be a mournful proof of spiritual declension if our conversation yielded none of the graces of the Spirit. It is all very fine to plead as some have done that they are doing *inside* work; if their fruit is all within they will have to be cut down that it may be got at. A true epistle of Christ is not written in invisible ink, and then sealed up, but it is known and read of all men. A tree of the Lord's right-hand planting bears fruit to his honour and glory, visible to those who are round about him.

Lord, make me one that can bear to be looked at. Make my inward grace to be so vigorous that my outer life may be fruitful to thy praise. May no one have to enquire about the sap; may they see so many baskets of fruit that they may be quite sure about the life of the tree.

THE MADMAN OF ATHENS

As the madman at Athens challenged all the ships that came into the harbour for his own, so carnal men claim an interest in heavenly things which are none of theirs. Deceived hearts believe they are

*running to heaven when they are posting[1] to hell; like rowers in a
boat, they look one way, and go contrary.*

Religious delusions may be very comfortable while they last,
but what will be the misery of their breaking up! To have all
your fancied godliness vanish like the mists before the sun will
be grievous indeed. In proportion to the confidence inspired
will be the despair involved. The poor madman in Bedlam[2] in
the olden time placed a straw crown upon his head, and issued
orders like a Caesar; it was his madness which made such a
farce a comfort to him. In the next world the sinner's madness
will be over, he will be sobered by his despair: what then will
he think of his former fancies and fond self-flatteries! What an
awaking, from the dreams of bliss to the realities of hell!

O my soul, see thou to it that all thy hopes are well grounded! Call not Christ thine, and heaven thine, if they are not so.
Do not play the fool with eternal things, but get a sure title to
everlasting blessedness.

THE UNFAITHFUL STEWARD

*We shall be called to an account, what we have done with our time,
and talents, and interests, and opportunities: 'At his coming our
Lord will require his own with usury' (Luke 19:23). Ah, unfaithful
ones, what will you say, when you cannot shift and lie? Will this
be an answer: I spent my time in serving my own lusts? This will
not avail you. If a factor (or steward), that is sent to a mart or
fair, should stay guzzling in an inn, or ale-house, and there spend
all his money, which was to be employed in traffic, could he excuse
himself by pleading that he was busy with his cups? Oh, what a
dreadful account will poor souls make, that have spent their time*

---

[1] Galloping, as if riding swiftly from one staging post to another.
[2] A nickname for the Bethlehem Royal Hospital, London. The institution was
once representative of the worst excesses of asylums.

either doing nothing, or nothing to purpose, or that which is worse than nothing, even sin which will undo them forever!

Come, my heart, call thyself to account. What hast thou been at? Hast thou served thy Lord, or hast thou wasted his goods and his time? The Lord will require this of thee before long, therefore require it of thyself. How would it fare with thee if the judgment-day commenced tomorrow, and on leaving thy bed in the morning thou shouldst find the dread assize already commenced? Say, my soul, if thou wert at this instant called away, how stand accounts between thee and thy Lord?

THE SUNFLOWER AND THE AQUEDUCT

As the flower of the sun doth follow the sun, and openeth and shutteth according to the absence of that luminary; so doth the heart of a Christian move after God.

The divine nature within us followeth hard after the divine nature, and longeth to drink in its warmth and light. Everything acteth according to its nature. '*We say,* "Aqua in tantum ascendit";[1] *and it is true that neither water nor nature riseth higher than its spring-head and centre.*'

So when self is our principle and end, we rise no higher than ourselves; but when God becometh the life of our soul we follow after him, and rise far above the highest point to which nature could conduct us. His grace in us strives to rise to the point from which it came, and it will never rest till it does so. This argues a high destiny for the believer, and is the foretaste of it. Hence the need to have a good and true beginning, and to draw our life from the eternal fountains above; for, apart from this, there will be no rising up to heaven.

---

[1] Latin: Water climbs up (or gets up) only so far.

How sweet it is to find our mind and heart turning God-ward, as the heliotrope[1] seeks the sun! To find our joys begin and end with manifestations of Jesus' love! It is well to pine till the Lord's face be revealed, and only to flourish when he imparts his gracious influences. It is wise to turn away from all things in which God is not evidently present, but carefully to follow each movement of his shining face that we may always front his love, and bask in the beams of his favour.

Whatever partakes largely of the light of Jesus should be prized by us, whether it be fashioned after our own favourite model or no: the sun is there, and we must turn to it. 'Anything of Jesus' should be a sufficient attraction to us. A gleam of his sunlight should be prized, for it is far more than we deserve; and we should joyously receive it as the crocus drinks in the rich gold of the spring sun, and brims its cup therewith. What will it be to dwell above, where the light no more goeth down, and the flowers feel no cold drops of the night?

A DECAYING ROOT HAS WITHERING BRANCHES

As when the root of a tree perisheth, the leaves keep green for a little, but within a while they wither and fall off; so love, which is the root and heart of all other duties, when that decayeth, other things decay with it. The first works go off with the first love; at least, are not carried on with such care, and delight, and complacency, as they should be.

Swiftly other works follow, withering in their turn; for the fatal blow has been struck, and failure of every good thing is

---

[1] A plant cultivated for its fragrant purple or blue flowers which are used in perfume. The name 'heliotrope' derives from the old idea that the inflorescences of these plants turned their rows of flowers to the sun.

but a matter of time. Could the love of saints to Jesus utterly die out, all their virtues must die also, for love is the root of all. The outward form of piety might survive, as the wretched counterfeit of holiness, but what would be its worth? Even this in many cases passes away, for some men are bravely consistent in their wickedness, and do not care to keep up the name to live when the life of God is not within their souls.

Our main concern must be as to the root. The heart must be alive with gracious gratitude, or the leaf cannot long be green with living holiness. How is it with thee, my soul? Is there root-life in thee? Is Jesus precious? Is the Father's name most sweet? Does the Holy Spirit move thee to ardent affection? A chill love, whose very existence is questionable, means a miserable experience. He who doubts his own love to Jesus generally doubts Jesus' love to him. O love, be thou the living root in me, and, through thy quickening and nourishing energy, may the branches of my consecrated life grow exceedingly!

ONE NAIL DRIVES OUT ANOTHER

Men will not be frightened from self-love; it must be another more powerful love which must draw them from it; as one nail driveth out another.

This is true philosophy. Love to God can alone expel the love of sin. Many forget this, and set to work extracting the old love: a very tedious task; impossible, indeed, with such poor tools as we possess. They torture the body and torment the mind, but the old nail of self-love is rusted in, and will not stir. They might sooner break up the fabric of their manhood than tear out its old deep-seated affections; the self-nail has been driven well home, and clinched besides, and what can we do?

It is wonderful to see how love to Christ fetches out the love of self from its lodging. At the first it shakes and loosens it; by and by it drives it a little from its place, and at last it drives it out altogether. Self is at first somewhat denied, then it is chastened and kept under, and finally it is crucified with Christ so completely that the man finds pleasure in warring against it, and glories in the submission of the flesh to suffering and loss.

O blessed hand of Jesus, drive in the nail of divine love! Smite hard, Lord. Force out the rusted iron of my selfishness. Let not a fragment of it remain. Love alone can vanquish love. Thyself alone can conquer self in me. No secondary force will suffice. My God, thou must display thy Godhead's power of love, or my vile heart will never part with self.

THE PERFUMED GALE

As the odours and sweet smells of Arabia are carried by the winds and air into the neighbouring provinces, so that before travellers come thither they have the scent of that aromatic country; so the joys of heaven are by the sweet breathings and gales of the Holy Ghost blown into the hearts of believers, and the sweet smells of the upper paradise are conveyed into the gardens of the churches. Those joys which are stirred up in us by the Spirit before we get to heaven are a pledge of what we may expect hereafter.

Oh that we had more of these heavenly gales laden with the spices of Immanuel's land! Gracious Lord, cause such a celestial wind to awake at this very hour! I am already accepted in Christ Jesus, adopted, and beloved in him: this is a foretaste of heaven. In him I am secure, immortal, triumphant: these also are heavenly privileges. In Jesus I have peace, and rest, and profound confidence: is not this also something of paradise?

In my Lord I have fellowship with God, and exceeding joy in his love: surely the wind is blowing from the glory quarter, and has taken up much of the aroma of the beds of spices whereon the saints recline. The Holy Ghost hath revealed unto us in our inward experience much of the bliss which the Lord hath prepared for them that love him. The life of the believer on earth is the same as that which will be in him throughout eternity, and the joy with which the Lord favours him below is of the same nature as that which shall fill him forever. When Jesus reveals himself to my soul, the winds are blowing from heaven; I can discern the fragrance. All around me delight is poured forth, and my heart is singing all the time.

DREAMS, BUT NOT DREAMS

Carnal men hear of the beauty of holiness, of the excellency of Christ, of the preciousness of the covenant, of the rich treasures of grace, as if they were in a dream. They look upon such things as mere fancies, like to foolish dreams of golden mountains, or showers of pearls.

'This their way is their folly.' When scientific men describe to us their curious experiments and singular discoveries, we know them to be persons of credit, and therefore accept their testimony: why do not men of the world do us the like justice, and believe what we tell them? We are as sane as they, and as observant of the law of truth; why, then, do they not believe us when we declare what the Lord has done for our souls? Why is our experience in the spiritual world to be treated as a fiction any more than their discoveries in chemistry or geography? There is no justice in the treatment with which our witness is received.

Yet the Christian man need not complain, for in the nature of things he may expect it to be so, and the fact that it is so is a confirmation of his own beliefs. In a world of blind men, an elect race, to whom eyes had been given, would be sure to be regarded as either mad or false. How could the sightless majority be expected to accept the witness of the seeing few? Would it not touch their dignity to admit that others possessed faculties of which they were destitute? And would it not be highly probable that the blind would conspire to regard the men of eyes as fanatical dreamers or deluded fools? Unrenewed men know not the things which are of the Spirit of God, and it is by no means a strange thing that they should deride what they cannot understand. It is sad that those who are dreamers in the worst sense should think others so, but it is by no means so extraordinary as to cause surprise.

O my Lord, whatever others may think of me, let me be more and more sensible of thy presence, and of the glorious privileges and hopes which are created in the heart by thy grace! If men should even say of me, as of Joseph, 'Behold, this dreamer cometh', it will not grieve me so long as thou art with me, and thy favour makes me blest.

ARROWS SHOT AT RANDOM

Continued meditation brings great profit to the soul. Passant and transient thoughts are more pleasant, but not so profitable. Deliberate meditation is of most use because it secures the return of the thoughts. Sudden thoughts pass away from us, and, as a rule, they do not return to benefit us; as children shoot away their arrows at rovers, and do not look after them; or as a ball stricken in the open field goes out from us, whereas a ball struck against a wall doth return to our hand again.

We need more meditation, more of this shooting of thought-arrows at a mark on which they will strike and stick, more of this throwing the thought-ball at the wall that we may catch it again. This would create for us a better style of teachers and preachers, and train a more solid race of Christian men and women. People do not think, and yet thinking is living, and one of the nearest approaches to death is to be without thought. Gentle reader, do you never think? Are you too busy to meditate? Is your time occupied from morning to night? Then stay a moment while we whisper in your ear: if you are very busy, think and pray all the more, or your work will wear and weary you, and drag you away from God. For your work's sake, break away from it, and give the soul a breathing time. Get a holy subject and keep to it till you have drawn somewhat from it to feed your soul upon, and then you will do your lifework with less fatigue because you will have more strength to spend upon it.

THE BURNING-GLASS

When the beams of the sun are contracted by a burning-glass, upon one spot, then they cause fire; so when our thoughts are concentrated on one object they warm the heart and at last burn the truth into it.

This is the reason why so many sermons and addresses are so cold and ineffective; they are not sufficiently focused upon one point. There are many rays of light, but they are scattered. We get a little upon many things, while what is wanted is one great truth, and so much upon it as shall fix it on the heart, and set the soul blazing with it. This is the fault of many lives: they are squandered upon a dozen objects, whereas if they were economized for one, they would be mighty lives, known in the present and honoured in the future. 'This one thing I do' is a necessary motto if we are to accomplish anything.

Our friend lay basking in the sunshine, and the beams of the sun did not disturb him for a moment. In a mirthful moment we crept to his side, and holding up a burning-glass, we formed a little bright spot on the back of his hand. He started in an instant as if touched with a hot iron, and was some little time before he quite appreciated our lecture upon concentrated energies. He did not invite a repetition of the interesting experiment, but confessed that he should throughout life dread a man whose strength all converged to one point, and that when next he wished to arouse a careless mind, he would try what concentration would do.

Great Lord, teach thou me how to accomplish somewhat for thy glory; and, to that end, enable me to live for thee with my undivided being, that what little light and heat I have may be so focussed that I may burn my way to successful service.

THE ALL-SUPPORTING NAIL

The creatures hang upon God as a garment upon a nail; take away the nail and the garment falls down.

The emblem is simple but accurate. All the weight falls upon the nail, and all the need of the creature's existence hangs upon the Omnipotent One. What power must he have from whom all power is derived! All that we see around us of force and might is but God in action. There is no such deity as 'Nature': nature is the Lord at work.

Do all things depend upon God? Then the law of faith is, after all, no novelty, no intrusion, no exception to general rule. A sort of passive faith is the life of all created things. Dependence is the faith of irrational objects, and the believer's trust is this dependence gifted with eyes and will. It should then be an easy thing for my creature-life to hang upon its Creator. Had it not been for sin, faith would have been my very nature, dependence upon God a constitutent quality of my existence. Who, then; are they that laugh at faith? Rationalists? Nay; irrational men, at war with one of nature's first and most essential laws. Let them laugh on, for my heart is well assured that confidence in God is the highest reason, and trust in my Maker the finest common sense.

O Lord! I bless thee that the nail on which creation hangs can never fail, for thou faintest not; neither will my confidence be put to shame, for it hangs where hang the worlds. Till thou dost thyself cease from thine almightiness, my soul's hope is safe beyond question, for it rests only upon thee.

THE WATCHMAKER

He that makes a watch, can mend it when it is broken and disarranged.

So it is certain that the best physician for the body is the Maker of the human frame. This is too much forgotten, and faith is placed in men and medicines, and the great Lord is forgotten. We would not have men decline the aid of physic[1] and surgery, but yet we count it a sort of idolatry to trust in these and make no appeal to the Lord himself. It is unwise to neglect the means, but be not so utterly foolish as to leave out of mind the *first cause* and true *author* of all good. It is best to trust in the Lord and use medicine too, but of the two evils—faith in God and no use of means, or use of means and no faith in God—we should certainly prefer the former.

With regard to the soul, none can do anything to purpose

---

[1] Medicine.

in putting it into order save the Creator himself. All merely human attempts at the repair of the spiritual nature are a kind of tinkering which injures more than it benefits. The Lord can set mainspring, and balance-wheel, and lever, and hands in good working order. He can cleanse, repair, and regulate; and what he does is done to purpose. We have known a child wash a watch till it was spoiled, and so may a reformer purge a man till he makes a hypocrite of him. An ingenious young man repaired a watch so that it would never go again; and so may the superstitious impress men with foolish fancies till they lose all capacity for true religion. God himself must put his hand to the business, or it will be a total failure.

Lord, with all my imperfections and irregularities, it gives me joy to know that I am in thy hands, and that thou wilt set me right. No case has ever baffled thee; neither will mine. Thou wilt yet make me perfect in every good work to do thy will.

THE DISH FOR ME

As at a feast, when there is a dish for which we have a great liking set upon the table, though all the company be welcome to partake of it, yet we say, 'Here is a dish for me.' So should you apply and take to yourselves your own portion of the word. Though it be propounded generally, yet, when God directeth the tongue of his messengers to speak expressly to your case, you should say, 'This is for me.' This is all the calling by name which you can look for.

How often has this been the case when reading the word of God, or hearing it! We have felt an inward relish and delight in divine truth, and our spiritual instincts have taught us that it was intended for us. A man may be misled by his natural appetite, but the spiritual man's holy taste never deceives him. If he can feed upon the word, this is clear evidence that it is 'food convenient for him', and that the Lord intends it for him. The Holy Ghost has said, 'Eat ye that which is good, and let your soul delight itself in fatness', plainly indicating that the truth which gives delight to the renewed soul may be safely feasted on, and that we have full license to enjoy it without stint.

My heart, here is good news for thee! Be not slow to avail thyself of the divine permit. At the feast of love, eat the fat and drink the sweet, and bless the Lord who satisfieth thy mouth with good things.

A PRINCE IN A DITCH

If you saw a man labouring in filthy ditches, and soiling himself as poor men do, would you believe that he was heir-apparent to a crown, called to inherit a kingdom? Who will believe in your heavenly calling when you stick in the mud of worldly pleasures, and are carried away with carking[1] care for secular interests?

Princes should behave as princes. Their haunts should be in palaces, and not amid dung-heaps. How, then, is it that some who profess and call themselves Christians are found raking in questionable amusements to discover pleasure, and many others groping amid sordid avarice to find satisfaction in wealth? What are they at to be thus disgracing the blood royal? How dare they drag the name of the 'blessed and only Potentate' through the mire? A prince of the blood acting as a beggar would dishonour not only himself but all the royal house. Nobility has obligations. Race, which is the eminent nobility of saints, lays them under heavy bonds to act as the true aristocracy of the universe. Come, my soul, dost thou carry thyself royally? I am made a king by Jesus Christ—are my bearing and conversation answerable to the dignity laid upon me?

[1] Causing distress or worry.

Lord, thou must teach thy poor child. He has so long been a vagabond and an outcast that unless thou teach him the majestic manners of thy holy courts, he will dishonour both himself and thee.

VICTIMS LED TO THE SLAUGHTER

The heathen were wont to hang garlands around the necks of the beasts which were about to be slain at the altar, and to crown them with roses as they led them to sacrifice.

Many are thus decked with the ornaments of wealth and mirth who are on the way to the slaughter. Ungodly men may be garlanded with social distinctions, scientific attainments, and courtly honours, and yet be no better than bullocks devoted to the axe, at the altar of the god of this world. How little availed the roses to the creature doomed to die! If men were wise they would regard with equal disesteem those earthly honours and possessions which do but deck out a condemned criminal, and adorn a wretch over whom the wrath of God is hovering. O silly men, to rejoice in the tokens of your destruction, and to glory in your shame!

Lord, it is better to bear thy cross, and march heavenward with the blessed burden, than to be smothered in flowery pleasures and to be led down to hell. I pray thee, bring my unregenerate neighbours to be of the same mind.

THE GIDDY THINK THE EARTH MOVES

The earth is never the more unsettled because to giddy brains it seemeth to run round.

Even so the salvation of the saints is sure, though to their trembling hearts it may seem to be in terrible jeopardy. A passenger on crossing the Channel is none the less in safety because he himself feels ready to give up the ghost with the nausea brought on by the rolling of the vessel. Our feelings are poor judges of facts. Some who felt sure of heaven are now in hell, and others who had almost lost hope are now glorified in heaven. My brain may whirl and make me think all things are running round, and yet I know those very things to be steadfast as the hills, and therefore I do not believe my feelings, but trust the facts; and so, when my poor silly heart imagines that the eternal promises will fail, I must chide its folly, and fall back upon the everlasting verities.

Yes, Lord, thou art immovable and immutable! This I know of a surety. Therefore give me grace never to doubt thee, or to distrust thy faithfulness to all those who put their trust in thee.

METEORS NOT STARS

Meteors are soon spent, and fall from heaven like lightning, while stars keep their course and station.

When a meteor darts across the sky children say that a star has fallen, but it is not so. Look through the telescope, and you will find Jupiter, and Saturn, and Venus, each one in its place, shining as usual; yea, even the tiniest satellite is in its predestined sphere, fulfilling its times and seasons. So, too, we hear men say that a Christian has fallen from grace, a saint has become an apostate. This also is an error. The saints are in their places still, for it is written, 'the righteous shall hold on his way': those who have fallen were meteors, not stars; professors, but not genuine possessors of the heavenly light. The seven stars are in a hand out of which nothing falls: 'all the saints are in thy hand'. Jesus says, 'he that believeth in me hath everlasting life', and therefore we are sure that they will not die.

O my blessed Saviour; give me no temporary salvation! Make me a star whose brightness shall never be quenched. To be enlightened for a time will not serve my turn; grant me light which Satan cannot extinguish. Let me be saved in the Lord with an everlasting salvation.

ALL BLOSSOMS DO NOT BECOME FRUIT

Plenty of blossoms do not always foretell great store of fruit.

Few knit out of the many flowers which make promise of apples. It has ever been so, and he is an unwise man who dreams that his trees will be exempted from the universal law. The same rule holds good in all earthly matters. Out of many hopeful results which we look for from our plans and labours some must fail us. Because we make appointments for ourselves, and forget the appointments of God, we meet with many more disappointments than would otherwise fall to our lot. It is of no use reckoning that every egg in our basket will become a chicken, for it will not so happen, and our over-anticipation will be the cause of needless sorrow to us. Every prudent merchant reckons upon a certain amount of bad debt and loss in his trading, and when it comes he writes it off as a part of his estimated charges, and is not broken-hearted: our wisdom lies in doing the same with all earthly hopes, and even with the visible results of our service for the Lord. Whether this or that will prosper we must leave with the Master, it is ours to sow with unwearied hand both at morning and at night.

THE LEAVEN IN THE BREAD

Jude saith we are 'preserved in Christ Jesus'. There is a close union between Christ and us: we are 'in him', and because of this union we are eternally preserved. Look! As it is impossible to sever the leaven and the dough when they are once mingled and kneaded together; so Christ and a believer, when they are united together, there is no parting them any more, and while one lasts the other must endure.

This is indeed the sure ground of the final preservation of the saints: their union with their Lord is of an indissoluble nature, so that the apostle inquires, 'Who shall separate us?' It is as the union of the body with the head, which cannot be sundered without death to both. 'Because I live ye shall live also' is our guarantee of life eternal. What more do we require? If Christ be in us, and we in him, the union is of the most intense kind, and the security which follows from it is of the most certain sort. 'He that is joined to the Lord is one spirit'; what closer and more abiding union can be imagined?

Lord, let there be no doubt as to my union with thee. Cause my fellowship to be so constant and so sweet that the oneness of soul to thy sacred person may be most evident. So shall I be with thee here, and with thee where thou art for ever.

A SAYING OF THE FATHERS

I remember one of the Fathers bringeth in the flesh, saying of believers, 'Ego deficiam, *I will surely fail them and make them miscarry; and the world.* Ego decipiam, *I will deceive them and entice them; and Satan,* Ego eripiam, *I will snatch them and carry them away; but God saith,* Ego custodiam, *I will keep them, I will never fail them nor forsake them.' Here lieth our safety and security.*

In other words, the flesh saith, 'I will deceive'; the world, 'I will defile'; the devil, 'I will destroy'; but the Lord saith, I will defend'; and that one word of God takes the sting from all the rest. The flesh is as a drawn sword, the world as a sharp spear, and Satan as a poisoned arrow; but the Lord God is a shield, and this baffles all. The flesh is much, the world is more, and Satan is most of all; but God is all in all. The flesh must die, the world must pass away, Satan must be overthrown; but the word of our God abideth forever; and as the word of God is the life of the saints, they shall also abide world without end. What a rest this affords us when we are looking out of the windows of the future! The Lord will be our succour in the days to come!

THE TIGHT-ROPE DANCER

They weaken Christian comfort who make believers walk with Christ like dancers upon a rope, every moment in fear of breaking their necks.

Those who deny the doctrine of the final perseverance of the saints deserve this censure. We cannot tell whence these brethren derive their comfort. Our notion of trusting Christ includes in it a reliance upon him for the present and the future as well as for the sins of the past. It is to us the glory of the gospel that it gives us now, at this very moment, a present and everlasting salvation. Once grasped in the hand of Jesus, what can pluck us thence or cause us to perish? Tight-rope dancing suits not our poor head, we prefer to be 'safe in the arms of Jesus'.

My soul, let others say what they will, do thou accept thy Lord's word for it, and believe that he will keep the feet of his saints. A temporary, questionable salvation may suffice those who know not thy Lord; but as for thee, do thou abide by his eternal, unchangeable love, and fear no final fall.

OLIVIAN'S DYING SAYING

Olivian, when dying, comforted himself with that promise (Isa. 54:10),
'The mountains shall depart, and the hills be removed; but my
kindness shall not depart from thee.' Being in the agonies of death,
he said, 'Sight is gone, speech and hearing are departing, feeling
is almost gone, but the lovingkindness of God will never depart.'
The Lord give us such a confidence in that day that we may die
glorying in the preservation of our Redeemer.

To this end let us live in the like assurance. It is certain that
God can never leave those who put their trust in him, and it
becomes us to be certain of this certainty. The security of the
saints is grounded, not upon their own faithfulness, but upon
the faithfulness of him to whose keeping they have committed
their souls. If the Lord can depart from his people they will
assuredly depart from him and perish; their comfort is that he
has said in his covenant, 'I will put my fear in their hearts, and
they shall not depart from me.' Our soul may live and die on
this one sure promise.

THE PLASTER AND THE HAND

The gospel is a sovereign plaster, but Christ's own hand must make
it stick.

How true is this! The wounded heart cannot by its own
unaided power avail itself of the promise though it be evidently
adapted to its need. Instead of grasping consolation, the soul
refuses to be comforted. Nor can the most loving of ministers
apply the balm; awakened consciences are usually more cunning at putting from them the reasons for hope than we are in
applying them. They think us flatterers when we bring them
cheering news. It will even happen that when a gracious word

seems to strike them and to stick upon their minds, they will with a cruel diligence and suicidal resolution tear it off lest it should work their cure. Abundant facts prove that according to our author's statement—

> When wounded sore the stricken soul,
>   Lies bleeding and unbound,
> One only hand, a pierced hand,
>   Can salve the sinner's wound.

Therefore, O Lord, doth my soul love thee because thou didst not only provide a salvation for me, but thou didst also apply it to me; and at this hour thou dost not only lay up comfort in store for me, but thou dost actually cheer and sustain my spirit. Thou art both Physician and physic, Comforter and comfort, yea, thou art all in all.

BONES STRONGER FOR HAVING BEEN BROKEN

Our reconciliation with God is like the soldering of a vessel, which is henceforth strongest in the crack; or as a leg broken, if well set, it is the stronger: so are we upon firmer terms than we were in innocency; there was before the fall a possibility of being at odds with God, which is now taken away.

This is a gracious fact. Under the covenant of works it would have been always possible for obedience to fail, and then the reward would have been forfeited; but now, under the new covenant, our Lord Jesus has settled and fixed all that was contingent in it by perfecting his part of the agreement, and therefore all the rest stands sure, and all believers must receive covenanted mercies. Adam might have fallen, and we in him, even had he stood for a thousand years. The second Adam has ended his probation both for himself and all his seed, and now nothing can intervene to deprive his people of the earned and purchased inheritance. Innocence seemed sure, but perfection is surer. It is something not to have broken the law; it is far more to have fulfilled it and honoured it, so as to be able to say as our Lord has said, 'I have finished the work which thou gavest me to do.' Fitly and justly did Watts say:

> He raised me from the deeps of sin,
> The gates of gaping hell,
> And fix'd my standing more secure
> Than 'twas before I fell.

My soul, be thou doubly diligent to magnify thy Saviour's name. If the bones which God has broken shall rejoice, much more the bones which he has set. If he rejoices more over the lost sheep which he has found than over that which never went astray, count thyself the happiest and most indebted of beings to be thus prized by thy gracious God.

DIRTY CORNERS

Sluttish[1] corners are not seen in the dark. Things are naught that cannot brook an open investigation.

Lord, let me have a religion which will bear the light of day, the light of self-examination, the light of the throne of judgment. If I hide my sin, how can I prosper? If I cannot bear to be judged of men, how shall I endure to be judged at thy appearing?

THE CLUCKING HEN

As a hen when she hath found a worm, or a barleycorn, clucks for her chickens, that they may come and partake of it with her; so

---

[1] Unclean, dirty, filthy.

a man acquainted with Christ, who hath tasted that the Lord is gracious, he cannot hold, he will be calling upon his friends and relations to come and share with him of the same grace.

It is so much an instinct with real Christians to do this, that those who do not so may well question their own sincerity. Common humanity leads a man to inform his fellow of that which will benefit him, and how can he be a gracious man who is not even commonly humane? In certain crafts and trades there are selfish reasons for keeping their knowledge a secret, but nothing of this kind can appertain to the profession of godliness. Having found this honey, so abundant and so free to all-comers, nature itself bids us call our brethren to see our treasure, and urge them to partake in its sweetness.

Hasten, reader, to call in thy friends and neighbours to rejoice with thee if thou hast indeed found the Lord Jesus.

THE ECHO

We love him because he first loved us. Love is like an echo, it returneth what it receiveth: there is no echo till the sound is heard. Our love to God is a reflex, a reverberation, or a casting back of God's beam and flame upon himself. The cold wall sendeth back no reflex of heat till the sun shines upon it, and warms it first; so neither do we love God till our soul is first filled with a sense of his love.

Hence the impossibility of producing love while we are under a legal spirit; it will not come to order, it will only rise to the bidding of its like. Love alone begets love. Purchase price for it there is none; the bribe would be scorned.

Love is not the result of effort on our part. As the fountain rises freely in the valley, pouring forth its crystal flood with spontaneous eagerness, so doth love sparkle and flash forth in the soul. Secret reservoirs, far up in the mountains, supply the water-springs; and eternal deeps of boundless love in the everlasting hills supply the love-springs of the believer's soul. Is it not written, 'All my fresh springs are in thee'?

O my heart, take care that thou answer to the Lord like an echo! When he saith, 'My love', do thou answer with the selfsame title. Be as the rocks which glow beneath the heat of the sun, and give forth warmth themselves. Love as long as thou livest, for love is the cream of life, and all of it is due to thy Lord.

COURTIERS' PRIVILEGES

It would be a great favour if a king should give leave to one of his meanest subjects to have the key of his privy chamber, to come to him and visit him, and be familiar with him when he pleaseth. How would such a favour be talked of in the world!

Yet this is but a faint image of what the believer is admitted to. He may come not merely to the palace of mercy, and the throne of grace, but to the very heart of God. Confidences such as ours surpass all the familiarities of friendship, and yet they are permitted, nay commanded, between the all-glorious Lord and our poor sinful selves. We may well copy the example of David when he went in and sat before the Lord, and said, 'Who am I, O Lord God, and what is my house? And is this the manner of man, O Lord God?' The intimate intercourse between the glorious sovereign of the Song of Solomon and his sunburnt bride is an inspired symbol of the near and dear communion between Christ and his people. What can be more honouring to the soul, and what can more wonderfully prove the boundless condescension of the Lord? He stoops like a God! There is as much of deity in the favour which he displays to the undeserving as in the matchless splendours of his celestial courts. Happy are the people who have such a God; shall they not accept with rapture the goodness which he sets before them so benignly?

O my most tender God and Father, I can never fully estimate the stoop of thy majesty in deigning to love me, nor the greatness of thy generosity in inviting me to have fellowship with thee. Give me, I pray thee, grace to value such priceless goodness, and every day to live in habitual fellowship with thee. Since thou makest me free of thy courts, teach me how to be a resident courtier, going no more out forever.

WATER POURED INTO A PUMP

Love must be paid in kind. As water is cast into a pump, when the springs lie low, to bring up more water, so God sheddeth abroad his love into our hearts, that our love may rise up to him again by way of gratitude and recompense.

How idle is it, then, to hope to chide ourselves into loving God! The price of love is love; the origin of it is not found in law or in a sense of duty, but in love, or a return of gratitude. When the sun of eternal love melts the glaciers of the soul, then the rivers of affection flow; but if the rocks of ice could all be broken to shivers with hammers, not a drop of affection would stream forth. Only a sense of divine love will ever create love to God in the heart.

How vain also is the attempt to recompense the mercy of God by mechanical acts of religion or works of legal service! 'Love must be paid in kind.' No other coin is current in love's empire but that which bears her own image and superscription. Do what we will, even to martyrdom, if we have not love, it profiteth us nothing. In this case it is specially true, 'If a man should give all the substance of his house for love, it would utterly be contemned.'

Come, my heart, does thy love run dry? Then pray the Holy Ghost to shed abroad the love of God within thee. Pour this living water into thy dry pump, and thou wilt soon pour forth a plentiful stream.

THE FELLOW-COUNTRYMAN

A man who is travelling in foreign lands is glad to meet with his own countrymen.

This we know by experience. Sweet is the music of the English tongue when heard amid the clatter of foreign speech. We feel our heart warmed at the sight of a costume which we can recognize as covering a true Briton. Such are the feelings of a Christian when he falls in with a true believer, and by his speech and conduct knows him to be a citizen of heaven. He detects him at once as being, like himself, 'a stranger in the land'; he seeks him out and cultivates his company, and in that company he finds a solace for his loneliness among the aliens around him. Those who dwell in warm-hearted churches, surrounded by Christian society, little know the value of a single godly friend to those who dwell among worldlings. To such, a man of God is more precious than the gold of Ophir. Think for a moment: if you had been condemned to dwell in a lions' den, what a relief it would have been to find a Daniel sitting among the ferocious creatures! Such is the consolation which a single holy companion may yield to a lonely soul compelled to sojourn among those who know not God.

Lord, make me one whom thy saints may be glad to meet; and, on the other hand, when I pine because I am exiled from my heavenly home, permit me to hear the voice of a fellow-countryman that I may be of good cheer.

WAITING FOR THE KEY OF THE HOUSE

He that made the soul hath most right to dwell in it; it is a most curious house, of God's own framing, and there ought he to dwell. But he will not enter by force and violence, but by consent; he expecteth love to give up the keys (Rev. 3:20)—'Behold, I stand at the door, and knock: if any man hear my voice, and open the door, I will come in to him, and will sup with him.' Why should Christ stand at the door and knock, and ask leave to enter into his own house? He hath right enough to enter, only he waiteth till we open to him.

Here our author admirably expresses the Lord's respect to the nature and constitution which he has impressed upon man. Inanimate matter obeys the divine law by force, but a human being can only obey God with his will, since unwilling obedience would be no obedience at all. There can be no such thing as unwilling love, unwilling trust, or unwilling holiness. Voluntariness enters into the essence of a moral act. Having, therefore, so fashioned man, the Lord doth not forget this fact, but ever treats man as a free agent. The divine compulsions of his grace are only such as are congruous with a willing and nilling creature. Man is sweetly led to repentance and faith, and by mighty arguments drawn to trust and love the Lord Jesus. We do not surrender our hearts to Jesus otherwise than with our own full and free consent. We are right glad to become his disciples, and to be taught the way of service. He does not break in like a burglar, but he enters the castle of the soul like a conqueror to whom the governor in all lowliness hands the keys.

My heart, it is hard for a theologian to explain how grace overcomes the will, and yet never violates it, and yet thou dost understand it perfectly by experience. Christ's love wooed thee and won thee, and led thee captive, and yet never was a will more free than thine when thou wast altogether bound to thy Beloved.

THE PRINCELY SUBSTITUTE

If a prince, passing by an execution, should take the malefactor's chains, and suffer in his stead, this would be a wonderful instance indeed.

The deed would ring through all history, and be quoted as an amazing instance of heroic pity; and well deserved would be all the words of praise and sonnets of admiration which would record and eulogize it. Yet our Lord Jesus did this and infinitely more for those who were not merely malefactors, but enemies to his own throne and person. This is a wonder of wonders! But, alas, it meets with small praise. The most of men around us have heard of it and treated it as an idle tale, and multitudes more regard it as a pious legend, worthy to be repeated as a venerable fable, and then forgotten as an unpractical myth. Even those who know, believe, and admire, are yet cold in their emotions with regard to the story of the cross. Herein is love which ought to set our hearts on fire, and yet we scarcely maintain a smouldering spark of enthusiasm.

Lord Jesus, be more real to our apprehensions, and so be more completely the Master of our affections.

TRYING THE KEYS

As one that would gladly open a door, trieth key after key till he hath tried every key in the bunch, so doth God try one method after another to work upon man's heart.

His persevering grace will not be baffled. He frequently begins with the silver key of a mother's tearful prayers and a father's tender counsels. In turn, he uses the church-keys of his ordinances and his ministers, and these are often found to move the bolt; but if they fail, he thrusts in the iron key of trouble and affliction which has been known to succeed after all others have failed. He has, however, a golden master-key, which excels all others: it is the operation of his own most gracious Spirit by which entrance is effected into hearts which seemed shut up forever.

Wonderful is the patience and long-suffering of the Lord, or he would long since have left hardened and careless sinners to themselves. *He* is importunate, whether we are so or not. We take pains to resist his heavenly grace, but he abideth faithful to his own name of love.

O Lord, we bless thee that thou hast opened our hearts, and we pray thee now that thou hast entered, abide in our souls forever, as a king in his own palace-halls!

LIFE PROVED BY GROWTH

Where there is life there will be growth, and if grace be true, it will surely increase. A painted flower keepeth always at the same pitch and stature; the artist may bestow beauty upon it, but he cannot bestow life. A painted child will be as little ten years hence as it is now.

What need there is to observe the wide distinction between the picture and the living thing! Of painted likenesses of Christians we have more than enough; nor is the manufacture of portraits a difficult operation: what we want is the real thing and not the artistic imitation. Manton saith well that *growth* is *the* test. Many professors must be forever beginning again:

they stick where they were, or thought they were. They were anxious about their souls, and are so still. They were trying and wishing, and with tries and wishes they are resting contented. If they were saved and knew it, they would find themselves making some measure of advance: not always advancing at the same rate, for all life is not equally rapid in its growth, but still progressing somewhat, forgetting the things behind, and reaching forth to that which is beyond.

Reader, how do you stand under this test? Come, search yourself, and see whether you are adding to your faith, courage; and to courage, brotherly kindness; and to brotherly kindness, love. If there be no growth, it may be, nay, surely it must be, that you are not a child born into the family of God, but a pretty picture, which may adorn a room, but which cannot perform any of the actions of life. It is a sad thing if such be your case, for heaven is not a portrait-gallery; it is the home of loving, living souls, whom grace has quickened with eternal life.

THE OPENED TREASURY AND THE BAGS

If a mighty king should open his treasure, and bid men come and bring their bags, and take as much as they would; do you think they would neglect this occasion of gain? Surely no; they would run and fetch bag after bag, and never cease. Thus doth the Lord act toward us in the covenant of grace.

He makes over all its fulness to his people, and saith, 'All are yours.' We are not straitened in him. The bags will come to an end long before the treasure is exhausted. Let us come, then, to the throne of grace with enlarged desires and widened expectations: the Lord does not stint us, why should we put ourselves upon short commons? 'He saith, eat and drink, yea, drink abundantly, O beloved.' Why, then, do we sit at the table and starve, or rise from it hungry? Let us by faith suck of the abundance of the sea of grace, and partake largely of the hid treasure which the Lord has laid up for us.

THE PHYSICIAN IN THE GARDEN

Plutarch, in his treatise on growth in moral virtue, wherein are many things applicable to growth in grace, saith that a man that hath made some progress in virtue is like a physician, who, when he comes into a garden, doth not consider flowers for their beauty, as gallants do, but for their use and virtue in medicine. So the grown believer doth not consider speech for its fineness, but fitness and seasonableness for present use.

The same holdeth good also concerning growth in grace; the more we grow the more we regard the spiritual part of the word, and such Scriptures and truths as are of practical use and personal concern. Hence it is that experienced believers cannot put up with the mere ornaments of speech which yield so much satisfaction to youthful minds. They want solid, practical, gospel doctrine, and they must have it. Their craving is for herbs for their healing, and not for bouquets for their button-hole. My heart, go thou with the wise men, and learn from them what is the way of wisdom.

BARKING DOGS CATCH NO GAME

Hard speeches have an evil influence in controversy, and do exasperate rather than convince. The dog that followeth the game with barking and bawling loseth the prey; and there is not a more likely way to undermine the truth than an unseemly defence of it. Satan is mightily gratified, if men had eyes to see it, with the ill managing of God's cause.

This lesson is a needful one. Zealots are apt to mistake hard words for arguments. The more in earnest we are, the more are we tempted to speak bitterly, and to overlook the better side of our opponent's cause. Many who think with us applaud us most for those very utterances which deserve the censure of the wise; and this foolish commendation is apt to egg us on in the same unprofitable direction. They would be more judicious if, while approving our zeal, they hinted that we might use a sweeter method and be none the less strong.

We hope as we grow older to be able to hunt more quietly, with surer scent but with less barking. Certainly as we grow in grace we shall more carefully distinguish between holy ardour which is kindled by the Spirit, and carnal heat, which is the wild-fire of unrenewed nature. God grant that as we grow prudent we may not also become lukewarm; else we may gain one way and lose another. We are poor creatures, for when we try to avoid an evil we generally swing like a pendulum to the opposite quarter, and commit another folly. The middle point, the golden mean of virtue, we do not readily reach.

TAKEN IN THE BRIERS

Most that are acquainted with God are taken in the briers. Jesus Christ in the days of his flesh had never heard of many, if their necessities had not brought them to him.

Free grace is a harbour into which few ships ever run except through stress of weather. 'Then they cry unto the Lord in their trouble': that is to say, when they are well-nigh wrecked and are altogether at their wits' end. Till the end of the creature is reached, men will not seek to their Creator, even as the prodigal never thought of home till he had spent all, and there was a mighty famine in the land. Our author refers to Manasseh who was taken among the thorns, and surely he was an instructive type of the great majority of those who are saved from sin.

Lord, be pleased of thy great mercy to overrule the vast amount of poverty and suffering which is now in this land, that men may be driven to thee thereby. Let thy black dogs fetch home thy wandering sheep. Let thy fierce, breaking tempests compel full many a wanton voyager to reef the sails of pleasurable sin, and steer for the haven of forgiving love.

CHESSBOARD

Be watchful; the world is the devil's chessboard; you can hardly move backward or forward, but he is ready to attack you by some temptation.

Those who play at the game of chess know that great circumspection is needed. Your opponent is working toward a design of which you know nothing, and while you imagine that you are doing exceedingly well he is entrapping you. The game of life, as against Satan, is one in which his age, his long practice, his superior skill, and his unscrupulousness give him an immense advantage over our poor self-conceited folly. Lord, help us, lest we lose our souls while we are dreaming of happiness. Thou knowest our adversary, be pleased to deliver us out of his hand.

THE DUMB BEGGAR

A dumb beggar gets an alms at Christ's gate if he can but make signs, when his tongue cannot plead for him.

This is a cheering sentence for the many poor souls who feel that they cannot find words wherewith to pray. Sit down at mercy's gate, and show your sores, and groan, and sigh. Let your rags ask for raiment, and your hunger plead for bread. Wounds are eloquent orators with a tender-hearted surgeon; expose your wounds to Jesus, and he will bind them up. Misery is mercy's best constraint. When the psalmist could not pray a set prayer, he says, 'I opened my mouth and panted.' He declares in another place that he panted like a thirsty hart:[1] there is nothing articulate in panting, and yet no one ever misunderstood the meaning of the act. Come, then, ye dumb beggars, and learn the language of signs. Come and pant, come and spread your misery before the eyes of mercy, and doubt not that he who knows the thoughts of the heart will readily understand you and speedily grant your desires.

CALVIN AND HIS LORD

'What if my master should come and find me idle?' said Calvin to his friends, who demanded of him why he wasted his body in such constant labours. Few are like-minded so as to put this question to their souls, 'Am I as I would wish to be should Christ come?'

This question may serve as a test as to our manner of life: Am I in such a state as I would wish to be in should my Lord appear? If we can answer this to our comfort, all is well; but if not, by all means let us mend matters, get out of our deshabille[2] and stand ready to meet our coming Lord. Bravely did Calvin fight on under a heap of disorders, and if we would be approved at the last we must imitate him in a constant diligence, born of 'seeing him who is invisible'.

Lord, make me to hear thy footfall evermore, and cause me so to live as though I heard thee at the door.

---

[1] A thirsty deer; a reference to Psa. 42:1: 'As a deer pants for flowing streams, so pants my soul for you, O God.'
[2] The state of being partly or carelessly dressed.

INVENTION OF FRESH WEAPONS

As in war, as the arts of battery and methods of destruction do increase, so also doth skill in fortification; so in the church, God still bestoweth gifts for the further explication of truth.

We are glad to see our author writing so cheerily, for at this present it seems to us that our adversaries have been far more acute in assailing the gospel than the church in defending it. Still on God's side it is true that though his ministers may not be as faithful as they should be, yet he raises up one and another to stand as bulwarks for the truth, and so, after all, the grand old cause is not quite overborne. To the end of the campaign it will be so, and there is no real cause for despair, or even for despondency. The fortress of the gospel is still unconquered. Her motto is *Invicta*.[1] The gospel has survived the brutal ignorance of many ages, and if now the world has changed its fashions and professes itself to be wise, the same eternal system of truth will continue to baffle its designs. The assaults of sceptics are a gain to believers, for they produce a clearing and opening up of the truth. Opposition directs attention to neglected doctrines, and heresy calls for orthodox replies, and so our defences become stronger as our enemies become more furious. Happy citizens, to be thus shielded from the foe.

HOMEWARD BOUND

A poor beast that is going homeward goeth cheerfully.

See how the horse pricks up his ears and quickens his pace when you turn his head to his stable. The proverb saith that even the dull ass doth the same. Much more then should intelligent Christian men feel the attractions of their heavenly

[1] Undefeated, unconquered.

home. Courage, brothers and sisters; we, too, are homeward bound. Every hour brings us nearer to the many mansions. We are not going from home, or we might hang our heads: our way is toward the Father's house on high, therefore let us rejoice at every step we take.

MARTHA COMPLAINING OF MARY

St Bernard hath a pretty note of Martha's complaining of Mary, that she sat at Jesus' feet, while herself was employed in all the business of the family. 'Oh', saith St Bernard, 'that is a happy family where Martha complains of Mary!' 'Oh, how few families do thus complain! The world eats up our time, our care, and our thoughts, and God hath but a little share, little worship, little reverence.

For the most part in our households Mary might well complain of Martha, for family cares still cumber many and keep them away from Jesus' feet. Very seldom are Christians nowadays too much in the closet, too much with their Bibles, too much at prayer-meetings. Alas, the most of them are all hack[1] for the world, the shop, or the evening party. Martha, Martha, we may well complain to the Master of thee, for thou leavest him alone, and forsakest his teaching, and all for this poor, cumbering world!

Lord, help us to balance our duties, and thus may we serve thee after the best manner, through thy grace.

THE COMET AND THE SUN

We gaze more on a comet than on the sun.

This is the reason why erratic teachers are for a while popular, and attract public attention. It is given out that they are

---

[1] Hired out as an overworked drudge.

'some great one', and all the town is staring with open mouth. The nine days' wonder is every day's talk. The new teaching is something marvellous, and the old creed is to be driven out of the land. New lights are to eclipse the old; at least, so we are told. Let us wait a while, however, and the comet will have vanished, and the half-forgotten fixed stars will be seen to be shining on with unfading splendour.

May the Lord give us such fixed and established judgments that no novelties of doctrine may ever dazzle us. Children are fond of new toys; let us be men and keep to the tried word of the Lord.

VIOLET AND NETTLE

Laden boughs hang low. The nettle mounteth above its fellow weeds, but the violet lieth shrouded under its leaves, and is only found out by its own scent.

Walking one day by a stream we were conscious of a delicious perfume, and only then did we perceive the little blue eyes which were looking up to us so meekly from the ground on which we stood. Virtue is always modest, and modesty is itself a virtue. He who is discovered by his real excellence, and not by his egotistical advertisement of his own perfections, is a man worth knowing: the other is a mere nettle who is sure to be forgotten, unless indeed his blustering pride should sting some tender spirit, and secure a wretched kind of remembrance.

O that I may ever be more gracious than I seem to be. Never may it be any concern of mine to be observed of men, and yet let me so live that I need not fear to be read and known of all.

THE SWOLLEN ARM

Certainly a proud spirit is no great spirit, any more than a swollen arm can be accounted to be strong.

Many mistakes are made on this matter both as to men and language. Boasters are by foolish persons reckoned at their declared value: no mistake can be greater; a proud spirit is of necessity small and mean in the judgment of truth. Language is thought to be forcible because it is hard, severe, and blustering; and yet there is little power in such speaking except to provoke opposition and furnish motives and weapons for the opposer. Judge, then, between swelling and strength: avoid the one and prudently aim at the other. True humility is beloved of God, and he ever comes to its aid.

I must be less and less in my own esteem if I would have power with God and prevalence with men. It seemeth not so, and yet so it is. Lord, write the lesson on my heart.

ONLY A LINK

The first appearances of error are many times modest. There is a chain of truths; the devil taketh out a link here and a link there, that all may fall to pieces.

The argument of 'charity' is used to screen those who are robbing us of the gospel. We are bidden to be cautious how we condemn those who only differ on small points; whereas the truths which they would take away from us have important bearings upon other truths, and cannot be denied without a serious break-up of the whole doctrinal chain. Let us not give up a single link of the divine system, for if we did so, we should prove traitors to the whole plan of revealed truth.

In these times the illustration given above is exceedingly

instructive. Satan knows that we would never consent to give up a wheel of the gospel chariot, and therefore in his craftiness he only asks for the linch-pins to be handed over to him. May God grant wisdom to his servants that none of them may be beguiled by the cunning of the adversary. Long ages may have to rue the defalcations[1] of this day, if we sell the precious gospel to its foes. Until the Lord shall come we are put in trust with the gospel: will we be fraudulent trustees? Can we dare to play fast and loose with that which concerns God's glory, and the destiny of immortal souls?

THE LUNGS

Some graces, like the lungs, are always in use.

'Pray without ceasing'; 'be thou in the fear of the Lord all the day long'; and such like exhortations appertain to continuous duties. Thus David says, 'I have set the Lord always before me'; he was always living in the presence of God. Other parts of the human frame are exercised occasionally, but the lungs are always at work, and, even so, certain of the graces are in active motion in their appointed seasons, but faith never ceases to believe in the Lord Jesus, for it is essential to spiritual vitality. Hence we ought never to go where we shall be out of the atmosphere of heaven. Lungs must have air, and cannot endure a dense smoke or a poisonous gas; nor can faith bear error, false doctrine, and evil conversation. Since we always need the pure air of heaven, let us not go where it cannot be found. Who in his senses would desire to have been in the Black Hole of Calcutta? Who wishes to dwell where drunkenness and loose living abound? How can faith breathe in such a suffocating atmosphere?

[1] Defalcation is the misappropriation of funds by a person trusted with its charge.

Lord, keep thou my faith alive, that it may keep me alive, and that I may live to thee.

FRUIT WITHOUT THE SUN

Fruit that hath but little sun can never be ripe.

We have had practical proof of this, for during the year 1879, there being a scant measure of sunshine, the fruit was never properly ripened, and was therefore destitute of flavour and sweetness. Whatever might be its outward appearance, the berry was insipid and altogether unlike what the sun would have made it had he smiled upon the swelling fruit.

Thus, without communion with God, no soul can develop its graces, neither can those graces become what they should be. No measure of care or effort can make up for the light of the Father's face; neither can attendance upon means of grace nor the use of religious exercises supply the lack. Fellowship with God we must have, or the essential honey of love will be deficient, the bloom of joy will be wanting, the aroma of zeal and earnestness will be missed. We may have the virtues by name, and we may exhibit some feeble, insipid imitation of them, but the secret savour and mystic richness of grace will not be in us unless we abide in the full light of divine love.

Lord, evermore be as the sun unto our souls, that we may be as fruit fully ripe, attaining to all the perfection and maturity of which our nature is capable.

FIRE! FIRE!

When a fire is kindled in a city we do not say coldly, 'Yonder is a great fire, I pray God it do no harm.' In times of public defection we are not to read tame lectures of contemplative divinity, or fight with ghosts and antiquated errors, but to oppose with all earnestness the growing evils of the world, whatever it may cost us.

If men valued truth as they do their goods and their houses, they would not regard error with such cool contentment. The cant of the present day cries, 'Charity, charity.' As if it were not the truest charity to grow indignant with that which ruins souls. It is not uncharitable to warn men against poisonous adulterations of their food, or invasions of their rights; and surely it cannot be more uncharitable to put them upon their guard against that which will poison or rob their souls. Lukewarmness of love to truth is the real evil to be deprecated in these times. We have new doctrines among us, full of practical mischief, and against these there is need to raise an earnest outcry, lest they gain so great a head that both church and state should be set on fire.

Lord, arouse thy watchmen, and bid them arouse all thy saints, for the times are full of danger.

THE GLASS WITHOUT A FOOT

We derive all our strength from Christ. We are like glasses without feet; they cannot stand of themselves; neither can we.

Such glasses are not ordinarily used now, but they were common enough in former times. A man must hold the glass in his hand, or it would be of no use to him, for he could not set it down on the table, since it could not stand alone, but rolled over, and spilt its contents. We are something in the hand of Jesus, but nothing out of it; we cannot even hold the water of life unless our Lord holds us. What poor creatures men are, and yet they dare to boast!

THE STONE AND THE CHIP

A great deal of fire falleth upon a stone and it burneth not, but a dry chip soon taketh fire.

According to our condition we are affected by the fire of the gospel. Hearts of stone are not kindled by the most vehement preaching of the word, nor will they ever be till grace works a change in their nature. The same sermons which are powerless with them are, through divine grace, most potent with souls prepared of the Lord to feel the flame. The failures of ministers are often traceable to the sinful state of their hearers—what is a man to do who labours to kindle a fire with stones? Must he not labour in vain? He may blow as long as he pleases, and burn his heart out with fervour, and yet his hearers' hearts will not catch the flame; and he may even die in very anguish; but so long as the natural mind remains what it is he cannot effect his purpose.

Lord, I thank thee not only for the heavenly fire, but for the power to be affected by it. It is thy grace which makes me capable of grace, and unto thee be all the praise.

THE ANT-HILL

The world is a great theatre, and the spectators are God and angels. I confess we little think of it; there is a foolish levity in our minds. As to us, the world is like a hill of ants; you stand by, and they run up and down, and do not think of your being there; so the Lord stands by and observes all our motions, and we run up and down like busy ants, and do not think of God's presence among us. We live in a great hurry and clatter of business, and have but few thoughts of God. The Psalmist gives a description of carnal men in these words (Psa. 86:14), they 'have not set thee before them'.

Lord, let me not be a mere ant on the world's hill; but as thou hast given me an understanding, help me to use it upon thyself, that so I may rise to the true level of an intelligent and immortal being. How can I disregard my God, my Father, my all? How can I be taken up with these trifles whilst thou art so near me, asking my love, and proving thy right to it by daily loading me with benefits? What a mere insect I am! Why am I thus? Why should I live like an emmet[1] when thou hast made me a little lower than an angel? I shall never rise to what I ought to be unless thou reveal thyself in me and to me by thy good Spirit. Deliver me from that foolish levity of which thy servant speaks, which makes me fill my mind with contempt-ible vanities, and let me seriously remember thee, and the day when I shall stand before thy judgment-seat.

WANDERING SHEEP NEED GENTLE HANDLING

Though swine or dogs be driven with violence, yet poor stray lambs must be brought home, as the shepherd brought home his lost sheep 'upon his shoulders rejoicing', Luke 15. Many well-meaning men may err; be not too severe with them, lest prejudice make them obstinate, and so from 'erring brethren', they become heretical.

Sound advice this. It is true that certain troublesome here-tics need to be rebuked sharply that they may be sound in the faith, but discretion is needed, and a loving spirit to guide the discretion: the sheep must not be driven as if they were swine. The tendency of stern orthodoxy is to act toward an erring one as cruel fathers do when they whip their boys without mercy, for they drive ten devils in while they think they are whipping one out. A doubter may be worried into a heretic before we are aware of it. Certain minds will learn anything from those they love, and nothing from those who are masterful with them. The gentleness of Christ is a choice qualification for a pastor.

[1] Ant.

Heresies are better kept out by a full gospel than driven out by fierce controversy. Sheep may be worried into worse strayings, but they can be held by their teeth most securely if they are led into plentiful pasture. O for the Holy Spirit's direction in dealing with weak and unstable minds.

DRY STICKS KINDLING THE GREEN

Two dry sticks will set a green one on fire. Can you blame the children of God, then, if they mourn and enter their protest against the iniquity of the times?

They see how the prevalence of sin affects those who would fain be innocent, and how the fashion of evil sweeps along with it those who at first had better manners; and this frets them sorely. We tremble at the mischief which can be done by men who are hardened in iniquity; those dry sticks, so eager for the flame, are our terror; when such are laid together we know how fierce will be the burning. Companionship in evil leads to a high pitch of sin. Hands joined in hand draw on with great force those who seemed reluctant to go in the way of evil. O that our young people would be warned of the danger of bad example! If we could keep the green sticks out of the way of the dry we should have little to fear for our sons and daughters; but, alas, the wicked are often more attractive than the righteous, and fair speech and gay habits fascinate the inexperienced. The amiable but undecided of our youth are beguiled by the pleasant manners of worldly people, and before they are aware they become like their betrayers.

Lord, save us from evil men, and when we are called in the order of providence to be in their presence, let us remember that we are also in thy presence, and so let us escape the contagion of their company.

TUNING AN INSTRUMENT

If we could learn to frame our minds to our estates, as the skilful musician letteth down the strings a peg lower when the tune requireth it, we should pass to heaven more comfortably.

Yes, we are as a rule pitched too high. We look for more in this life than it will ever yield us. If we could be satisfied with less we should be less dissatisfied. It is a great pity when men try to live above their means, for it often ends in their hardly having the means to live at all. Probably there is as much happiness in one station of life as in another if it is suitable to us, and we are able to fill it: the misery of life must be when a man has a little less than he needs and a great deal less than he aspires to. Contentment is the crown jewel of a happy life. We shall have enough, for the promise guarantees us our portion; why need we fret after more? 'Here little and hereafter much', as Bunyan says, is best for us.

O Lord, grant me grace to live above this world; and wherein I must live upon it, and think about it, help me to have few desires and no cares. Tune my nature so that without fail my life may make music to thy praise.

PRINTERS' PROOFS

O ye ministers of the word, consider well that you are the first sheets from the King's press; others are printed after your copy. If the first sheet be well set, a thousand more are stamped with ease. See, then, that the power of religion prevail over your own hearts, lest you not only lose your own souls, but cause the ruin of others.

Correcting for the press is work which has to be done with great care, since thousands of copies will be faulty if the proof-sheet be not as it should be. So should the minister of a congregation be seriously earnest to be right, because his people will imitate him. Like priest, like people; the sheep will follow the shepherd. What need there is that the pastor should order his steps aright lest he lead a whole flock astray! If the town-clock be wrong half the watches in the place will be out of time.

We have all an influence over others. Even the least one among us has some individual beneath his power to whom he serves as an example, for whom, indeed, he is a sort of proof-sheet. O that the good Lord would make us correct in all points, lest we be propagators of sin through the influence of our faults. By self-examination let us labour to correct the proofs.

THE LAPWING

Usually complainers do least. The crafty lapwing will go up and down fluttering and crying, to draw the fowler from her own nest. We have some secret nest of our own, and we are loath it should be rifled and exposed to public view, and therefore we raise an alarm about other matters.

This we may be doing without being aware of it, for self-deceit is easy. We may be amusing ourselves with zeal for political reforms when in truth our own personal habits need reforming, or we may be exclaiming against the errors of the church while our own private life far more needs our attention. It is a pity to be cheating our own selves.

Our author, however, is very shrewd in his judgment of complainers. Our own experience leads us to the conclusion that critics of others, and noisy talkers of all kinds, have usually some design of their own, and are working to their own hand. If we were to press them home we should probably discover that they are no better than they should be. Their pretence of being wounded and hurt by the sins of others is a crafty scheme for drawing away observation from their own failings. Lapwings are plentiful enough all around us, and not a few are still deceived by their practices.

O Lord, save me from all deceit, and, above all, prevent my deceiving myself.

THE CHANGED BED

A sick man thinketh to have ease in another bed, in another room; carry him thither, his pain continueth. If a carnal man had lived in the prophets' times or the apostles' times, he would have been the same as now (see Matt. 23:29, 30). A brier is a brier wherever it groweth; change of times will not avail without a change of heart. Adam sinned in Paradise; the apostate angels in heaven; Lot was unchaste in the mountains, where were none but his own family; in a howling wilderness, where they had no outward enticements, the Israelites were given to fleshly lusts.

This is a needful rebuke of a very common folly; let the reader see that he fall not into the error. We ought not blame our occupation, but our disposition. We may not saddle our poverty or our wealth with the sin which is purely of ourselves, for this is only an oblique way of blaming God for our faults. Change of place is not wanted, but change of heart. If, dear friend, you are unholy where you are, you would be the same in any other position in life. The fault is not in your stars, but in yourself, that you are still an impenitent sinner. Lay this to heart; abandon all idle excuses and seek your Saviour.

DEEP FOUNDATIONS

The Lord diggeth deep when he meaneth to raise the building high; and when he would give men to know much of Christ, he first bringeth them out of themselves by godly sorrow.

We see many to be but low and mean in point of grace, not rising like towers toward heaven, but lying low upon the earth: these have never been digged out by a deep sense of sin, nor excavated by profound soul-trouble, and hence it would not be safe to build high with so shallow a foundation. If we could read the secret history of dwarfed Christians we should find that they never had much humbling of heart. They tell us there is as much of a tree under as above ground, and certainly it is so with a believer; his visible life would soon wither were it not for his secret life, and his high enjoyments would fall over to his ruin were they not balanced by his inward humiliations. There must be deep foundations if we are to have high walls; we must be emptied of self, and everything of human strength, or we shall never be filled with the love of God.

O my heart, be ready to be trenched deep if this be the necessary preparation for being built up aloft. Welcome pain and down-casting if edification is to follow.

GOOD DIET IN UNHEALTHY PLACES

When the air is infectious we are the more careful of our diet.

In sickly times and places men endeavour to keep up the strength of their bodies by nourishing food, and they strive to avoid sickness by wholesome meat. In this they act wisely, and according to the rules of prudence. An equal care should be exercised over our souls. When the very air seems to be laden with error and vice, believers should set a double watch as to what they hear, and where they go. Sin is as subtle and as deadly as the foul gas which bears within it the seeds of plague, and therefore the utmost caution must be used that we keep as far from its occasions and temptations as we possibly can. We must also live nearer to God than ever, and feed more upon Christ, and seek more of his Spirit than at any former time, that we may be fortified against the unusual dangers of the age. So shall we be error-proof and vice-proof, and, though a thousand fall at our side, the spiritual death shall not come nigh unto us. Errors, like diseases, prey upon the feebler sort, and though they bring no good even to the strong, yet these are able to cast off their deleterious influences, even as a man in armour shakes off the arrows which else would wound him grievously. To be strong in the Lord is the best preservative against the ills of our age, and the perils of our surroundings.

O Lord, we would dwell in thy secret place, that abiding under thy shadow we may live unharmed even where Satan's seat is, should thy providence there pitch our tent.

HEAVEN'S CEMENT

Love is a grace that will make us industrious for the good of others, and therefore we read of the 'labour of love' (1 Thess. 1:3). It is **gluten animarum,** *the glue of souls, the cement and solder of the church: the jointing that runneth throughout all the living and squared stones (Col. 3:14). By this souls are mingled, and all mutual offices are cheerfully performed.*

O for more of this sacred cement! The walls of many churches gape with huge cracks for lack of it. Building with untempered mortar is an ancient fault, but nowadays some build with no mortar at all. Professors seem to be piled together like a load of bricks, without life, love, or living truth to unite them; and the promise is forgotten, 'I will lay thy stones with fair colours.' Will not our reader, if he be a believer, endeavour to furnish his portion of the sacred cement of love, which is the perfect bond? This will be far more useful than complaining of the lack of unity, for this complaint often creates the evil which it deplores. Critics pick out from between the stones the mortar, of which there is little enough already; but loving hearts fill up the cracks, and do their best to keep the structure whole. 'Blessed are the peacemakers.'

How am I acting? Am I a bond in the building, or do I, like the foolish woman in the Proverbs,[1] pluck down the house with my hands? O Lord of peace, make me more and more a lover of peace.

LAY-FIGURES

You would all judge it to be an affront to the majesty of God if a man should send his clothes stuffed with straw, or a puppet dressed up instead of himself, into the assemblies of God's people, and think that this would do instead of his personal presence. Yet our clothes stuffed with straw would be less offensive to God than our bodies without our souls. The absence of the spirit is the absence of the more noble part.

Think of this, ye whose hearts are with your flocks and herds, and shops, and ships, when you are in your churches and chapels. Will ye longer insult the Lord who will have only those to worship him who worship him in spirit and in truth? A mind stuffed with vanity and unbelief must be worse than clothes stuffed with straw. Reader, have you never set up this abomination before the very eyes of the Eternal?

CLOWNS AND PRINCES

It is not a wonder for a clown, that hath not been acquainted with dainties, to love garlic and onions; but for a prince, that hath been acquainted with better diet, to leave the dainties of his father's

[1] Prov. 14:1.

*table for such base feeding, that were strange. I do not wonder
at carnal men, that they are delighted with carnal objects: they
never knew better; but for a child of God, that hath tasted how
gracious and sweet God in Christ is, to find sap and savour in
coarser fare, this is wonderful.*

Yet were our author now alive he might weep his eyes out as
he saw professing Christians craving for the ball-room and the
theatre. The carrion which professors can now feed upon is dis-
gusting to the very thought of a real Christian. Entertainments
are got up among religious people which are unworthy even of
decent worldlings. Many true hearts are deeply wounded by
this terrible degeneracy. Were it not for a small remnant we had
been as Sodom, and been made like unto Gomorrah.

PAINT FOR PAINT

*A ministry that stayeth in the paint of words will beget but painted
grace.*

If it is not a real, hearty ministry of grace, inspired by the
Holy Spirit, it will end in nothing. Fine words neither wound
nor heal. Oratory may amuse, but it cannot convert; and
rhetoric may astonish, but it will never save. We must have
more than mere words, however striking—paint will not
do; we want living preaching, by men in downright earnest,
attended by the living Spirit, or else life will never be created or
sustained by it. What is the use of colouring the cheek of the
dead? The hue of life is a mockery while death reigns within.
That is evil preaching which creates the semblance of piety, but
never imparts the substance.

Lord, save me from being the imitation of a Christian,
the produce of a mimic gospel. Give me thoroughness and

sincerity, and let not my religion be a painted pageantry for me to go to hell in. Create in me a clean heart, O God!

SLUGGARDS HATE LIGHT

The lazy world would fain lie upon the bed of ease, draw the curtains and rest; and therefore light is troublesome to it. In these days men begin to tire of gospel music, and thirst and pant for the old unsavoury moral strains, which deal with sin in general, and do not irritate men by close personal applications.

Faithful preachers are like those men whose business it is to arouse slumbering workmen and call them to their labours. The sound is not welcome to those who desire a little more slumber; they wish no blessings upon the head of the noisy watchman. Yet if they be aroused and reach their work betimes they have a good word in the end for him who caused them to be up and doing. The watchman should not take notice of a hasty word from one half awake; he may rest content that he will have their good word by and by.

Manton was right in his suspicion that mere moral preaching would continue to have its admirers. Many nowadays reckon it a crime for the preacher to be rousing and personal; they prefer a good sound moralist who will tell servants their duty, and let their masters and mistresses sleep. O that men were wise, for then they would count him to be the best preacher who the most earnestly calls them out of their beds of sinful ease to seek and find salvation. None do this but spiritual, gospel preachers. Your 'moral' teacher pretends to be very practical, and yet if you watch for the results of his efforts, what will you see? When you have looked through a microscope you will only say, 'There is nothing', for truly there are no results worth mentioning. Sin is a serpent which these moralists cannot tame, charm they never so wisely.

Lord, help us to cry aloud, and spare not till the slumberers arise; and let us use thy truth as the best awakener. Let thy light shine on sluggards and awaken them. If these things suffice not, Lord, thunder at them, and by some means break their death-sleep.

THE LONG GARMENT

A garment which is too long trails in the mire and soon becomes a dirty rag; and it is easy for large estates to become much the same. It is a hard lesson to 'learn to abound' (Phil. 4:12). We say such a one would do well to be a lord or a lady; but it is a harder thing than we think it to be.

It is hard to carry a full cup with a steady hand. High places are dizzy places, and full many have fallen to their eternal ruin through climbing aloft without having grace to look up. The simile of the trailing garment used by Manton is simple, but instructive. Such robes raise a dust, and gather upon themselves all sorts of filthiness, besides being subjected to needless wear and tear. A man may have so much of this world that he misses the next. His long robe may trip him up in the race for the heavenly prize, and he may fall victim to the wealth he idolized. Alas, for the poor rich! Faring sumptuously every day, and yet full often strangers to that deep and peerless joy which belongs to those who, in the deep waters of poverty, find a boundless bliss in trusting God. When the rich are saved they should count it a miracle of grace, and feel great gratitude to him who enables a camel to go through the eye of a needle, notwithstanding his hump.

Lord, give me neither poverty nor riches; or, rather, be thou my riches, and give thyself to me. As for all else, I would leave myself without reserve in thy hands.

CRIPPLES MOCKING

If cripples mock us for going upright, we pity them.

If worldlings rail at us for endeavouring to lead godly and sober lives, we should, not be angry, but rather sorrow over their infatuation. No wise man will swerve an inch from his path to please those who are mad with sin, nor will he break his heart because idiotic sinners make a jest of his uprightness.

BIRD-CATCHING BY NIGHT

This is the devil's device, first to maze[1] people, as birds are with a light and a bell in the night, and then to drive them into the net. If you would keep to wholesome doctrine, keep to a form of wholesome words, and do not place religion in conceited speaking.

Would to God that this advice would be heeded! We have those about us who are forever inventing some new thing, and using the old orthodox terms in an altogether novel sense. Their hearers are first dazzled with the clever candle-light, and cannot make out what the novel brilliance means; and when they are thoroughly bewildered, a great noise and tinkling is made of pretended wisdom and deep thought, so that the poor souls are ready to fly anywhere and anyhow. Thus fowler's business is effectually done, and by this means, if it were possible, they would ensnare the very elect. The safest way for simple souls is to keep to a definite and decided gospel ministry. If you do not know the voice of the shepherd, do not follow him.

[1] To daze or confuse.

Of course you will avoid a wolf, for his howl is your warning; but be doubly careful to keep clear of the false shepherd, and, to make quite sure of your man, count him to be false who is not evidently true.

Lord, preserve my poor silly mind from being dazed and dazzled, and let me follow thy truth step by step even to the end.

DWELLERS IN MARSHES

In marshy countries we do not expect a clear air; so sensual persons have seldom any clear and elevated thoughts of God. Men given to pleasures can taste meats and drinks, but not doctrines.

Hence the folly of being swayed by their censures. Learned men are to be respected when they express opinions upon subjects which they understand; but when they are known to be without grace and spiritual light their opinions upon divine truth are not to be regarded. They have not the capacity to appreciate such things, and they had better let them alone. A blind man may be a first-rate musician, and in his own department he may be a master, but if he ventures to dogmatize upon colour and artistic portraiture he is more worthy of ridicule than of reverence. Carnal men have not the needful taste by which divine doctrine is discerned. Their minds are as to religion a mere marsh land, breeding fog and mist, and to hope for clear and expansive views of the gospel from them is in vain. May God of his great mercy uplift the great, sunken intellects of our day, and give a holy taste and discernment to those who now know nothing of the bread of heaven or the new wine of the gospel. Meanwhile it will be as well to take as little notice as possible of their opinions upon religion, which must of necessity be valueless.

THE UNFINISHED HOUSE

We shall not keep what we have received if we do not labour to increase it, as a house begun to be built goeth to decay, and droppeth down more and more, if we do not go on to finish it.

Have we not all seen what are commonly called house-carcasses standing in desolation, a blot upon the street, and a dead loss to the builder? Today the slates are falling, tomorrow the windows are broken, and anon timber after timber falls. Just such are they who having begun to build in the matter of religion have failed to count the cost, and so come to a stand-still, and speedily arrive at a ruin. We believe —*not* in the continuance of unprogressive grace, but in the perseverance and progress of saints even to the end. Blessed are they who have this persevering progress, for these are habitations builded of God. Others, who abide in their immovable self-content, are ruined by degrees, and prove themselves to be mere carcasses, within which the living graces have never taken up their residence. Remember this, O my soul, and pray the Lord to build thee up by his Spirit, and complete in thee the work of grace with power.

SOLDIERS AND SAILORS

If because you are Christians you promise yourselves a long lease of temporal happiness, free from troubles and afflictions, it is as if a soldier going to the wars should promise himself peace and continual truce with the enemy; or as if a mariner committing himself to the sea for a long voyage, should promise himself nothing but fair and calm weather, without waves and storms;—so irrational it is for a Christian to promise himself rest here upon earth.

Experience abundantly confirms this, and yet who would not be a soldier of the cross? And, being so, who would wish to be a feather-bed soldier, never flushing one's sword, or smelling powder? If there be no war there can be no victory; ease is therefore our loss and hindrance. What we need is not freedom from conflict, but abundance of faith. Trials would little try us if we had more confidence in God, and afflictions would have small power to afflict us if we laid up our heart's joy and confidence in the Lord alone. Nearness to God is the one desideratum.

O Lord, draw us very near thee, and then we shall dwell in peace though the whole world should battle with us.

BURNING A HOUSE TO KILL MICE

If a man should fire a house to destroy the mice in it, we should think him to be fairly mad.

Yet those who consider themselves to be reasonable men will set a church in a blaze about the merest trifle. Meeting after meeting will be called, and angry discussions provoked, and holy work overturned about the smallest mistake of the preacher, or the minutest fault of a deacon. One would think that heaven itself was endangered, and yet it turns out to be a question of infinitesimal importance. Societies which were doing great service have even been broken up by the crazy whimsies of good brethren, who made much ado about nothing, and did great harm in trying to do a little good.

But the mice are a nuisance! Of course they are, and we must buy a cat or set a trap, but we certainly shall not burn the house down when a simple means will accomplish our purpose. We aim at reformation, not at desolation. We see no wisdom in so perpetually improving a church or a good society that in the end it is improved from off the face of the earth.

Religion has been thought to be sick, and fools have doctored it till they brought it to death's door by their poisons. Prudence is to be used, even when our object is worthiest of zeal; and never ought we to endanger a really good thing for the sake of making it a little better.

Lord, make me wise as a serpent and harmless as a dove, and if I am called to protest against error or sin, help me to do it in the spirit of my Lord.

CLOSING THE FLOOD-GATES

Any fool can open the flood-gates, but when the waters have once broken out, who can recall them?

A question well worthy to be weighed by those who create strife. They can with a few hasty words set loose a torrent of anger and uncharitableness, and cause the sweeping away of much good service and sweet fellowship, but who shall rule, restrain, or call back the raging flood. O meddler, pause ere thy sad work be actually commenced, for woe unto that man by whom the offence cometh!

So, too, a stream of dangerous doctrine may easily enough be set flowing among a people. Doubtful words and curious questions may soon let out a ruinous deluge of infidelity and false teaching, and he who at the first drew up the flood-gate may never have dreamed what would come of it; he may even wring his hands at horror of his own deed, and yet may be utterly powerless to stay the mischief. Be cautious, therefore, O speculating teacher. Carry thine inventive faculties into a less dangerous region. Let the old barriers stand, and be not thou Satan's tool to do a mischief which an age may rue.

THE SPIDER

The blind hope that is found in men ignorant and presumptuous will certainly fail them; it is compared to 'a spider's web' (Job 8:14). The spider spinneth a web out of her own bowels, which is swept away as soon as the besom[1] cometh; so do carnal men conceive a few rash and ungrounded hopes; but when death cometh, or a little trouble of conscience, these vain conceits are swept away.

Let us not spin a hope of heaven out of ourselves, or our own works, feelings, or professions. Such a web of confidence may be very ingeniously contrived, but it must be very frail and will inevitably be swept away. What is a man full of self-righteousness but a dark room full of cobwebs? Good house-keepers do not care for the clever works of this poor insect, but are eager to destroy them, for they are a detriment, and not an ornament. Neither spiders nor their webs are acceptable to us; and even so we may depend upon it that when we have finished the web of our legal hopes and worked hard at our will-worship, God will have no more respect to us and our proud doings than we have to spiders and their constructions. Let proud Pharisees think of this and be humbled. The bee is our example, for she builds a house, but fetches all the material from abroad, and it is from the flowers of the garden, and not from herself, that she procures the honey with which she stores her cells. Spiders suck no flowers as bees do, their productions are from their own bowels. True believers get all the substance and sweetness of their hopes from the flowers of the promises, and dare not live upon themselves, or anything that they can do or be.

---

[1] Broom.

BIRDS ON THE WING

Birds are seldom taken in their flight; the more we are upon the wing of heavenly thoughts, the more we escape snares.

O that we would remember this, and never tarry long on the ground lest the fowler ensnare us. We need to be much taken up with divine things, rising in thought above these temporal matters, or else the world will entangle us, and we shall be like birds held with limed twigs, or encompassed in a net. Holy meditation can scarcely be overdone; in this age we fear it never is. We are too worldly, and think too much of the fleeting trifles of time, and so the enemy gets an advantage of us, and takes a shot at us. O for more wing and more use of the flight we have! Communion with Jesus is not only sweet in itself, but it has a preserving power by bearing us aloft, above gun-shot of the enemy. Thoughts of heaven prevent discontent with our present lot, delight in God drives away love to the world, and joy in our Lord Jesus expels pride and carnal pleasure: thus we escape from many evils by rising above them.

Up, then, my heart. Up from the weedy ditches and briery hedges of the world into the clear atmosphere of heaven. There where the dews of grace are born, and the sun of righteousness is Lord paramount, and the blessed wind of the Spirit blows from the everlasting hills, thou wilt find rest on the wing, and sing for joy where thine enemies cannot even see thee.

VALENTINIAN AND THE SPOTTED GARMENT

There is a story of Valentinian in Theodoret, that when he accompanied Julian the Apostate to the temple of Fortune, those that had charge of the house sprinkled their holy water upon the emperor, and a drop fell upon Valentinian's garment. He beat the officer, saying that he was polluted, not purged, and tore off the piece of his

garment upon which the drop lighted, hating, saith the historian,
'the garment spotted by the flesh.'

The man was decided and outspoken, and this may well make us lenient toward his rough way of showing it. The story is narrated, not that we may imitate Valentinian in his violence, but that we may regard it as a figure of the holy horror which ought to inspire us when so much as a spot of sin defiles us. We are to keep ourselves unspotted from the world; not only free from great smears and daubs, but even from spots. O for a deep hatred of sin, and a determination to part with anything and everything which bears its stain. Let us rend off a polluting habit and utterly abstain from it, however pleasing it may have been. Sins of the flesh especially are so apt to grow that the least approach to impurity must be regarded as a plague-spot; here there must be no dallying with evil, or winking at the appearance of it. The same is true of all other forms of evil, the smallest seed will bring forth a terrible harvest. From the least error, the least wrong, the least falsehood we must be purged if we would walk with Christ and be accepted of him as his 'disciples indeed'.

Lord, cleanse thou me, that I may be without fault before thy throne.

COURTIERS' COURTESY

Courtiers are more polite in their manners than ordinary subjects,
because they are more in their prince's eye and company. The
oftener we are in God's court the more holy shall we become.

The company of the Lord's holy servants raises the tone of our thought and makes us aspire after a sanctity beyond what we possess, and therefore we may be sure that communion with their Lord will be still more beneficial to us. If we learn good manners from the man, what may we expect from being with the Master! From Jesus we shall learn gentleness and love, purity and self-sacrifice, and so acquire the courtly manners of the Prince of Peace, shaking off at the same time the boorish ways which cling to us from having dwelt in Mesech and tabernacled in the tents of Kedar. There is no preparation for heaven like abiding with heaven's Lord.

Come, my heart, art thou now walking with God? How long since thou hast spoken with thy sovereign? Arise and get thee to his royal courts, and, once there, go no more out forever. Thy heaven and thy preparation for heaven both lie in thy Lord.

FINE-SPUN THREAD

When the thread of the gospel is too fine spun, it will not clothe a naked soul.

Nice distinctions and technical phrases may hide the fulness of the word of God, and the simple truth may be treated in such a philosophical manner that its strength and substance may be taken away. Some men preach the gospel, but there is very little of it. It is the right wool, but it is spun too fine. They give milk, it is true, but the water of their own notions so dilutes it that a man might sooner be drowned in it than nourished by it. O to preach a full gospel fully!—to give it out with the richness and freeness which poor sinners need. This is one of the great demands of the day. Men are very liberal in their views, but they are not liberal in dealing out the precious things of the gospel of Christ. Cold is this world and bitter are the blasts of conscience, and while they are shivering in their sins, poor awakened souls need all the gospel of grace, and all the grace of the gospel. O that our brethren would give up their fine spinning and wire-drawing of the doctrines of grace, and give us something substantial from the storehouse of the everlasting covenant, and plenty of it! Alas, too many despise the old-fashioned word, and in their heart of hearts hate the very doctrine which they pretend to uphold. We know some who have no more right in the Christian ministry than Mahometans, and yet they say they are followers of Jesus. We have not so learned Christ.

THE FRIGHTENED WOLF

A wolf may be scared from his prey, but yet he keepeth his preying and devouring nature.

He has not lost his taste for lambs, though he was obliged to drop the one which he had seized. So a sinner may forego his beloved lust, and yet remain as truly a sinner as before. He gives up the drink for fear of losing his situation, or dying of disease, but he would be at his liquor again if he dared. The fear of hell whips him off some favourite vice, and yet his heart pines for it, and in imagination he gloats over it. While this is the case the man in the sight of God is as his heart is: the muzzled wolf is still a wolf, the silenced swearer is still profane in heart, the lewd thinker is still an adulterer.

Something is done when a wolf is scared, or a transgressor driven out of his evil ways, yet nothing is done which will effectually change the wolf or renew the ungodly heart. A frightened sinner is a sinner still. Like the frightened dog, he will return to his vomit; and like the sow that was washed, he will wallow in the mire again as soon as opportunity offers. 'Ye must be born again':—this is the only effectual cure for sin. While the nature is unchanged it is but the outside of the cup and platter which is washed. 'Truth in the inward parts' is that which God desireth, and till that is given we remain under wrath. Any thief will turn honest under the gallows, and yet if he were set free he would rob the first house he came to. A scare is not a conversion. A sinner may be frightened into hypocrisy, but he must be wooed to repentance and faith. Love tames and grace transforms; may the God of all grace deal thus with each of us.

THE FALLEN SOT

A sottish drunkard, that is overpoised with his own excess, lieth where he falleth, and except some friendly hand lift him up, there he perisheth; and just so it is with sinners, they are pleased with their condition, and if they be not soundly roused up and awakened, they lie and die, and fry in their sins. Oh! then, pluck them out of the fire, warn them to flee from the wrath to come.

Be in earnest with them! Exhort, rebuke, entreat. Do not leave them to perish in their sins. Use a holy violence with them, and pull them out of the mire. Common humanity would lead us to help a sheep which had fallen into a ditch, and shall we not come to the rescue of an immortal soul? The sottishness and folly of the ungodly must not dispirit us; we must take that into the account, and we shall not wonder at their uncouth and ungrateful treatment of us. As a drunken man does not want to be helped, and curses those who would serve him, so is it often with those ungodly ones who most of all require our aid. Let us not be put off by them, but labour to save them even though they are resolved to destroy themselves. Whatever evil expressions they use toward us now, they will think and speak very differently if they are saved by our means. We will appeal from the verdict of their present drunkenness to the thankfulness of their future sobriety.

Blessed Master, make us more concerned to win souls, and

let us never give over, however bad men may be. How can we let them perish when we remember that thou wouldst not leave us to die in our sins, though we were as far gone as any of those around us?

THE CLOCK OF PROVIDENCE

There is a clock with which providence keepeth time and pace, and God himself setteth it.

So that everything happens with divine punctuality. Israel came out of Egypt on the selfsame night in which the redemption was appointed, and afterward wandered in the wilderness till the hour had come when the iniquity of the Amorites was full. Our time is always come, for we are in selfish haste; but our Lord when on earth had his set times and knew how to wait for them. The great God is never before his time, and never too late. We may well admire the punctuality of heaven.

Our trials come in due season, and go at the appointed moment. Our fretfulness will neither hasten nor delay the purpose of our God. We are in hot haste to set the world right, and to order all affairs: the Lord hath the leisure of conscious power and unerring wisdom, and it will be well for us to learn to wait. The clock will not strike till the hour; but when the instant cometh we shall hear the bell. My soul, trust thou in God, and wait patiently when he says, 'My time is not yet come.'

THE HOUSE ON FIRE

If a man set his house on fire, he is liable to the law; if it be fired by others, or by an ill accident, he is pitied and relieved.

We are to take up our cross when laid upon our shoulders by God's providence; but we are not to make trouble for ourselves. We are not to fill our own cup with gall and worm-wood, but to drink it off when God puts a bitter draught into our hand. We are to meet temptation and overcome it; but we may not venture into temptation on our own account, or we may have to rue our foolhardiness.

The figure of the burning house is a very apt one, and capable of many illustrations. A man who partakes of wine or strong liquors wilfully fires his own house and, whatever may be the result of his intemperance, he can only blame himself. He who reads sceptical works, or frequents infidel society, cannot be pitied if he loses faith and comfort, for he runs a wanton and useless risk. To be taken at unawares by a fierce temptation, is to be like a building fired by a malicious hand, and this is a grievous calamity; but to go wilfully into temptation is another matter, and is comparable to the crime of arson, in which a man collects combustible materials and secretly kindles them, that his house may be burned down.

Lord, evermore keep me from being my own destroyer. Let me not, like Absalom, grow my hair for my own hanging. 'Let not any iniquity have dominion over me.'

A KNOCK BORNE FOR THE SAKE OF A CROWN

A man will venture a knock that is in reach of a crown.

The ambitious will run all risks of cruel wounds, and death itself, to reach a throne; the prize hardens them against all hazards. Even so will every wise man encounter all difficulties for the crown of life; and when, by faith, he sees it within reach, he will count all afflictions light through which he wades to glory. 'If we suffer, we shall also reign with him.'

PROVISION FOR A JOURNEY

He that is in a journey to heaven must be provided for all weathers;
for though it be sunshine when he first sets forth, a storm will
overtake him before he cometh to his journey's end.

Very small must be the number who have had fair weather all the way to glory: it is questionable if ever one has been so favoured. Hence we ought, every one of us, to be prepared for tempest and hurricane, or we may be found in an evil plight in the day of our calamity. The presence of God is the only universal preservative. When he is with us the sun shall not hurt us by day, nor the moon by night. God, all-sufficient, meets every contingency, seen or unseen. Faith must take her God to herself, and then prudently look forward to occasions for making test and proof of the endless uses to which the divine presence can be turned. A man who has made ample provision for all weathers is rather glad than sorry to be driven to use what he has provided, and, even so, trials are well-nigh welcomed by the man who is fully armed against them. He feels that it would be a kind of waste to be well stored and then never have to draw upon the supply—a sort of superfluity to be fully armed and yet never to meet an enemy.

Have faith in Christ and you are ready for anything, thankful for everything, afraid of nothing. 'Ye are complete in him.'

MAKING A NOISE BY CRYING 'SILENCE'

A crier in the court, that is often commanding silence, disturbeth
the court more than they that make the noise; so, disputing with
our distractions increaseth them. They are better avoided by a
severe contempt.

That is to say, when Satan would disturb us at our devotions by injecting blasphemous thoughts or trifling ideas, we had better keep right on, and as much as possible disregard his interruptions. As blind Bartimeus cried all the more because officious persons sought to silence him, so should we be the more vehement in our supplications when the devil seeks to take us off from them. When he knocks let us fasten another bolt, and let him knock till he grows weary. Our business is with the Lord, and let us give our whole heart to seeking his face, for if we turn away to answer the enemy he will at once have gained his point. When he paints images on our fancy,[1] if we steadfastly refuse to look at them, he will cease from the unprofitable work, and betake himself to work upon some more foolish folk, who will turn aside from prayer to answer his vile insinuations. Let him howl as he pleases; if we do not regard him his pride will be hurt more severely than by any blow that we can aim at him.

> Satan trembles when he sees
> The weakest saint upon his knees.

Therefore, let us keep to our praying, and let him keep to his tempting till he has had enough of it, 'Get thee behind me, Satan' is as much attention as he deserves. Herein is wisdom, and he that hath understanding will learn from it.

RIPENING CORN

Before corn be ripened it needeth all kinds of weather. The husband-man is glad of showers as well as sunshine; rainy weather is troublesome, but sometimes the season requireth it.

Even so the various conditions of man's life are needful to ripen him for the life to come. Sorrows and joys, depressions

---

[1] Imagination.

and exhilarations, have all their part to play in the completion of Christian character. Were one grief of a believer's career omitted, it may be he would never be prepared for heaven: the slightest change might mar the ultimate result. God, who knows best how to ripen both corn and men, ordereth all things according to the counsel of his will, and it is our wisdom to believe in the infallible prudence which arranges all the details of a believing life. 'All things work together for good.'

LOOKING FOR AN EXPECTED GUEST

When we expect anyone, we turn our eyes that way, as the wife looks toward the sea, when she expects her husband's return.

Surely, then, if we look for Christ to come we shall keep our eyes heavenward, and our minds occupied with the country from which he cometh. If we mind earthly things, it will be evidence that the coming of the Lord has no power over us.

Yet a good wife does not sit idly by the sea watching for a sail, but she sets the house in order for her husband's return. She who should sit looking out of window, or studying almanacs, and have no provision made for the home-coming, would show but scant love for her lord. We should watch, but we should also stand with our loins girt, and do the duty of the hour, that when our Lord comes he may not blame our negligence in his service. If we know little of the prophecies, we can show our expectancy by keeping the precepts.

PAYMENT IN GOLD INSTEAD OF COPPER

Though Christ paid the same debt as that which is due from lost souls, yet, through the excellency of his person, it was done in a shorter time. A payment in gold is the same sum as a payment in silver or brass; only, through the excellency of the metal, it taketh up less room.

Thus do we clearly see how the one death of Jesus was a fit and full substitute for the eternal woe of many. How precious does it appear in that light! We are redeemed with a price inconceivable! Gold and silver are corruptible things in comparison therewith. How we ought to prize the adorable person of our Lord! What high thoughts we ought to entertain of him, seeing that it is 'by himself' that lie purged our sins! His own intrinsic excellence was the essential value of the great price which he had paid. Had he been less illustrious his sufferings had been insufficient. Precious blood! yea, more precious Lord Jesus, from whose preciousness the finished work derives its infinite efficacy.

SLOW SHOWERS ARE BEST

We would have speedy riddance of trouble, but God thinketh not fit to grant our request. Showers that come by drops soak into the earth better than those that come in a tempest and hurricane.

The gradualness and long continuance of a trial, which are its sharpness and bitterness, are also, to a large extent, the causes of its usefulness. If the affliction came and departed with a rush, we should be rather swept away by it than softened and saturated by its influence. To push a crucible among the glowing coals and snatch it forth again would answer no purpose in refining: the metal must tarry in the furnace till the fire has done its work.

Perhaps the reader has long lived in a perpetual drip of trouble, and now feels himself to be quite weary of the endless torture. Let him not faint under the lengthened process: the highest degree of benefit is accruing to him from the continuance of his adversity. In the later part of a trial every stroke tells with tenfold result, and operates with a greatly increased efficacy. It would be a pity for the Lord to stay his hand when it is working with such special and marked result. All the preceding affliction has only worked the heart into a fit condition to receive the master-strokes of the divine artist. The ground colours have hitherto been laid on, but the second and finishing touch is now being given; therefore, ask not the hand to cease, but rather pray that its work may be carried on with power, and the Lord's glory be seen in it all. It will not cease raining yet; and why should it so long as the soil is being softened, saturated, and fertilized by the falling drops? Let patience have her perfect work; and how can that be unless the tribulation runs its full time?

Lord, make me ready to tarry for the vision, however long it may be delayed. Thy way of trying me is the best. I would not hurry thy hand if I could.

GERMAN CHILDREN DIPPED IN THE RHINE

God seeth it fitting sometimes, at our first setting forth, as the old Germans were want to dip their children in the Rhine to harden them, so to season us for our whole course by plunging us in trouble. Saints must bear the yoke from their youth, or first acquaintance with God (Heb. 10:32), for this is good for them.

Some of us can endorse this opinion from our own experience. Sharp trials in our early days hardened us for our life's warfare. Abused and misrepresented both by good and bad, we learned to set small store by the judgment of men, so that when praise and flattery followed, we had an antidote for the poisons. Pain and depression of spirit, endured in early life, have prepared many to sympathize with the unhappy, and to live a life of benevolence. A baptism into fire is, for young converts, a terrible ordeal, and yet an incalculable blessing. The whole church endured this baptism for ages, and thereby gathered a strength much needed in these last days.

Let us never despise the chastening of the Lord. Should he seem to dip us in the Styx[1] itself, let us believe that it is for our good, and stand to Job's resolve, 'Though he slay me, yet will I trust in him.'

THE TRADESMAN MISSING HIS CUSTOMER

You that are tradesmen are troubled if you happen to be abroad when a good customer cometh to deal with you: the ordinances of God are the market for your souls; if you had not been abroad with Esau you might have received the blessing, and gone away richly laden from a prayer-meeting, from the word, and the Lord's Supper; but you lose your advantages for want of attention.

With what diligence should we use the means of grace, 'not forsaking the assembling of ourselves together as the manner of some is'; and when we are there, we should be like the shop-keeper—on the lookout for business; not half asleep, or wandering in our minds. If we were more lively at sermons, we should find them more lively. Nothing profits a man which is done carelessly; when our minds are not in our business we cannot prosper in it, and we may be even more sure that we cannot profit by sacred exercises if we are not intensely earnest in them. If customers call, and find the tradesman away, he loses all hope of gain; and when grace and blessing come, and our hearts are not on the watch, we miss heavenly treasure,

[1] A river in Greek mythology that formed the boundary between earth and the underworld.

and remain in a poor and miserable condition. My soul, bestir thyself. Lord, quicken thou me in thy ways.

READY TO SAIL

A Christian should be always as a ship that hath taken in its lading, and is prepared and furnished with all manner of tackling, ready to set sail, only expecting the good wind to carry him out of the haven.

Would to God it were always so with us. We are fully stored and equipped in Christ Jesus, and yet we do not always enjoy the holy quiet which ought to spring out of so divine a fact. All is well. Why do we not feel that it is so? Why do we fear to depart? There remains nothing for us but to obey the call, let loose the cable, and float into the heavenly haven; but we act as if it were not so, and often dread the time for commencing the last voyage. It is more important to be prepared to live aright than to be in an ecstasy at the thought of death; but, still, while we are ready for service, it is sweet also to be ready for glory. The thought of death should never put us in a flurry. It should be every-day work to die: indeed, we should be always dead with Christ. Where this is realized death is dead, and as children are not afraid of a dead lion, so we also are not disturbed at the prospect of departing out of this world unto the Father.

> All that remains for me
>   Is but to love and sing,
> And wait until the angels come
>   To bear me to my king.

THAT WHICH WILL FILL A SEA WILL FILL A BUCKET

God is satisfied with himself, and sufficient to his own happiness. Therefore, surely, there is enough in him to fill the creature. That which fills an ocean will fill a bucket; that which will fill a gallon will fill a pint; those revenues which will defray an emperor's expenses are enough for a beggar or poor man.

Good reasoning. God all-sufficient is assuredly more than sufficient for me. What said Paul? 'My God shall fill up all your needs, according to his riches in glory by Christ Jesus.'

CONTRARY TO BIAS

A man may act from a violent impression contrary to nature, as a stone moveth upward, or a bowl[1] thrown with great strength will so run that it is clear that the bias is overruled; so a wicked man may do a good action or two, as Saul forced himself; but the bent and natural inclination is another thing.

A fish now and then leaps out of the water, but it is not a bird; and a swallow touches the brook with its wing, but it is not a fish. Occasional actions and deeds done under pressure are no evidences of a man's condition one way or another. Even a life of pure morality may not be a sure proof of a gracious heart; for circumstances and surroundings may have restrained the natural tendency of the mind, and it may be secretly as impure as that of the man who riots in open crime. A young leopard seemed to be perfectly tame for years, but it once had an opportunity of tasting blood, and straightway its innate ferocity was aroused. Some men only need to be assailed by a fitting temptation, and we should soon see that Satan's power within them is in full force. The ball must be cured of its bias,

---

[1] As used in the game of lawn bowls, and which is weighted on one side.

or else the next throw may reveal its inability to move in a straight line; and so we must be renewed in heart, or our next action or thought may manifest our depravity.

Lord, make me to do good freely and naturally because I delight to do it; for nothing less than this will prove that thou hast renewed me by thy Spirit.

THE HOLDER OF THE KEYS KNOCKING AT THE DOOR

What strange condescension, that he who hath the key of David should knock at the Father's gate, and receive his own heaven by gift and entreaty!

These are Manton's words of surprise at the first sentences of our Lord's prayer in John 17: 'Father, glorify thy Son.' Even to Jesus it is said, 'Ask of me.' God had one Son without sin, but never a son who did not pray. The cry of 'Abba, Father!' is the mark of sonship. True prayer is the sign of a true-born child of God: 'Behold, he prayeth' is the token by which each heir of glory is known.

What, then, must be the condition of such as never pray? How dwelleth sonship in them? All who call upon the Lord in spirit and in truth may say, 'Our Father': it is as 'the Father' that God seeketh such to worship him.

O my heart, dread above all things a prayerless spirit! Thou hast not the key of David; how, then, canst thou enter into glory without knocking? He who had power to enter of himself yet asked that he might receive. Rouse thee, my soul, to renewed supplication, and may the Father hear thee at this hour, for Jesus' sake.

CHILD'S PLAY

To rule a kingdom is a nobler design than to play with children for pins or nuts.

What, then, is the folly of the worldling's choice when he prefers to be contending among men for earthly toys, instead of seeking those things which are above! How great the degradation of professing Christians when their minds are taken up with fashionable trivialities instead of living alone to glorify their God, and acting as those whom Jesus has made to be kings and priests! Who cares for pebbles when jewels glitter before him? Who would choose toys and rattles when the wealth of the Indies is offered him? Let us be no longer children or fools, but act as men who have put away childish things.

THE PRICELESS PRICE

The satisfaction must carry proportion with the merit of the offence. A debt of a thousand pounds is not discharged by two or three brass farthings. Creatures are finite, their acts of obedience are already due to God, and their sufferings for one another, if they had been allowed, would have been of limited influence.

Jesus alone, as the Son of God, could present a substitution sufficient to meet the case of men condemned for their iniquities. The majesty of his nature, his freedom from personal obligation to the law, and the intensity of his griefs, all give to his atonement a virtue which elsewhere can never be discovered. None of the sons of men 'can by any means redeem his brother, nor give to God a ransom for him'. Jesus only could stand in our soul's stead, and pay the dreadful price. What sinners we are! What a sacrifice has been presented for us! No brass farthings were our price; nay, gold and silver are called 'corruptible things' when compared with the precious blood which has paid our ransom.

PHIDIAS AND HIS NAME

Like Phidias, who in his image carved his own name, there is God engraven upon every creature.

Not in characters of human writing is it written, but in the character of the work. Phidias needed not to have written the word PHIDIAS in so many letters, for the master's hand had a cunning of its own which none could counterfeit. An instructed person had only to look at a statue and say at once, 'Phidias did this, for no other hand could have chiselled such a countenance'; and believers have only to look either at creation, providence, or the divine word, and they will cry instinctively, 'This is the finger of God.' Yet, alas, man has great powers of wilful blindness, and these are aided by the powers of darkness, so that, being both blind and in the dark, man is unable to see his God, though his presence is as clear as that of the sun in the heavens.

EXPEDIENT ABSENCE

It is better for us that Christ should be in heaven than with us upon earth. A woman had rather have her husband live with her than go to the Indies; but she yieldeth to his absence when she considereth the profit of his traffic.

The figure is well selected. Let us dwell on it a while, and think of the amazing profit which this journey of our best Beloved is bringing in to us. He is pleading in the place of authority: what an enrichment to us to have an intercessor at the throne of grace, through whom every true prayer is accepted! He is ruling on the seat of empire, arranging all providences for the success of his church: what a gain to have our head and leader raised above all principalities and powers! He is preparing a place for his people: what a boon to have such a forerunner, representative, and preparer! Moreover, by his departure we have received the Holy Ghost, of whose divine value what pen shall write! He is with us and in us, our instructor, quickener, purifier, and comforter.

Even upon these few points we are great gainers by his bodily absence; but there is much more. If our Lord judged it to be expedient that he should go, then expedient it is in the highest sense, and therefore let us solace ourselves in his present bodily absence from us 'till the day break, and the shadows flee away'.

THE EMPTY HOPPER

The mind is like a mill: when it wanteth corn it grindeth upon itself.

And this is the cause of much of the mental depression which afflicts mankind; many people have nothing to think of outside of themselves, and so their thoughts prey upon their own hearts. Occupation is the remedy for many an internal sorrow. The study of the Scriptures would prevent brooding over imaginary ills. Try it, good friend, and see! Fill the hopper of thy mind's will with holy instruction, and thou shalt get for thyself good corn instead of wear and tear and grit.

THE LOVING WIDOW

A woman, that only bemoaneth the loss of her husband in company, but banisheth all thoughts of him when alone, might justly be suspected to act a tragedian's part, and to pretend sorrow rather than feel it.

The moral is, that one who only has Christ upon his tongue in public, and has no thought of him when alone, is a mere actor and hypocrite. Secret religion is the very soul of godliness. What we are alone, that alone we are. Private communion with Jesus is a better sign of grace than all the outward sacraments that were ever attended. It is not likely that a hypocrite will delight in solitary devotion; there is nothing in it to pay him for his trouble; for his reward is the praise of man. Judgment upon ourselves will be much more likely to be correct, if we examine our hidden life than if we measure ourselves by that which is seen of men.

THE HUNTING DOG

A good dog hunts by sight as long as he can see his game; but when that is lost he hunts by scent.

So in prayer we are to pursue the blessing while we are encouraged to seek it, but we are not to cease when the likelihood of success is gone. We must hunt by a spiritual scent when sight quite fails us. The odour of the promise must direct our way when the mercy is numbered with the 'things not seen as yet'. It would be a sad degeneration if faith became nothing better than a conclusion drawn from preponderating probabilities: we must hope against hope, and believe in the truth of the promise against all likelihood of its performance, or we know nothing of the crown and glory of faith.

O for a quick nostril, that we may follow after those heavenly things which the eye seeth not and the ear heareth not! These will repay the chase; whereas the things seen of the eye turn out, when overtaken, to be mere gaudy butterflies which are spoiled in the act of grasping them.

THE DWARF

A child, if he should continue a child, and an infant still, would be a monster.

However pleased the parents had been with the little one when it was a babe, they would soon be deeply distressed if year after year it still remained a tiny thing: indeed, they would consider it a great calamity to be the parents of a dwarf. What, then, shall we say of those in our churches who never grow? They are no forwarder after fifty years! Infants at sixty years of age!

I have in my house a singular picture which is made up of the portraits of my sons, taken on their birthdays for twenty-one years. They begin in the perambulator,[1] and end as full-grown young men. This is interesting and according to nature; but, alas, I have spiritual children whom I wheeled about in the perambulator of tender comfort twenty years ago, and they are babies still, needing as much care as ever, and are as little able to run alone. Ah me! that so many who ought to be warriors are weaklings, that those who should be men of six feet high are so stunted as to be mere Tom Thumbs in grace.

O for grace to grow in grace, and especially in the knowledge of my Lord and Saviour, Jesus Christ! God save us from a life which does not grow, and from a growth which is not healthy.

WHETTING THE SCYTHE

Certainly the best of our hours should be taken up about the best business, and not in recreations. Those are to be blamed who as soon as they rise think about amusements, knit pleasure to pleasure, and wear away the scythe in whetting, not in working.

[1] Pram.

This is a specially wise hint. Doubtless many occupy the chief of their thoughts upon mere sport and pastime, and wear out their minds by anxiously considering that which can only be allowable as a relief from anxious consideration. To expend more pains upon their pleasures than upon their duties is the mark of ungodly men, and the sign of folly. That which should be a rest from thought is made to be the theme of thought, and so a second wear and tear is created by the very process which ought to have prevented it: the scythe is not only worn away by its cutting, but by its whetting.

Christian man, remember this. Let not allowable diversions become occasions for transgression. This they will be if they cause waste of time; for in such a case you will be reported to your Master as a steward who has wasted his goods. Nor will you be blameless if your recreations weary the brain and heart, and cause a new and unremunerative expenditure of force. Above all, you will be greatly censurable if there is the slightest tinge of sin about the amusement: 'Abstain from all appearance of evil.' 'Happy is he that condemneth not himself in that which he alloweth.'

SHIP BUILDING

He that buildeth a ship doth not make his work of such a sort that it may avoid all waves and billows, that is impossible; but he so builds it that it may be tight and stanch, and able to endure all weathers.

Even so the very frame and construction of the spiritual life were formed with a view to trials. Jerusalem was walled because enemies were expected; David built towers and armouries because he looked for war; and what mean the graces of faith and patience unless affliction is to be reckoned on? Our glorious leader would never have armed and armoured all his followers if there had not been allotted to them a wrestling with principalities and powers. See how Paul, in the same chapter in which he tells us of the panoply of God, reminds us of the adversaries whom we shall surely encounter.

Has the Lord made thee, my brother, to be strong in faith and brave in heart? Then be not surprised if thy stout ship is sent to traverse stormy seas. God doth not throw away strength by putting it where it will never be needed. Storms will surely come where grace is given to bear them, and through these storms grace will develop into glory.

ONE BIRD SETTING THE OTHERS CHIRPING

It is of advantage to others when we use vocal prayer, for it quickens them to the same exercise, as one bird setteth all the rest a chirping.

Often one who has been in the spirit of prayer has stirred his friend out of a cold and lifeless frame, and set him all on a glow. Yea, and a whole company of believers have been roused to hearty devotion by the fervour of one man.

The simile used by our author is very beautiful. Ere the sun has risen, one bird awakes, and, with a clear tuneful note, calls to his mate. Whereupon another follows in the same manner, and a rivalry begins between the first two songsters. These bestir birds of every wing, and in a few minutes the whole grove is vocal, the air is full of music, and the sun rejoices to arise amid a concert of happy minstrels. Earth has nothing sweeter than its spring sonnets, which make that season of the year like the first creation, when the morning stars sang together and the sons of God shouted for joy. Blessed is the bird which thus leads the choir, and happy is that praying or praising man whose holy expressions awaken his fellows to the like sacred exercise. It is well worth while to shake off natural timidity, which would make a good man to be as though he were dumb, and deprive him of half of his usefulness. To pray in private is essential, but to be able to pray in public is profitable. We are not to live unto ourselves in anything, and certainly not in those matters which are the crown and glory of our highest life: therein it is well to edify saints as well as to benefit ourselves.

Lord, open thou my lips, and my mouth shall show forth thy praise.

THE ROMAN SENATE AND CHRIST

The story goeth, that the Roman Senate, hearing of the miracles in Judea, decreed divine worship to Christ; but Tiberius the emperor crossed it, when he heard that he would be worshipped alone.

There is the edge of the controversy between Christ and the world. The Christian religion interferes with no man's liberty, but leaves every conscience free and accountable only to God; and yet it has no tolerance for false doctrine, and enters upon no compact or truce with error. It does not claim to be one form of truth which exists side by side with a dozen others, but it reveals Christ as 'the truth'. We do not believe in many ways to heaven, for we know that there is only one way, and we do not acknowledge two foundations for faith, for we know Christ to be the one and only foundation, and we dare not say otherwise. Christ is not one among many saviours, he is the only Redeemer of men. The popular fiction of 'comparative religions' is a delusion; there is but one truth, and that which does not agree with it is a lie.

In my heart, great Lord, many lords have had dominion aforetime, but now thy name alone shall bear rule over my nature. Let me never insult thee by enduring a rival; let me never ruin myself by dividing my allegiance.

LOOSE STONES IN THE FOUNDATION

It is dangerous when foundation-stones lie loose.

Indeed it is. Never was this danger greater. Men are denying the full inspiration of the Bible, frittering away the atonement, carping at justification by faith, and questioning the proper deity of our blessed Lord. It is the work of the Holy Spirit to establish, ground, and settle his people in foundation truths, and there is reason to fear from the dubious preaching of certain 'intellectual' persons that they have little or no acquaintance with his inward teachings. 'If the foundations be destroyed, what can the righteous do?' The ungodly may triumph, but we weep and lament when we see the glorious doctrines of truth assailed by those who, though they know it not, are the enemies both of God and man.

O Lord, visit thy church, and restore a martyr's faith among us. Meanwhile we rejoice that 'the foundation of God standeth sure'.

THE QUEEN CROWNED WITH THE KING

We are made prophets, priests, and kings: prophets meet to declare God's praises, priests fit for holy ministering, kings to reign over our corruptions here, and with Christ forever in glory. As the queen is crowned with the king, so shall the church reign with Christ.

What a joy it is thus to receive our honours in connection with our Lord! 'Crowned with the king'—this is a vast increase of joy! It makes our seat in the heavenlies the more glorious when we remember that we are made to sit there *together with him*. To rise in his resurrection, to live because he lives, to be crowned in his coronation, and to be glorified with his glory, this is a double, yea, a sevenfold bliss. The queen's coronation with the king is much more joyous to her than if she were crowned alone; for all her husband's honours are her delight, and give her, as it were, another coronation better than her own.

O Lord, it seems too great a thing that such a worthless, unworthy creature as I am should be glorified at all; but to be with thee and like thee is a greater glory than even heaven itself would have been if it could have been enjoyed apart from thyself.

THE CIVET[1] BOX

After the worship of the Lord's Day, and especially after the Lord's Supper, we should continue in devotion, and make the whole day a post-communion. As civet boxes retain their scent when the civet is taken out, so, when the act of visible communion is over, our thoughts and discourse and actions should still savour of the solemnity. Certainly it is an argument of much weakness to be all for flashes and sudden starts.

This retaining of their perfume by boxes and drawers in which sweet scents have been placed is a fragrant figure of the abiding nature of grace in a heart wherein it has once been stored up. If ordinances yield the influence designed by them, their savour will remain in our lives, and if our conversion be indeed a passing from death unto life, the effect of it will be seen as long as we dwell among men.

We cannot come away from real communion with Christ without carrying some of the delightful odour of his good

---

[1] A perfume obtained from the civet or civet cat of Africa and India.

ointments. Grace will reveal itself by its fragrance if it be genuine, and that fragrance will be a perfume of everlasting continuance, a sweetness indestructible. It should be said of every believer, in his measure, even as it is written of his Lord, 'All thy garments smell of myrrh, and aloes, and cassia, out of the ivory palaces, whereby they have made thee glad.' The hypocrite has a temporary perfume, with which he takes care to odourize himself when he goes into the outward sanctuary; but the true believer is, by grace, made inherently fragrant, and the heavenly spices have so thoroughly saturated his garments, that they shed their savour abroad even when he is engaged in his worldly calling, yea, as long as he lives, and wherever he goes.

Sweet Lord Jesus, do thou so anoint me that I may always bear about with me the fragrance of thine infinite perfections, and be a savour of life unto life among my neighbours.

BEGGAR WITH TREMBLING HAND

We give a beggar an alms, though he receives it with a trembling, palsied hand; and if he lets it fall, we let him stoop for it.

So doth the Lord give even to our weak faith, and in his great tenderness permits us afterward to enjoy what at first we could not grasp. The trembling hand is part of the poor beggar's distress, and the weakness of our faith is a part of our spiritual poverty; therefore it moves the divine compassion, and is an argument with heavenly pity. As a sin, unbelief grieves the Spirit, but as a weakness, mourned and confessed, it secures his help. 'Lord, I believe' is a confession of faith which loses none of its acceptableness when it is followed by the prayer, 'help thou mine unbelief.'

CYRUS AND THE RIVER

Cyrus, in Herodotus,[1] going to fight against Scythia, coming to a broad river, and not being able to pass over it, cut and divided it into divers arms and sluices, and so made it passable for all his army. This is the devil's policy; he laboureth to divide the people of God, and separate us into divers sects and factions, that so he may easily overcome us.

This needs no comment. What is needed is that by a spirit of brotherly love we promote the unity of all the churches, and the peace and concord of that to which we belong. May the peace of the church be 'as a river'. Unity is strength. 'Divide and conquer' is Satan's watchword to his myrmidons; but Christ teaches us that the world will be won when his disciples are one.

WINDOWS AND TILES WORTHY OF CARE

Some say—'fundamentals are few; believe them, and live well, and you are saved'. This is as if a man in building should be only careful to lay a good foundation, and care nothing for roof, windows, or walls. If a man should untile your house, and tell you the foundation and the main buttresses are safe, you would not be pleased. Why should you be more careless in spiritual things?

This is well spoken. The least particle of diamond is diamond, and the least grain of truth is truth, and therefore to be prized above the rarest gems. That which is not essential to salvation may yet be essential to comfort, and necessary to our complete spiritual manhood. Our Lord threatens those who teach men to disregard the least of his commandments that they shall be called the least in the kingdom of heaven. It becomes not servants to trifle with the smallest commands of

---

[1] A reference to *The Histories* written by the Greek historian Herodotus.

a perfect master. How can the church ever be a perfect house of God if one of the parts, which are 'fitly framed together', should through our neglect be left out? No, we must receive all the truth, that we may be built up 'a holy temple in the Lord'. Grave errors have been suggested and nurtured by what at first appeared to be trifling departures from scriptural rule, therefore we ought to give earnest heed even to minor precepts. Future ages may have to mourn over the defalcations of today, unless we are careful to do the building of the Lord's house with faithfulness.

Lord, make me watchful in little matters, lest I grow careless in weightier concerns. Thou didst speak concerning the pins and cords of the tabernacle, and ordain that all should be made to pattern, and by this I perceive that thou regardest even the small things of thy service; I pray thee, therefore, give me both clear light, a keen eye, and a tender heart, that in all things I may please thee.

FLINT AND STEEL

God's seasons are not at your beck. If the first stroke of the flint doth not bring forth the fire, you must strike again.

That is to say, God will hear prayer, but he may not answer it at the time which we in our own minds have appointed; he will reveal himself to our seeking hearts, but not just when and where we have settled in our own expectations. Hence the need of perseverance and importunity in supplication. In the days of flint and steel and brimstone matches we had to strike and strike again, dozens of times, before we could get a spark to live in the tinder; and we were thankful enough if we succeeded at last. Shall we not be as persevering and hopeful as to heavenly things? We have more certainty of success in this business than we had with our flint and steel, for we have God's promise at our back. Never let us despair. God's time for mercy will come; yea it has come, if our time for believing has arrived. Ask in faith, nothing wavering; but never cease from petitioning because the king delays to reply. Strike the steel again. Make the sparks fly and have your tinder ready: you will get a light before long.

CATCHING AT A BOUGH

As a man falling into a river espieth a bough of a tree, and catches at it with all his might, and as soon as he hath fast hold of it he is safe though troubles and fears do not presently vanish out of his mind; so the soul, espying Christ as the only means to save him, and reaching out the hand to him, is safe, though it be not presently quieted and pacified.

The soul's grasp of Jesus saves even when it does not comfort. If we touch the hem of his garment we are healed of our deadly disease, though our heart may still be full of trembling. We may be in consternation but we cannot be under condemnation if we have believed in Jesus; even as the man who has grasped the branch may be wetted, but cannot be drowned. Safety is one thing, and assurance of it is another. Whether the believer in Christ Jesus is able to rejoice in his safety, or is still under bondage to fear, the word of the Lord standeth true beyond all question—'He that believeth in him hath everlasting life.'

THE COIN AND THE PRINCE

In the Scriptures there is a draught of God, but in Christ there is God himself. A coin bears the image of Caesar, but Caesar's son is his lively resemblance. Christ is the living Bible.

We rightly call the Scriptures 'The word of God', and yet in the deepest and truest sense Christ only is 'The Word'.

What reverence, then, is due to him, and how important it is that we get beyond all the outward signs and symbols of religion, and even beyond the letter of Scripture, to the person of the Son of God himself. His promise of rest is to those who come to *himself*—'Come *unto me*, all ye that labour and are heavy laden'; for it is in himself that the divine power is centred. He tells us, 'He that hath seen *me* hath seen the Father'; but the eye of the mind has never yet beheld the glory of God, or known him in any true sense until it has gazed upon Immanuel, God with us; for he alone is 'the brightness of his Father's glory, and the express image of his person'.

God is in every covenant blessing, but not as he is in Christ, for 'in him dwelleth all the fulness of the Godhead bodily'.

A man had better have the prince for a friend than possess a thousand images of the king his father upon gold and silver; and so it is a happier thing for us to know that Christ is ours than to possess all other blessings, however much of God there may be about them. 'Christ is all', and he is more than all. To his people he is all in all, for such is God.

My soul, let this endear Jesus to thee beyond all else, and let it make thee urgent and eager to draw very near to him. Here lies thy way to God, for God is in him, and nowhere else canst thou ever find him. What a happy thing for thee that thy God, thy heaven, thy all, are treasured up in one so accessible to thee as thy Mediator and Friend.

THE ANGLER AND THE HUNTER

Till we sin Satan is a parasite; but when once we are in the devil's
hands he turns tyrant. As an angler, when the fish hath swallowed
the bait, discovers himself; or as a hunter lies out of sight till the
beast is gotten into the toils,[1] and then he shouts and triumphs
over his prey, so the evil one lets not his enmity be seen till he has
deceived his dupe.

How often have I seen this. A soul tempted by the pleasures of sin one day, and driven to despair by remorse for it the
next! Satan first acts as deceiver and then as accuser. While men
can be made to suck down sin he will make it sweet in their
mouths; but when the poison is down he makes it bitter in
their bowels. At the first he tells them that there is no punishment, and by and by that there is no mercy.

Lord, teach us how to baffle Satan's arts, and rescue men
from his wiles. No mere human wisdom can match his subtlety; instruct us, then, by thy Spirit that we may be as wise to
win souls as he is crafty to destroy them.

WEDGES

When a man cleaves a block he first pierces it with small wedges, and
then with greater; and so doth the devil make entrance into the soul
by degrees. Judas first purloineth and stealeth out of the bag; then
censureth Christ as profusely lavishing. 'What needs this waste?'
This was not only a check to the woman, but to Christ himself.
Lastly, upon Christ's rebuke he hates him, and then betrays him
to his enemies.

There is no dealing with the devil except at arm's length.
Those little wedges of his are terribly insinuating because they
are so little. Keep them out, or worse will follow. Occasional

[1] Nets or snares.

glasses lead on to drunken orgies; occasional theatre-going grows into wantonness and chambering; trifling pilfering soon grows to downright theft; secret backslidings end in public abominations. The egg of all mischief is as small as a mustard seed. It is with the transgressor as with the falling stone, the further he falls the faster he falls. Again we say— beware of the little wedges, for they are in crafty hands, and our utter destruction may be compassed by them. Even iron safes have been forced when little wedges have made room for the burglar's lever. Take heed of the plea, 'Is it not a little one?'

O my Saviour, let me not fall by little and little, or think myself able to bear the indulgence of any known sin because it seems so insignificant. Keep me from sinful beginnings, lest they lead me on to sorrowful endings.

THE RIDER AND THE FOOTMAN

We expect he should come sooner that rideth on horseback than he that travelleth on foot.

Privileges have their responsibilities. To whom much is given, of him much shall be required. Five talents must bring in more interest than one, or their possessor will prove to be a slothful servant.

How is it with us? Have we more talents than others? Then our Master asks, 'What do ye more than others?'

LIGHT CARRIED BY A BLACK MAN

A torch giveth never the less light though carried by a blackamoor; nor is the gospel less efficacious because managed by carnal instruments.

It is not God's will that anyone who is himself living in sin should proclaim the gospel, or be an officer in his church, and yet when it so happens, the gospel itself is still a divine light, and those who see it live thereby. The faults of the preacher are very grievous; but if the truth of God be delivered by him, we should not be so foolish as to reject the doctrine, though we censure the man. The church itself may be like Laodicea, in an ill state; but it is not for us to quarrel with the Scriptures on that account. Young persons are greatly stumbled when they hear of the fall of an eminent professor, and yet they need not be surprised, for there have been hypocrites in all ages. We must not rest our faith upon men nor believe in God because we have confidence in a minister; that would be a sorry reason for faith, and would vitiate its nature. No, if the torchbearer turns black as soot we will still rejoice in the light.

Fit is it, however, that none but gracious men should touch the work of the Lord; all others are intruders. 'Be ye clean that bear the vessels of the Lord.' 'To the wicked God saith, What hast thou to do to declare my statutes?'

THE RIVER LOSING DEPTH

Salvian observeth that the church, like a river, loseth in depth what it gaineth in breadth.

Yet Salvian could not prove that it needs to do so. It is to be feared that the case is occurring even now; but it ought not so to be. When the knowledge of the Lord shall cover the earth as the waters cover the sea, we shall look for depth as well as breadth, or the figure will not be complete. The New Jerusalem lieth four square, and the length is as large as the breadth; 'the length and the breadth and the height of it are equal'.

THE WOODEN LEG

Wicked men may supply the needs of an office, as Judas for a while did duty as an apostle. A wooden leg may be a stay to the body, though it be not a true member.

Quaint, but true. It is to be feared that our churches have many wooden legs, in the form of lifeless ministers, graceless deacons, and unregenerate elders. The body may move with these, but her walk must be limping, painful, slow, and ungainly. As for the wooden limb itself, its end is to be burned. It will be a fearful thing to turn out to be a dead member of a living body—a false arm, or a glass eye. Such shams can never be part of the body of Christ. O for living, loving, lasting union with the living Head!

THE MISFIT

A garment too short will not cover our nakedness, and a garment too long will be a dirty rag to trip up our heels. God is bound in covenant only to do what is convenient for us, and that we must leave to God to judge. The sheep must not choose the pastures, but the shepherd.

O for contentment! 'Too much', we see by the figure used above, has its inconveniences as well as 'too little'. *Enough* is the word, and God knows best when we are at that point. We see around us those who are much hindered in holy living by the fact of their being wealthy, and yet perhaps we are pining to run in their silken sack. Others we see who are impeded by their poverty, and yet this need not be, for some of the Lord's poor are far ahead of other runners, and keep up all the better pace because they have so little to carry. Come, my heart, be satisfied. It should be no hard task to thee to be content, seeing all things are thine, and thy Father acts as thy steward, and deals out daily 'things convenient' for thee. The garment which he puts around thee fits thee in every part; blessed art thou if thou canst wear it becomingly and praise him for it.

TIMBER. SHEEP. WAX.

We warp in the sunshine, a shower does us good. The dog is let loose that the sheep may run together. A piece of wax, when it is broken, put it together never so often, it will not close; but put it into the candle and the ends will stick close together.

Thus by three figures we see the danger of prosperity and the benefit of affliction.

The first metaphor is impressive. Timber warps if it be exposed to noontide heat, and men are all too apt to be influenced one way or another by success. Poor fools that we are, we cannot, while on earth, bear too much happiness. It is our tendency to warping which often necessitates our weeping. The Lord will sooner damp us with showers of sorrow than allow us to be spoiled.

The dog to fetch back the wandering sheep is a well-known illustration. Some need to feel the dog's teeth before they will mind him, and God has dogs which will bite if barking is not enough. Our good Shepherd will sooner worry us with the dog of affliction than leave us to the wolf of apostasy.

The broken stick of wax prettily shows how we need suffering if we are to be set right after the fractures of temptation. How well the broken heart of a sinner unites with the heart of the suffering Saviour! There must be melting, or there will not be union. Blessed be God for any experience by which he unites our heart to fear his name.

THE TRAIL OF A SNAIL

As a snail leaveth a frothy slime upon the fairest flowers, so do unthankful persons leave their own slime upon the rich mercies of God vouchsafed to them.

Pining for things denied them, they undervalue favours bestowed upon them. Like Israel in the wilderness, if they cannot have flesh to feed their lusts they call even angels' food 'light bread'. By feasting to the full, and wasting their substance in luxury, many persons do more mischief with the bounties of providence than slugs and snails can do among the plants in a garden. Yet, when their festivals are over, or even while their wine is yet on the board, they grumble and murmur as if they were more hardly done by than any other men upon the face of the earth: thus a second time they besmear God's goodness by their thankless conduct. They abuse the gift and then abuse the Giver. They climb the wall, and spurn the ladder by which they climbed; they drink, and then defile the spring; they rise upward to the sky, and then, like clouds, obscure the heavens.

My God, grant that I may never abuse thy gifts, nor even dare to use them without gratefully praising thee for them. Moses warned the Jews that the lizard, the snail, and the mole are unclean, and I would not be like to any one of them. David said concerning the wicked, 'As a snail which melteth, let every one of them pass away.' God forbid that I should come under that curse, and so pour out my life in complaining, leaving behind me a trail of repining wherever I may move.

THE WOLF AND THE PICTURE OF A SHEEP

A wolf doth not worry a painted sheep, nor does the world annoy a mere professor. But when any are holy indeed, and of a strict innocency, they are hated, and contradicted, and spoken against.

No one fights with a statue, but living soldiers are often in the wars: living Christians are sure to be assailed in one way or another. Let us therefore for once gather figs of thistles, and find comfortable fruit upon the thorns and briers of persecution. The world is no fool; it would not be so fierce against us if it did not see something about us contrary to itself; its enmity therefore is part evidence that we are the children of God. When we see wolves worrying the picture of a sheep we shall expect to see the ungodly scoffing at those who are like them. 'If ye were of the world, the world would love his own.'

SMALL VESSELS AND A GREAT FOUNTAIN

Our communion with Christ is not now full. There is a defect both in the pipe and in the vessel; we cannot contain all that he is able to give out, nor can the means convey it all to us. The means are as narrow conduits from the fountain, or as creeks from the sea. The fountain could send forth more water, but the pipe or conduit can convey no more.

Yet the means of grace could convey much more than we are usually ready to receive, and Dr Manton must not blame the pipe so much as the poor, cracked earthen vessel, so narrow at the mouth, and so stinted in every direction. Ministries and ordinances would be far more profitable if we were prepared to be profited. At the same time, if we dwell where outward privileges are scanty, we need not therefore be famished. Our Lord can pour his grace into us altogether apart from the means: we are not straitened in him—the straitness is in ourselves alone. We are shallow and narrow creeks, and how can the great sea of divine love pour its fulness into us? O Lord, enlarge our hearts till we shall be 'filled with all the fulness of God'.

TRAVELLING MUCH MORE DIFFICULT THAN
LOOKING AT MAPS

When we look at towns on a map, we think the way to them easy, as if our foot were as nimble as our thoughts; but we are soon discouraged and tired, when we meet with dangerous and craggy passages, and come to learn the difference between glancing at the way and serious endeavours to traverse it. So in matters of religion, he that endeavours to bring Christ and his soul together, before he hath done, will be forced to sit down and cry, Lord, help me!

He means that faith is no such child's play as some dream: it appears easy enough, and yet when the awakened soul comes to seek the Lord in earnest, it finds out its own insufficiency. It is well when this discovery comes speedily, and is clearly made, so that the heart early in the morning casts itself on God for everything, and does not waste the day in searching for water in its own broken cisterns. We need as much to look to Christ *for* faith as *by* faith.

Our author also sets forth the difference between theory and experience. Grace in the book is one thing, and grace in the heart is another. To build on paper by drawing elaborate plans has been the amusement of many a fool who could not lay one brick upon another. We must beware of resting in mere words and confiding in head-knowledge, and we must come to solid, substantial facts. A man may dream that he is among the stars, and may suddenly wake to find that he has battered his face against the post of his bed: dreaming, doting, and theorizing are poor substitutes for *real* experience of divine things.

KNOCKING THE BARREL

By knocking upon the vessel we see whether it be full or empty, cracked or sound; so by the knocks of providence given us in affliction we are discovered.

The figure may be varied by remembering the manner in which wheels are tapped with a hammer on the railway, that their soundness may be tested. Not only does affliction thus try our characters, but prosperity does the same. Approbation is a testing blow to many a man; for he who could have borne opposition gallantly too often yields at the touch of praise, and is found to be empty, vain, and devoid of stability.

When we are afflicted it is wise to watch the result upon ourselves. Can our faith bear trial, or is it a mere counterfeit? Do we love a taking as well as a giving God? Do we cleave to Christ when under a cloud, or is our religion only a fair-weather amusement? Heart-searching may thus be greatly helped, and we shall run less danger of self-deception. It will be an awful thing to be mere empty barrels, and never know it till death deals a blow with his rod of iron, and we answer to it with hollow sounds of despair.

THE BROOK AND THE RIVER

A traveller may easily pass over the head of a brook; but when he goeth down, thinking to find it narrower, it is so broad that he cannot pass at all. Every delay brings on a new degree of hardness of heart on our part, and a new desertion on God's part.

Never will his sin be less powerful than at this moment,

though the ungodly man should wait for fifty years. The domination of evil is ever growing, never waning. Manton well points out the two dangers of delay—our own hardening, and the Holy Spirit's withdrawal. Either of these may well cause fear and trembling in self-confident hearts.

Today let the anxious soul pass the brook by God's gracious help; tomorrow the stream will be hard to ford, and anon the torrent will sweep all before it. Tarry not, O thou who wouldst be saved.

COMMERCE

Divers countries have divers commodities, and one needeth what another produceth; one aboundeth with wines, some have spices, others have skins, and commodities of other kinds; and all this is so ordered that by commerce and traffic there might be society maintained among mankind. So God in his church hath given to one gifts, to another graces, to each one somewhat which is not possessed by his fellow, to maintain a holy society and spiritual commerce among themselves.

Brethren who will not commune with one another upon spiritual subjects are as traders who shut up their shops and will neither buy nor sell. Too wise to be taught, and too idle to teach, they live isolated lives, like the man in the iron mask, without joy to themselves or benefit to others.

We shall all be beggars together if we shut ourselves up like hermits, and cry 'every man for himself'. We have seen a little of this 'protection' in spiritual goods, and we witness that it tendeth to poverty. Fellowship is pleasant, mutual help is profitable; let us not look every man on his own things, but every man also on the things of others. Time was when they that feared the Lord spake often one to another, and that was the best of times. Let us hold mutual discourse upon our experiences, make pleasant exchange of our knowledge, and aid each other by our gifts. Among idolaters we read that 'the carpenter encouraged the goldsmith, and he that smoothed with the hammer him that smote the anvil', and surely such co-operation ought to be even more evident among the servants of the true God. We wish it could be said of all church work, 'They helped every one his neighbour, and everyone said to his brother, "Be of good courage."' When shall all rivalry cease, and every Christian seek to advance the interests of his brethren? We want no more 'exclusive brethren', whoever they may be; but we need communicating brethren, whose fellowship is with the Father, and with the Son, and with all the saints.

THE BIRD AFRAID OF THE SCARECROW

If an unregenerate man should leave off sin under fear of death or hell, it would not be out of hatred to sin, but out of the fear of the punishment, as the bird is kept from the bait by the scarecrow.

Much of this scarecrow work is going on around us, and if it prevents the stealing of the wheat we may be glad of it. Still, it is a poor state of things for a man to refrain from sin merely and only because he is afraid of smarting for it. If the heart *would*, but the hand *dares not*, the person will be judged by what he desires rather than by his actions. We are before God what in our hearts we wish to be. The raven is not a dove so long as it longs for carrion, even though it may sit in a cage, and act like the gentlest of birds. Christ did not come to scare us from sin, but to save us from it. Even if there were no hell, true saints would hate sin, and strive after holiness.

ON THE TREE AND IN THE STILL

The rose is not so sweet on the tree as in the still.

Yes, Mr Manton, it is just as sweet, but it does not so fully pour forth its perfume. Thanks to the fire, the fragrance cannot lie latent when the leaves are distilled. Thus is it with the believing soul under adversity, the heart then yields up to God the sweetness which else had laid dormant.

Some of us owe more than we can tell to what Manton calls 'the still'. The furnace, the anvil, and the hammer have been the making of our lives under the guiding wisdom of the great Worker's hand. We cannot enjoy the process while we undergo it; but the results are such that we are ready to fall in love with suffering. O rose, were it not for the still, thine essence had not made fragrant the robes of queens; but now art thou in king's palaces, and a drop of thy soul's inmost ichor[1] is of more worth than gold. Even so, we had never been so near our Lord, the Prince Immanuel, had we not, after our measure, been made to drink of his cup, and to be baptized with his baptism.

We bless thee, O Lord, for all that thou doest, whether thou load us with favour till we are as flowers gemmed with dew, or pluck away our beauty, and sever us from our delights till we are as roses cut off and cast into the still. All that thou doest is good, and for all thou shalt be extolled.

CALLING OFF THE DOG

A stranger cannot call off a dog from the flock, but the shepherd can do so with a word; so the Lord can easily rebuke Satan when he finds him most violent.

Lord, when I am worried by my great enemy, call him off, I pray thee. Let me hear a voice saying, 'The Lord rebuke thee, O

[1] A discharge from a wound.

Satan; even the Lord that hath chosen Jerusalem rebuke thee.'
By thine election of me, rebuke him, I pray thee, and deliver
me from the power of the dog.

HEWING STONES AND PRUNING VINES

*There is more squaring, and hewing, and hacking used about a stone
that is to be set in a stately palace than that which is placed in an
ordinary building; and the vine is pruned when the bramble is
not looked after, but let alone to grow to its full length.*

This should reconcile believers to their chastisements. It is
a well-worn figure; but it is well put. Brambles certainly have
a fine time of it, and grow after their own pleasure. We have
seen their long shoots reaching far and wide, and no knife has
threatened them as they luxuriated upon the commons and
wastelands. The poor vine is cut down so closely that little
remains of it but bare stems. Yet, when clearing-time comes,
and the brambles are heaped for their burning, who would not
rather be the vine?

Ah, Lord! Let me never sigh for ease, but always seek for
usefulness. Square me till I am fit for a place in thy temple;
prune me till I yield my utmost fruit. I know not what this
prayer may involve; but if I did, I would pray to be helped to
pray it, and I would entreat thee to fulfil it to the letter.

THE SINGER

*In a choir or concert of voices he is commended that sings well.
Whether he sings the bass, or the mean, or the treble, that is
nothing, so he singeth his part well; but he is despised and disal-
lowed that sings amiss, whatever voice he useth. Even thus doth
God approve, accept, and reward his people that serve and glorify*

him in any state, whether it be high or low, rich or poor, eminent or obscure.

Yes, it is not our rank or estate, but the right using of our position which is the point to be thought of—the point by which we shall be judged at the last. If called in poverty to sing bass, blessed is he who sings so as to please the ear of God; he shall be fully as accepted as his neighbour who exalts his voice upon a higher key. So long as the music of his life was true to the score of duty no man will be censured because his notes were not so strong, or high, or many as those of another in the company. It is not the loftiness of our place, but the worthy occupying of it, which will bring acceptance to our work before the Lord.

O, my great Master and Teacher, help me to remember this, and let me be far more anxious to sing my part correctly than to sit in this seat or that, among the rich or the great.

WAGONS NOT MOVED BY WIND,
NOR SHIPS DRAWN BY HORSES

The wise use right means, such as will bring them to their desired end. We do not use to draw ships in the sea with horses, nor draw wagons with the wind. We must not use contrary means, nor insufficient means. We cannot go to the bottom of a well that is thirty foot deep with a line that is but ten foot.

Why, then, do men try to win heaven by their own merits? This short line will never reach so far. Why do they endeavour to save souls by noise and carnal excitement instead of crying for the Spirit of God? What is this but refusing to spread the sail for the heavenly breeze, and relying upon the tramp of horses, and the strength of flesh and blood? How is it that so many look to obtain blessing through ceremonies of man's invention? This is an endeavour to move a mountain by dancing before it.

If the means must be adequate to the end, then nothing short of the merits of Jesus can cause a sinner to enter heaven, and nothing but the power of the Holy Ghost can make men new creatures in Christ Jesus. If the means must be adapted to the end, then we must have mercy to comfort misery, love to rescue lost sinners, divine goodness for despairing hearts, and power from on high for souls dead in trespasses and sin.

Next time we hear a man try to convert people by fine language, we shall remember Manton's saying, that wagons are not moved by wind.

THE PRICK OF A PIN AND A HEAVY BLOW

The prick of a pin maketh a man start, but a heavy blow stunneth him. David, when he cut off the lap of Saul's garment, his heart smote him; but when he fell into adultery and blood, he was like one in a swoon.

Thus it is that a slight departure from right will startle the unsophisticated conscience, while a gross sin may stun it into a horrible insensibility. Much serious thought is suggested by this most striking simile. Among other things it teaches us to dread a benumbed or swooning conscience, for it may have been brought into that condition by a terrible sin. Better far to be morbidly sensitive, and condemn one's self needlessly, than to be hardened through the deceitfulness of sin. A quick and tender conscience is among the best gifts of grace; let those who have it guard its delicacy with jealous care.

Lord, let my conscience be as tender as the apple of my eye.

As well-balanced scales are tremulous at the fall of a single grain of dust, so let the minutest sin set me on the move. Never, I beseech thee, permit me to become heavy with the intoxication caused by a deep draught of evil: 'Keep back thy servant also from presumptuous sins; let them not have dominion over me.'

TO DIE FIGHTING

Sometimes God letteth his people alone till their latter days, and their season of fighting cometh not till they are ready to go out of the world, that they may die fighting and be crowned in the field. But first or last the cross cometh, and there is a time to exercise our faith and patience before we inherit the promises.

It has been observed that many of those who begin their spiritual career with severe mental conflicts are afterward filled with peace, and are left unmolested for years. Others have their battle in middle life, and find the heat of their noontide sun to be their severest trial; while a third class suffer, as our author tells us, at the very close of their pilgrimage. No rule can be laid down as to the varied experiences of the saints; but we suspect that few make the voyage to heaven over a perpetually glassy sea; the vast majority, at some time or other, are 'tossed with tempest and not comforted'.

What if we also must die fighting? We shall fall amid the shouts of victory. How surprising will heaven be to us! One moment almost wrecked, and the next in 'the Fair Havens'. Wrestling one moment, and resting the next with the crown about our brows! 'At eventide it shall be light.'

TRADING ON A MAN'S WORD

If a man promise, they reckon much of that; they can tarry upon man's security, but count God's word nothing worth. They can trade with

*a factor beyond seas, and trust all their estate in a man's hands
whom they have never seen; and yet the word of the infallible
God is of little regard and respect with them, even then when he
is willing to give an earnest of the promised good.*

It is noteworthy that in ordinary life small matters of business are transacted by sight, and articles valued by pence are paid for over the counter: for larger things we give cheques which are really nothing but pieces of paper made valuable by a man's name; and in the heaviest transactions of all, millions change from hand to hand without a coin being seen, the whole depending upon the honour and worth of those who sign their hands. What then? shall not the Lord be trusted? Ay, with our whole being and destiny. It ought to be the most natural thing in all the world to trust God; and to those who dwell near him it is so. Where should we trust but in him who has all power and truth and love within himself? We commit ourselves into the hands of our faithful Creator and feel ourselves secure. 'Blessed is he that trusteth in the Lord, and whose hope the Lord is.'

THE CHILD AND THE FATHER

*A young child does not know his father's strength. We are poor, weak
creatures, and cannot conceive fully of the perfections of God; we
know not what the power of God can do for us.*

It would be the height of absurdity for the child to think and speak of its father as if he were a child too, and could do no more than the boy's playmates. Yet this is the common error of the children of God. We do not raise our thoughts to a godlike level. We think our own thoughts of God, and straightway we doubt. Oh, that we rose to God's thoughts, and tried to conceive how *HE* looks upon matters! Surely he taketh up the isles as a very little thing, and the mountains he weighs in scales. If our troubles were set in the light of God's power, and love, and faithfulness, and wisdom, they would become to us small burdens: why should we not so regard them? Why must we reckon as children? Why not compute our load by our Father's measurement, and then see how easily it will be carried? Estimating divine strength by human standards is one of the childish things which we must put away.

O Lord, forgive me for having often limited the Holy One of Israel, and teach me never again to judge after the flesh.

THE GILDED POTSHERD

A gilded potsherd may shine till it cometh to scouring, then the varnish is speedily worn off.

May this never be my character, but may I be solid gold, which will bear not only rubbing but burning. Alas, when I am impatient under affliction, or cowardly under persecution, or weary in holy service, have I not good reason to suspect myself? It may be that my religion is only, a mere surface film, and not part and parcel of my being; and if so, it will go ill with me. I shall ere-long be like a broken vessel, cast away upon the dunghill of everlasting contempt.

O Lord, of thy mercy save me from being a mere piece of gilded clay, by giving me truth in the inward parts.

HOLDING ON WITH THE TEETH

He who is spoken of in the story first holds the boat with his right hand, and that being cut off, he takes hold with his left hand, and when that is cut off, he fastens on with his teeth. So when one help is cut off, and then another, yet faith doth fasten upon God as long as it hath his word to fasten on. When God makes breach after breach, then to depend upon him is faith indeed.

Well may we maintain our hold upon our God, come what may; for who else is fit to be our soul's holdfast? With us it must be Christ or nothing, for other refuge there is none. Trying times make us desperately resolved to trust in the Lord at all hazards. A sense of sin snatches away one promise, and another; and then we betake ourselves to such words of grace as were expressly given to the most unworthy: there we resolve to perish, if perish we must. Our grasp at such times does not embrace much of the truth, but it is intense, and takes fast hold on what it has reached. We cannot, we will not, let go the Saviour. Like Joab, we will die at the horns of the altar, if we must die. He who, like the man in the story, has lost both his hands and yet holds by his teeth, is safe enough: God will never leave such a man to drown. Let us refuse to despair, or even to despond; since there is no just cause for distress while we can truly say, 'Though he slay me, yet will I trust in him.'

GONE AT THE ROOT

As when the root of a tree perisheth, the leaves keep green for a while, but within a while they wither and fall off; so love is the root and heart of all other duties, and when that decayeth, other things decay with it.

What would the virtues be if they could remain without love? A sounding brass and a tinkling cymbal. But, as a rule, they do not long remain. First one drops off and then another, like falling leaves; and by and by the man is as a bare branch, only fit to be cut down and cast into the fire. Some, who once professed great things, have now hardly enough rags of morality left decently to go to hell in, and all because they were without true love, and therefore were rotten at the core.

Evil in the heart is a deadly wound, but it is usually unperceived till it has done its work. No axe has been lifted against the man's morals, no great strokes have gashed his visible character, and yet the end has been certain, the ruin has been complete: the spiritual life-sap ceased to flow, the branch of usefulness withered, and at last the tree fell over, to lie prone among the spoils of death. We have seen it—seen it so often, that our most solemn warnings are reserved for secret declensions. There is something nobler in falling by the woodman's strokes than in perishing by a little worm at the root. The meanness of decaying into corruption, while standing in the midst of a church, is awful. Lord, have mercy upon us, and keep us from this evil. Amen.

CHESSMEN IN THE BAG

As chessmen are all thrown into the bag together, so in the grave there is no distinction; skulls wear no wreaths, and corpses carry no marks of honour.

The bishop and the knight tumble into the box with the pawns, and the king and the queen fare no better. Death is a terrible leveller. It is a pity that some men carry their heads so high above their fellows all the day, for they will have to sleep at night in the same bed of clay with those whom they despise. With uncouth verse the poet tells the like story:

> Beauty, and strength, and wit, and wealth, and power,
> Have their short flourishing hour;

And love to see themselves and smile,
And joy in their pre-eminence awhile.
Ev'n so in the same land,
Poor weeds, rich corn, gay flowers together stand:
Alas! death mows down all with an impartial hand.

THE BITER BITTEN

Persecution and oppression are like an iron in the fire, which, heated too hot, burneth their fingers that hold it.

The nations on the continent which drove out the Huguenots were ruined in their trade by the loss of their most intelligent and industrious artisans. The Romish Church itself became the object of popular hatred by its burnings of godly men and women. As Pharaoh was glad at last to be rid of the Israelites whom he had oppressed, so are persecutors frequently pleased if they can sneak out of their persecutions, and wash their hands of the business. Playing with edged tools is dangerous work, and so is slandering the saints of God. Hammers have smitten the patient anvil until they have been worn out, and have become more weary of the anvil's endurance than it was of their blows.

If any reader is opposing the church of God, let him consider what he is doing. He will find it hard to kick against the pricks. It will end as did the famous battle of the tow with the fire, and the stubble with the flame. No honour is to be gained by the conflict, but a blot will fall on the persecutor's escutcheon, and his portion shall be everlasting contempt.

THE GIANT AND THE STRAW

A giant striking with a straw cannot put forth his strength with it. So in blessing, no creature nor ordinance can convey all the goodness of God to us.

The best preacher is no better than a straw, in and of himself. God shows his omnipotence by accomplishing anything with such poor tools as we are. Were he not Almighty the infirmities of his servants would cause him to fail in every design in which he employs them. As it is, the fact of *our* unfitness should greatly enhance our sense of *his* glory. This feebleness on the part of the fittest instrument makes it imperative that the Lord's own Spirit should work in men's hearts over and above his working through the means. New hearts cannot be created by mere human voices: these are more qualified to call beasts to their fodder than dead souls out of their spiritual graves. The Holy Ghost must himself breathe life and infuse strength into men; for his ministers are little better than the staff of Elijah, which was laid upon the dead child, but neither hearing nor answering resulted from it.

The figure of a giant using a straw as a cudgel is not, however, perfect unless we picture him as able to strengthen the straw, till he strikes with it as with a hammer and dashes rocks in pieces; for even thus the Lord doth by his feeble servants. Hath he not said, 'Fear not, thou worm Jacob, and ye men of Israel; I will help thee, saith the Lord, and thy Redeemer, the Holy One of Israel. Behold, I will make thee a new sharp threshing instrument having teeth: thou shalt thresh the mountains, and beat them small, and shalt make the hills as chaff. Thou shalt fan them, and the wind shall carry them away, and the whirlwind shall scatter them: and thou shalt rejoice in the Lord, and shalt glory in the Holy One of Israel'?

O thou Almighty One, continue to display thine omnipotence by using me, even me, the least and feeblest of all thine instruments.

EVERYTHING ACCORDING TO ITS NATURE

A bowl used on the green must be made round before it can run round; a musical instrument must be framed and strung, and put in tune before it can make melody; a tree must first be made good before we can expect any good fruit from it.

Precisely so; and yet this fact is seldom considered. Men are loath to believe that their errors arise out of themselves, and that they must themselves be improved before their lives will be bettered. Their circumstances and associations are blamed, whereas the fault lies in themselves, only they will not believe it. They will not admit that there is a bias in the ball itself, but they blame the hand which threw it; the harp-strings they will not attend to, but complain of the musician's touch; the tree they will not chide for bearing crabs, it is the soil, the season, or the gardener. Most guilty men, when their crimes are exposed, blame their ill-luck, and not their evil hearts. The world has come to call an unchaste woman 'unfortunate'; and this is but one open expression of what it secretly believes as to all sin: it reckons our transgression to be our misfortune rather than our fault. We are poor erring mortals, and are more to be pitied than punished—this is the secret creed of mankind, and there is a floating tradition abroad that we ourselves are right enough, but our position renders error unavoidable.

When will our fellow-men give up this falsehood, and perceive that if the vessel leaks, it is because it is broken; and if foul water drips from it, it is because its contents are unclean? Oh, that they would blame themselves, and seek a change of heart; for nothing short of this can set the matter right.

ALEXANDER AND APELLES

Alexander would be painted by none but Apelles, and carved by none but Lysippus. Domitian would not have his statue made but in gold or silver. God, the great king, will be served with the best of our affections. When we care not what we offer to God, how will he accept us?

It is but ordinary manners that, when we entertain a friend who is greatly our superior, we should at least do our best and set before him all that our house and purse can afford, with many an apology that it is no better. If our queen came to sup with us, we should do our very best to please her majesty; how much more ought we to be devoutly intent to offer fit homage to the King of kings!

O my Lord, teach me to give thee the choicest product of my being, and instruct me how to do this in the most acceptable manner. May I never play the sloven with thee. Angels cannot serve thee as thou deservest to be served, and shall I think to please thee with haphazard offerings? If I sing to thee, make me earnest and hearty in spirit, and as musical in utterance as my harsh voice permits. When I pray, forbid that I should even seem to be chill and dull. If I am honoured to preach thy gospel, may I plead for thee with my whole heart, and speak even to a few as zealously as if thousands waited for my words. It is meet that the best should have the best; that thou, the most loving of Lords, shouldst have my most loyal services.

TWO WAYS OF PUTTING OUT FIRE

Fire is quenched by pouring on water or by withdrawing fuel; so the Spirit is quenched by living in sin, which is like pouring water on a fire; or by not improving our gifts and graces, which is like withdrawing fuel from the hearth.

Many are found carefully avoiding outward sin, and yet they daily neglect the gifts of grace! What folly! Will it not come to the same thing in the end with the fire upon my hearth whether I pour water on the logs or refuse to place fresh brands thereon? It will die out with equal certainty, whichever is my mode of procedure. So will it be with the fire in my heart. To be careless is as dangerous as to be disobedient. Not to do good is to do evil. Sins concerning neglected grace and omitted duty are as mischievous to us as actual wrongdoing.

This is a caution to thousands; possibly to the reader; certainly to the writer. Oh for grace to attend to the state of the inward fires, lest Satan should get an advantage over us by our neglect! Though he may have been foiled in every attempt to lead us into active rebellion against God, the enemy may yet prevail by bringing us into a negative state of indifference and apathy. There is a passive disobedience, which is exceedingly injurious to the soul. The Lord save us from this great peril. Let us hear him say, 'Quench not the Spirit', and yet again, 'Stir up the gift which is in thee.'

SETTLING THE EXPENDITURE

When a man hath allotted so much for building a house, so long as he keeps within the bounds of his allotment he parteth with his money freely; but when that is gone he parts with every penny with grudging. It is good to make Christ large allowance at the first so that we do not afterward grudge our bargain and contract.

Good, Dr Manton! Very good! When some of us began with the Lord Jesus we meant to place all that we had at his disposal, and ever since it has been a great joy to feel that everything we are and have belongs to him. What we can give to his cause we regard as children do their spending money; we lay it out with eagerness, and wish it were a hundred times as much. No silver slips from our hand so joyfully as that which goes to God. No gold is so readily parted with as that which is spent upon his cause. Grudging is far from us, when God's cause is near to us. Surely, some of our friends started with other notions, and put the Lord on short commons at the first estimate, for they need to be hardly pressed ere they will give to his cause.

Dear reader, is this so with you? Do you look a score times at every sixpence you spend upon the Lord? If so, revise your contract. Make your Beloved a more liberal allowance. 'He that soweth sparingly shall reap also sparingly.'

THE SHAKING OF THE TREE

When the tree is soundly shaken, rotten apples fall to the ground; so in great trials guile of spirit will fail.

This, then, is the purpose of affliction: first, *to test me*, that I may see how far my supposed graces are real and vital. Those which are not sound will soon be lost; only the living and growing graces will remain. Can I bear the test? How have I borne it?

Secondly, trials *relieve me*, for it is a hurtful thing to the tree and to its living fruit to be cumbered with rottenness, in which may breed noxious worms, which when they multiply may come to be devourers of the tree's life. We are enriched when we lose fictitious virtues. Stripping of filthy rags is an advance toward cleanliness, and what are counterfeit graces but mere rags, worthy to be torn off and cast into the fire?

In the end such a result of affliction also *beautifies me*, for as rotten apples disfigure the tree, so would the mere pretence of virtue mar my character in the sight of God and good men. It is always better to be openly without an attainment than to bear the form of it without in reality possessing it. A sham is a shame: an unreal virtue is an undoubted vice.

Lord, I thank thee for shaking me, since I now perceive that all this good and much more is designed by the process, and is, I trust, in some measure accomplished thereby. Oh that thy Holy Spirit may bless my adversities to this end, and then they will not be adverse to me, but the very reverse!

THIRSTY MEN DRINKING WITHOUT LOOKING

As men in a deep thirst swallow their drink before they know the nature of it, or discern the taste of it; so when we are under a great thirst, or under great famishment as to spiritual comfort, and have great troubles upon us, we take up with comfortable notions of Christ and salvation by him, and easily drink in these and other truths, catching at them without looking into the grounds or reasons of them. Afterward we see the need of care and watchfulness of soul, to strengthen our assent and fortify ourselves against those doubts of mind which shake us. Then we desire to settle our hearts in those supreme truths which in our necessity we accepted without discussion.

This is a very natural figure. See how the thirsty man turns up the cup and drinks the contents at a draught; he cares little what it is, so that it quenches his raging thirst. 'Behold, he drinketh up a river, and hasteth not: he trusteth that he can draw up Jordan into his mouth.' But now, mark him in cooler moments! He is careful of his drinking, lest he be made top-heavy, or become nauseated. A simple, receptive faith is a fine thing for the speedy removal of the soul's thirst; but if it were not soon qualified by spiritual discernment it would lead to credulity, and the man would be ready to take in anything which might be set before him. The rapid believer would soon become the victim of superstition. The more study of the Scriptures, and testing of doctrines thereby, the better. Careful investigation may save the mind from being injured by poisonous teaching, and it will certainly endear the truth to us, and strengthen our confidence in it.

What a draught was that which some of us had at the first! Little enough we knew; but our enjoyment of what we did know was intense! Lord, thou hast now revealed to us the ingredients of that divine cup; grant that this may give us a new and deeper joy; but do not allow us to forget the bliss of satisfied thirst because we are gifted with fuller knowledge. Such a gain would be a loss most serious.

CHILDREN CARRIED BY THEIR FATHER

We must look upon Christ as a father carrying all his children on his back, or lapped up in his garment, through a deep river, through which they must needs pass, and, as it were, saying to them, 'Fear not, I will set you safe on land.' Look upon Christ wading with all his children through the floods of death and hell, and saying, 'Fear not, worm Jacob; fear not, poor souls, I will set you safe.'

This is not very poetically put. It is the old Christopher story in a more common dress. The good Lord waits at the river to bear us over, lest the water-floods prevail against us. He hath made, and he will bear, even he will carry. Here is our safety: He shall gather the lambs with his arm, and carry them in his bosom. O my gracious Lord, be pleased to carry me among thine own in life and in death. Yea, set me safe on the further shore to sing forever of thy saving power.

GOING TO BED TO RISE AGAIN

A man goes to bed willingly and cheerfully, because he knows he shall rise again the next morning, and be renewed in his strength. Confidence in the resurrection would make us go to the grave as cheerfully as we go to our beds; it would make us die more comfortably, and sleep more quietly, in the bosom of the Lord than we rest in our own beds.

This is a choice word; a flower which smells sweet, and blossoms in the dust. It needs not a line from us; it only requires the Holy Spirit to enable us to enjoy its fragrance.

THE KING'S LODGING

If an earthly king lie but a night in a house, what care is there taken that nothing be offensive to him, but that all things be neat, clean, and sweet? How much more ought you to be careful to get and keep your hearts clean, to perform service acceptably to him; to be in the exercise of faith, love, and other graces, that you may entertain, as you ought, your heavenly King, who comes to take up his continual abode and residence in your hearts!

We know a house in which an empress rested for a very short time, and the owner henceforth refused to admit other inmates. Such is his devotion to his royal guest that no one may now sit in her chair or dine at the table which she honoured. Our verdict is that he makes loyalty into absurdity by this conduct; but if we imitate him in this procedure in reference to the Lord Jesus we shall be wise. Let our whole being be set apart for Jesus, and for Jesus only. We shall not have to shut up the house; for our beloved Lord will inhabit every chamber of it, and make it a permanent palace. Let us see to it that all be holy, all pure, all devout.

Help us, O Purifier of the temple, to drive out all intruders,

and reserve our soul in all the beauty of holiness for the Blessed
and Only Potentate.

BANKRUPTS

*A man is a man, though he be a bankrupt; he has a being, though
his well-being is lost.*

So a believer may be truly alive unto God, though by his
carelessness he has lost all the wealth of the spiritual life, and
has fallen into soul poverty. Such a man should not despair,
but with deep humiliation he should begin again. A tradesman
who has failed will take to a humble calling to earn his bread,
and so should a Christian who has broken down in his spiritual
estate take a lowly position, and with all diligence labour to
glorify the Lord better than before.

O my Lord, give me good speed in heavenly business,
lest I fail, and do an injury to thy cause. But if I have already
made a miscarriage of my life's endeavours, then set me on
my feet again, for I am still thy child. 'I have gone astray like
a lost sheep; seek thy servant; for I do not forget thy commandments.'

INFECTED AIR

*The devil is called 'the prince of the power of the air'. Infected air is
drawn into the lungs without pain, and we get a disease before
we feel it, and so die of a pestilential air.*

Thus doth Satan injure and destroy men's souls by an influence so subtle and painless that ere a man is aware of it he is
inflicted with error or iniquity, and falls a victim to the evil.
Whole cities have been carried off by pests arising from causes
which the sick ones never suspected, and whole classes of men

perish from wild passions which only the devil could have excited to such a pitch. No gas is so impalpable, so penetrating, so all-pervading, so deadly, as the influence of Satan. In these days it is not polite to speak of him; it would seem that he is so much respected by his own children that they cannot endure to hear a word against him. The common doubt of his existence is a proof of his powerful cunning; nothing will serve his turn better than for silly men to dream that he is dead or incapacitated. He laughs in his sleeve, for he is surrounding the very men who deny him, and for him they live and move. His subtlety slays without leaving the stain of blood to alarm other victims: who knoweth the depth of his cunning! Alas, that so many should be so ignorant of his devices as to be unsuspicious of the deadly influence which he breathes into the moral atmosphere!

May the health-giving Spirit of the Lord preserve all new-born hearts, so that they may pass through this pestiferous world unharmed. Surely we may give a spiritual as well as a natural meaning to that promise in the psalm, 'Thou shalt not be afraid for the pestilence which walketh in darkness. A thousand shall fall at thy side, and ten thousand at thy right hand; but it shall not come nigh thee.' Doth not the Scripture expressly say, 'Sin shall not have dominion over you'? Under the protection of this assurance we may pursue our callings in the midst of this evil generation, and yet remain in vigorous health of soul. God grant it, for Jesus' sake. Amen.

INFECTION EASY

We easily catch an infectious disease from one another, but no man receiveth health from another's company.

Too true. Evil communications inevitably corrupt good manners; but good communications do not so necessarily improve evil manners. We more readily learn evil than good, and we are also more forcible in communicating sin than virtue. Both as to the giving out and the receiving, the aptness lies on the wrong side. What a proof of our natural depravity! What a change must grace work in us before we shall be fully like our Lord Jesus, who was incapable of being inoculated by sin, but abundantly able to communicate goodness; for healing virtue proceeded from him. When shall we become dissemina-tors of holiness by our very presence? When shall we dwell where every companion shall minister to our soul's health? Such a place Jesus is preparing for us, and thither is he bring-ing his redeemed ones.

THE EVERY-DAY SUIT

Godliness is not a holiday suit, but apparel that is for constant wear.

This illustrates a very important truth. Some people seem to fancy that they can put their religion on and off as they do their Sunday clothes. Such religion is better put off once for all. He who is not godly every day is not godly any day. We should aim at serving God with all our hearts on the Sabbath, in songs, and prayers, and sermons; but if these are to be acceptable, we must also serve God on all the week-days in an honest, upright, holy conversation. True Christians will endeavour to make their houses temples, their meals sacraments, their garments vestments, and all their days holy days. That profession which is merely on the surface, like the gilt upon the gingerbread at a country fair, is too poor a thing to enter heaven.

Lord, make me to wear thy righteousness within me, and

then I cannot leave it off. Make me like the king's daughter, 'all glorious within'. Weave thy grace into the warp and weft of my being. Even on earth let me ever be with the Lord.

WORKING BY CONTRARIES

God many times worketh contrary to outward likelihoods. When the bricks were doubled, who would look for deliverance? As the Hebrew tongue must be read backward, or as the sun going back ten degrees in Ahaz's dial was a sign of Hezekiah's recovery, so is providence to be read backward. Joseph was made a slave that he might be made a favourite. Who would have thought that the dungeon had been the way to the court, that error is a means to clear truth, and bondage maketh way for liberty?

Thus have we found sickness work for our health and poverty promote our wealth. Our worst days have turned out to be our best days, and our low estate has lifted us on high. When storms come we may welcome them, for they bring blessing on their wings; but when our calm is long and deep we ought to be on our watch, lest stagnation and disease should come of it. Science talks of curing by likes; but the heavenly Physician heals both by likes and by contraries; in fact, he bends all things to his gracious purpose. To judge his proceedings is folly and ingratitude. What can we know? Especially what can we know of his design and purpose while his work is yet on the anvil? Our judgments at their best are only moderated foolishness. We are neither prophets nor sons of prophets, and it would be wise if we would no more speculate upon the results of divine operations, but firmly believe and patiently wait till the providence comes to the flower and to the seed, and God becomes his own interpreter.

LIFE IS THE MAIN MATTER

A corpse may be laid in state, and sumptuously adorned, but there is no life within.

Adornments are out of place in the chamber of death; they do but make the scene the more ghastly. We have heard of a dead prince who was placed upon a throne, dressed in imperial purple, crowned, and sceptred! How pitiful the spectacle! The courtiers mustered to so wretched a travesty of state must have loathed the pageantry. So is it when a man's religion is a dead profession; its ostentatious zeal and ceremonious display are the grim trappings which make the death appear more manifest. When, like Jehu, a man cries, 'Come with me, and see my zeal for the Lord', his false heart betrays itself. The more he decorates his godliness the more does the hypocrite's spiritual death appear. It is not possible to supply the lack of the divine life. There is an essential difference between a dead child at its best and a living child at its worst, and it needs no Solomon to see it. Unless the Spirit of God shall give life, sustain life, and perfect life, none of us can ever dwell with the living God. This is the point to look to: the vestments and trappings are a secondary business.

WINDFALLS

When the tree is shaken the rotten apples fall.

When religion is at a discount, and godliness is derided, then hypocrites and unsound professors desert the cause. It is astonishing what a little shake will get rid of the commonplace members of our churches. Let but a minister die, or remove, or a couple of leading men fall out—off they go. A warm south wind, blowing from the cathedral, or the manor house, or the public house, and dropping a gentle shower of gifts, will cause many rotten ones to fall into the lap of bribery. Sound believers, who are full of life, and untouched by the worm of insincerity, hold to the church of God in all weathers. May more of these be produced every year to God's glory!

Rougher winds than these try other professors. Stagnation in business, pressure for money, and the temptation to speculate fetch down many rotten Christians. The fashion of the world, the luxuries of life, and the habits of wealthy society also shake off others from their visible profession. When they fall, the loss is all their own: the church may apparently lose by their apostasy, but it is not a real injury; in fact, it may be in God's sight a gain to it. God thinks no better of a tree for being burdened with rotten fruit, nor of a church for being swollen in numbers by base pretenders.

Lord, make me true to the core, and keep me so.

THE BAKER AND HIS OVEN

The baker watcheth when his oven is hot, and then putteth in his bread.

Thus should we seize the best opportunity for a good work. Let us pray most when we feel we can pray best; and labour most in our holy calling when God is giving us precious opportunities, for the old proverb bids us make hay while the sun shines. To everything there is a season, and much depends upon seizing that season, and utilizing it. Oh, worker for God, take the tide at its flood, and the occasion at its full! Preach the gospel at all times, but specially bring it in when men's minds are tender through affliction or thoughtfulness. If the oven be cold, heat it; but when it is heated, do not lose your fuel. Work up the conversation till it reaches a fit stage for bringing in the Lord Jesus and saving truth; but be sure that you never get men's minds ready, and then fail to do that which you are aiming at. As the baker would not forget to put in the bread, so never forget to introduce the word of faith, the gospel of our salvation, before the interview is over. Have we not already suffered many a hot oven to cool? Let us mend our ways, and be more diligent in our Master's business.

THE BENUMBED SNAKE

It is true that natural corruption doth not break out in all with a like violence; but a benumbed snake is a snake; a sow washed is not changed. As when the liver groweth, other parts languish, so great lust intercepteth the nourishment of other corruptions.

It seems, then, that there may be a winter to our corruptions as well as to animal and vegetable life, and then the sin which dwelleth in us may be quiet, as though frozen into a rigid powerlessness: but what of that? The weather will change, and then the nest of vipers will be all astir again, each one with venomed tooth aiming to destroy. Experience has also taught the wise observer that sin may be bound by sin, and one ruling passion may hold the rest in check. One man is kept from licentiousness by covetousness: he would be glad to revel in vice if it were not so expensive; another would be a rake and a spendthrift, but then it would not be respectable, and thus his pride checks his passions. This restraint of sin by sin is no proof that the nature is one jot the better, but that it puts on a fairer appearance, and is more likely to deceive. When Satan casts out Satan it is a deep game; but we must not be deceived by the diabolical trick. When the devil's work seems good it is at its worst.

Nothing will answer with inbred sin but the killing of it. When Joshua had the five kings in the cave at Makkedah, he was not content to shut them in with great stones. No, he took special pains to fetch them out, and hang them up. The condemned race must die, and then Israel can breathe freely. Sin will be our death if we do not put it to death. Checks and restraints are of small value; what is needed is the root-and-branch cure—crucifixion with Christ. To cure sin by sin is a mere piece of stage-playing, which will never answer before God. We need to be purged of the cause of sin, yea, of all sin, or we can never enter heaven.

O thou destroyer of the serpent and his seed, break the head of sin within me, so that it may never lift up its usurped power within my soul. Let the sword of the Spirit do a thorough work within my nature, till not a single rebel lust shall remain alive in the wide domains of my being. Furbish thy sword, O Captain of the Host, and do thine office within me, for I cannot rest till sin is slain.

BUTTERFLIES

As children catch at butterflies the gaudy wings melt away in their fingers, and there remaineth nothing but an ugly worm.

Such is the end of all earthly ambitions: they cost us a weary pursuit, and if we gain our desire it is destroyed in the grasping of it. Alas, poor rich man, who has wealth but has lost the power to enjoy it! Alas, poor famous man, who in hunting for honour has learned its emptiness! Alas, poor beautiful woman, who in making a conquest of a false heart has pierced her own with undying sorrow! A butterfly-hunt takes a child into danger, wearies him, throws him down, and often ends in his missing the pretty insect; if, however, the boy is able to knock down his victim with his hat, he has crushed the beauty for which he undertook the chase, and his victory defeats him. The parallel is clear to every eye. For my part, let me sooner be the school-boy, dashing after the painted fly, than his father worrying and weary-ing to snatch at something more deceptive still.

Lord, it is time I had done with all butterfly-hunting, for my years are warning me that I may hope soon to be among the angels, and see greater beauties than this whole creation can set before me. I am now bent on pursuing nothing but that which is eternal and infinite. Keep me to this resolve, I pray thee.

SPECTACLES USELESS TO THE BLIND

When unrenewed nature putteth on the spectacles of art she is still blind.

Nowadays men must needs be philosophers, and reason and argue; but their conclusions as to spiritual things, wherein they come into conflict with divine revelation, are not one whit more to be respected than the conclusions of utter ignorance. Blind men blunder enough in the dark; add light, and they see no better; add spectacles, and the case is not altered; what is needed is the seeing eye. Till God gives eyes it is in vain for opticians to lend their glasses. So unregenerate men, when they are ignorant, are full of error; set them in the light of the gospel, they are in truth no wiser, for they have no spiritual perception of it; then add learning and sharp reasoning, and the case is by no means altered; they see no more than before, for they are still stone-blind. We have in this day many famous learned men, whose talk about the things of God is as idle as that of illiterate blasphemers. Whatever they know as to other matters, they can know nothing of divine truths, for they have no faculty with which to perceive them. Let them put on their great goggles of science, they see no more of spirituals with them than without them.

Lord! let me not go about to fit spectacles to blind eyes; but whenever I meet with a birth-blind Bartimeus, help me to bring him to thee, for it is a mark of thy Messiahship that from thee the blind receive their sight.

AT HOME, YET NOT AT HOME

Jerusalem from above is the mother of us all. Heaven is the believer's native country, and therefore, though the man be at home, yet the Christian is not; he is out of his proper place.

Hence our position is a paradox. We were in literal fact born out of our native country, and whilst we are at home we are abroad. We can say, 'Lord, thou has been our dwelling-place in all generations', and yet we often cry, 'Oh that I knew where I might find him!' We are exiles in spirit while we are at home in the body; and we shall never be at home till we have left our native land, and have returned to the country which we have never yet seen. We are living paradoxes and contradictions, and it is no wonder that men know us not, for we scarcely know ourselves.

HORSE WITH HALTER

A beast escaped with a baiter is easily caught again; so a lust indulged will bring us into our old bondage.

Nothing is harder to bury than the tail of a habit; but unless we do bury it, tail and all, the viper will wriggle out of its grave.

A clear, clean, and complete escape is the only true deliverance from an evil practice which has long been indulged. A drunkard is not safe from the drink while he takes his occasional glass with a friend. A man who allows himself any one sin will be sure to allow another; where one dog comes into the room, another may follow. A fish is not free for his life while a hook is in his mouth, and a line holds him to the rod. However thin the connecting medium, it will be the death of the fish, if it holds; and, however slight the bond which links a man to evil, it will be his sure ruin.

Oh for grace to war with every sin! So long as one Amalekite remains, Israel is not free from peril from the accursed race. Let us, like Samuel, hew the delicate Agag in pieces before the Lord. He may have a gentle speech and pleasing manners, but he is the very king of the band, and must not be spared. We must not let our heart go after one of its idols, or it will be in bondage to it, and afterward in servitude to every other form of sin.

Lord, set me free from the last link of my chain. Suffer me not to drag behind me even a fragment of my fetters. Free to obey, free to be holy—this is what I crave!

THE SUNBEAM ON THE DUNGHILL

God can by no means be looked upon as the direct author of sin, or the proper cause of that obliquity that is in the actions of the creatures; for his providence is conversant about sin without sin, as a sunbeam lighteth upon a dunghill without being stained by it.

This is a grand truth most clearly set forth. It will help us to answer many a gainsayer. Evil is in God's world, but God is good, and only good.

IRON IN THE FIRE MADE LIKE FIRE

In a stamp impressed, the wax receiveth only the form and figure, without any real quality; as a golden seal leaveth no tincture of gold, nor a brazen seal the property of brass. In a glass, besides figure and proportion, there is a representation of motion, but no other real qualities. But here, as iron in the fire seemeth to be fire, we are like our Lord in holiness and happiness.

Thus, my soul, be thou in Christ as the iron in the fire, thyself transformed into his very nature and spirit. Is it so with thee now? Alas, not as it should be. Yet he that hath wrought us to the self-same thing thus far is the Lord, and he will not cease his work till he hath perfected it. Refining fire, go through my heart until I, also, burn and glow. Lord, I cry to thee for this, and surely that which is already in my desire will soon be in my possession. I leave myself in thy hands. Change me wholly into thine image, I beseech thee.

THORNS AND BURRS

Ears of corn do not catch our clothes and hang about them, but thorns and burrs will do so.

In passing through the midst of this crooked and perverse generation, we are far more likely to learn evil than good. It is well to keep our clothes well brushed when traversing this world's dusty roads, for it is not a fragrant spice, but a defiling dust, which we gather in our journeying. Often have we gone for a walk and brought home mire upon our shoes, but we never remember to have come home with our clothing improved by our perambulations. The tendency of all around is to soil us, and mar the beauty of our holiness. The Lord help us to be very careful on this point. May we be among those of whom there were a few even in Sardis, 'who have not defiled their garments'; for the Lord Jesus says of them, 'they shall walk with me in white, for they are worthy'. What a walk will that be! What joy had Enoch in such a walk on earth! What honour will be given us by such a walk in heaven!

SERVANTS AND HEIRS

A servant must have something in hand, he must have his pay from quarter to quarter, or from week to week. He is not expecting to receive his master's possessions, and, therefore, seeks a present wage; but an heir waiteth till the estate falls in to him, and looks not for present gains.

Thus may we discern between the mere hireling and the true-born child: the one deserts the Lord's service when it does not pay down on the nail; the other never expects reward till glory shall crown his labours. It is a sad thing for any sort of people when Jesus can say of them, 'Verily, I say unto you, *they have* their reward.' They cannot expect to be paid twice, and as their account is discharged in full, what have they to look for?

Blessed shall we be if we are enabled to imitate the example of the Lord Jesus, who served the Father in the spirit of Sonship. Love made him rise above all idea of present recompense: he waited the Father's time, and he still waits for his complete reward till the hour of his Second Advent shall arrive.

'A servant', according to Job, 'earnestly desireth the shadow of evening', when his task will be ended; 'and the hireling looketh for the reward of his work': this is nothing more than natural, for they have no interest in the work beyond their pay. But the heir loveth his father, and worketh and waiteth patiently, for the father saith to him, 'All that I have is thine.' In serving the cause of God we are really serving ourselves, for we are partakers in this great cause, even as the interest of sons is one with that of their father. Can we not, therefore, 'both hope and quietly wait for the salvation of the Lord'?

HOUSES AND SHIPS PREPARED FOR STORMS

He that buildeth a house, doth not take care that the rain should not descend upon it, or the storm should not beat upon it: there is no fencing against these things, they cannot be prevented by any care of ours; but he takes care that the house may be able to endure all weathers without damage. And he that buildeth a ship, doth not make this his work, that it should never meet with waves and billows; that is impossible; but that it may be tight and stanch, and able to endure all tempests. A man that taketh care for his body, doth not desire that he meet with no change of weather, hot or cold; but he prepareth his dress that his body may bear all inclemencies. Thus should Christians do: they should not so much take care how to avoid afflictions as to be ready to bear them with an even and quiet mind.

Let me then seek steadfastness that I may stand in every storm, strength that I may brave every tempest, and all the graces of the Spirit that I may be happy in every condition. I may not pray to be kept from the flood and the wind, but that my house may be built upon a rock. I may not ask that no tempest may assault my bark, but that Jesus may be always in the vessel. I may not beg the Lord to change the arrangements of his providence, and neither try me with the heat of prosperity nor the cold of adversity, but I must see to it that I buy of him raiment that I may be clothed amid all the changes of my circumstances.

Herein is wisdom. Let us learn it, even as the prudent woman of the Proverbs had learned it, of whom we read, 'She is not afraid of the snow for her household: for all her household are clothed with scarlet.' Better to be prepared for trial than to be flying hither and thither to avoid it. Come, my soul, thou must make a passage across a rough sea, nerve thyself to it by grace divine, and the Lord shall yet be glorified in thee. A battle awaits thee. Do not attempt to run from the fight, but look to thine armour, and unsheathe thy sword.

HEART-DISEASE THE WORST DISEASE

What would we think of a man who complained of the tooth-ache, or of a cut finger, when all the while he was wounded at the heart? Would it not seem very strange?

Yet men will lament anything sooner than the depravity of their hearts. Many will confess their wandering thoughts in prayer, but will not acknowledge the estrangement of their hearts from God. They will be sorry for having spoken angrily, but not for having a passionate heart. They will own to Sabbath-breaking, but never lament their want of love to Jesus, which is a heart-matter. The evil of their hearts seems nothing to them: their tongues, hands, feet are all that they notice. What! will they cry over a cut finger, and feel no fear when they have a dagger thrust into their bowels? Oh, madness of sinners, that they trifle most with that disease which is the most dangerous, and lies at the bottom of all other ills. God's great complaint of men is that they set up in their hearts idols which they themselves think nothing of (Ezek. 14:3, 5). Certain in our day are so far gone that they even deny that the human heart is diseased. What then? It does but prove the intimate connection between the heart and the eyes. A perverted heart soon creates a blinded eye. Of course a depraved heart does not see its own depravity. Oh that we could lead men to think and feel aright about their hearts; but this is the last point to which we can bring them! They beat about the bush, and mourn over any and every evil except the source and fountain of it all.

Lord, teach me to look within. May I attend even more to myself than to my acts. Purge thou the spring, that the stream may no longer be defiled. I would begin where thou dost begin, and beseech thee to give me a new heart. Thou sayest, 'My son, give me thine heart.' Lord, I do give it to thee, but at the same time I pray, 'Lord, give me a new heart'; for without this my heart is not worth thy having.

THE JUDGE'S VERDICT ALONE TO BE REGARDED

It is no matter what standers-by say of the runner, so the judge of the race doth approve of his running.

Yet we all make too much of the approval or disapproval of our fellow-men, who are, after all, only the spectators, and not the umpires, of the race. What folly this is! What injuries it inflicts! We are elevated by human opinion if it be favourable to us, and this betrays us into the weakness of pride; which weakness soon shows itself in faint-heartedness, when that unstable opinion veers round, and blows a cold blast of fault-finding. If we were steadily 'looking unto Jesus', this would not happen, and our running would be more regular and less disturbed. Be it our endeavour to live above men, in the conscious presence of God. Who and what are men that we should live upon the breath of their nostrils? Their judgment is a small matter; the judgment of God is all in all. Lord, thou hast said, 'Walk before me, and be thou perfect', and from this I learn that I cannot hope for perfection unless I set thee always before me, and rate thine approval at an infinitely higher price than the judgment of those about me. Enable me to say with thy servant David, 'I have set the Lord always before me; because he is at my right hand, I shall not be moved.'

PRUNING UNPRUNED TREES

Trees long unpruned have the more cuts of the knife when the gardener begins with them.

The ground is strewn with their offshoots, and they present a sorry figure: one might even think that the gardener was quite destroying them. So have we seen our Father, who is the husbandman, cut and slash terribly with those who have been long prosperous, and have, therefore, borne little of the fruit of grace, and much of the wood of worldliness. See how their wealth diminishes, their health declines, their family sickens! Providence multiplies their trials till they feel that the hand of the Lord is gone out against them. Does the gardener hate the apple tree when he prunes so remorselessly? Far from it: he knows it to be a choice tree, and, therefore, he would have fruit from it: he would not thus wear away his knife upon a crab. Abounding trials prove their own necessity and the Lord's sagacity. If it clearly appears that we have not been able to bear seasons of worldly ease, it is the stern order of heavenly love that we must lose the unprofitable luxuriance of our unregulated joys. Is it not well that it should be so?

O Lord, I thank thee for all the wounds thou hast hitherto seen it wise to inflict upon me. If I, too, have enjoyed too much repose, and have spent my strength unprofitably in consequence thereof, I rejoice to think that I am in good hands. Deal with me even as thou wilt. I ask not for affliction, but

I beg thee to make me fruitful unto thyself, let the means be what they may.

LIKE WILL TO LIKE

Everything tendeth to the place of its original. Men love their native soil; things bred in the water delight in that element; inanimate things tend to their centre; a stone will fall to the ground though broken in pieces by the fall.

Thus I may judge of my nature by my inclination. What delights me? For where my delight is my heart is. If I take pleasure in the ways of the world, then I am of the world. If I find myself at home in sin, then I am still the servant of sin. Doubtless many hasten to evil with such desperate speed that they will be broken in the fall; yet to evil they must needs go, and he who would hinder them gets a wound for his pains. Come, my heart, what sayest thou of thyself? Art thou inclined to holiness or to lewdness, to grace or to covetousness? How much hangs on this! Yet take heart, for if thou hast a nature which came from heaven it will rise to heaven. If Jesus is the source of thy life, that life will rise as high as the place where Jesus dwells. Is not this a rich encouragement?

SAILING LONG, BUT NOT FAR

A man may abide long in the world till he be eaten out of life by his own rust, or droppeth like rotten fruit; but he cannot be said to have a long life; as a man may be long at sea, but if he is driven to and fro by the waves he cannot be said to make a long voyage when he is at last driven back into the port out of which he sailed at first.

Yes, life is not to be measured by mere lapse of time, but by the real headway which a man makes. The mass of mankind voyage to no known port, but are the sport of winds and waves.

Compass or chart they no more consult than do the seabirds or the dolphins. Thus it happens that in advanced years men are no forwarder than in youth, for they never continue in one line, having no object before them: they have not *lived*, but existed. Nothing has been attempted, much less accomplished; their years have rusted them into infirmity, but otherwise they are unaltered. Here's the respect which makes calamity of so much wasted life.

O my blessed Lord, preserve thy servant from spending his sojourn here after the manner of the idler. Let mine be a real life. May I not be a mere strainer of meat and drink, or a walking clothes-horse, or a cipher; but may I so live on earth that it may seem wise to thee to bid me continue my life forever.

DOUBLE BENEFIT

A malefactor that hath a leprosy on him needs not only a pardon, but a medicine; and in a broken leg, not only ease of the pain is desirable, but that the bone be set right. So we need both justification and sanctification.

Justification saves the malefactor, and sanctification cures him of his spiritual disease: are they not equally desirable? Who would wish to miss the one or the other if in need of them? Pardon removes the pain of our broken bones, but spiritual renewal reduces the fracture. Let us not be content with half a gospel, but obtain a whole Christ for our broken hearts. Renewal of life is every way as desirable as forgiveness of sin. As well be full of guilt as full of guile. If a child has eaten unhealthy food, it is well to cure the disease which is occasioned by it, but it is equally desirable to break him off the habit which led him to such foul feeding.

Lord, thy poor servant is by nature both malefactor and leper; and nothing will serve my turn but a double-handed blessing. I pray thee absolve me, and cure me too. Let me know of a surety that both these blessings are mine beyond all question, mine in immediate and experienced possession.

GRAVEL IN THE SHOE

Who will pity the man who complains of soreness and pain in walking, and yet doth not take the gravel out of his shoe? If you wound and gore yourselves, no question but your smart and trouble are real, you do not complain in hypocrisy; but who is to be blamed? Your business is to remove the cause.

Many of the trials of our spiritual life are preventable: if we indulge a sin we invite a sorrow. Others are curable: if we refuse a remedy we rivet a disease. All that we can do for ourselves we are bound to do. We must put away evil habits, and not content ourselves with whining out our regrets. We must get away from temptation, and not sit near the fire and complain of the heat. There is too much of this insincerity abroad. What should we have thought of the prodigal if he had lamented his destitution, but had continued in the far country? What do we now think of the drunkard who mourns over the redness of his eyes, and yet tarries long at the wine; or of the lascivious man who bemoans his vice, and yet frequents the house of the strange woman?

By gracious instruction, I pray thee, O Lord, teach me to be practical in going to the bottom of things, that I may not waste time in regretting evils which it is my duty to prevent. Let me not mourn my doubt, and yet refuse to believe thy faithful word; neither permit me to cry over my chastisement, and yet continue in my folly. Lord, make me to know wisdom. To this end, make me mindful of little things. Help me to look to the little stone, or tiny dust in my shoe, for this may cause me many a blister, and even lame me, so that I cannot hold on my way.

AN UNUSUAL COMPLAINT

I have read in the lives of the Fathers of a devout man that, being one year without any trial, cried out, 'Domine, reliquisti me, quia non me visitasti, hoc anno', — Lord! thou hast forgotten me, and for a whole year hast not appointed me upon any exercise of patience.

We would not recommend any one of our readers to unite with this devout but mistaken expression. We should count it all joy when we fall into divers trials, but, at the same time, we ought to be thankful if we do not fall into them. If a cross be laid upon us, let us take it up cheerfully; but it would be folly to make a cross for ourselves, or go out of our way to look for one. He must be a very foolish child who begs to be whipped. 'Lead us not into temptation' is a prayer of our Lord's own teaching, and we prefer to keep to it rather than follow this devout man in what reads very like a prayer for temptation. Those who cry for chastisement will have enough of it before all is over. Be it ours to leave our correction and probation in our Lord's hands, and never let us be so unwise as to desire more trials than his infinite wisdom appoints us.

THE TAP AND THE LIQUOR

The tap runneth according to the liquor with which the vessel is filled.

The tongue babbleth out that which occupies the mind. We shall never hear much pious conversation till we have more thorough conversions. Taps will never run with pure water while the barrels are bursting with fermented liquors. Change the contents of the heart, and you alter at once the droppings of the mouth. From a sweet fountain of thought we shall have sweet waters of talk. Even the involuntary utterances of gracious men are gracious: the mere drippings of common speech reveal the heart of the man. The leakings of a tap show the contents quite as surely as the proper runnings of it.

Lord, grant that even my dreams may be pure, that my playful thoughts may be godly, and my chance words acceptable before thee. Fill me with thyself, and then nothing but good can come from me.

BRASS FARTHINGS AND GOLD IN THE POCKET

He that hath in his pocket more store of gold than of brass farthings will at every draught bring out more gold than farthings.

Of course the hand fetches out the various kinds of coins in proportion as they exist in the place from which it takes them. Now, our works are our hand, and this, by action, fetches out of us that which is in us. In a child of God there is a measure of natural evil, and a more abounding measure of grace; and so it will come to pass that, in his life, holiness will be more conspicuous than sin. His life has its failings, but much more its virtues. Peter brought out brass farthings of boasting and impetuous folly at times; but he also brought forth so much true gold that his Lord said, 'Blessed art thou, Simon Barjona.' When he had received the Holy Ghost he brought out much more gold; but even then a farthing came out now and then, for Paul withstood him because he was to be blamed.

When the believer's tongue also makes a dip into the pocket of the heart there may come forth some of those wretched brass farthings in the form of idle words; but much more will the gold be poured forth in edifying discourse. Paul saith that foolish talking is not befitting, but he commends giving of thanks; now, if somewhat of our folly has come forth in our talk, let us give heed that far more of our gratitude shall be brought out also. We ought daily to grow richer in grace, and so have more gold, and less of the baser sort.

Lord, help me to get rid of these miserable brass counters, and do thou fill up their places with the precious metal of thine own holiness and truth. Am I not thy child? Wilt thou not supply me within with that which will be fit to be brought out into my life? Oh that I might be 'filled with all the fulness of God', that my poor empty things may no more appear!

RAVENS LOVING THE SCENT OF CARRION

If you would be free from sin, avoid the temptations that lead to it.
If ravens or crows be driven away from carrion, they love to abide
within scent of it.

This last sentence is a grim parable, but all too true. If human nature cannot yield an ell[1] to self-indulgence, it will give its full inch. We have seen those who dared not enter the devil's house linger long and lovingly around the doors. The old woman in the fable, who could find no wine in the jar, yet loved to smell at it. It is a clear proof of the love of human nature to evil that, when restrained from actual sin, men will rehearse their former exploits, and dote on the lusts which they indulged years ago. If they cannot have a fresh dish from Satan's garden they will have 'the cauld kail het again' sooner than go without.

[1] A unit of measurement, originally a cubit (18 inches or 45 cm).

Our author gives sage advice at the outset, when he says—to avoid sin, avoid temptation. He who would not be wounded should keep out of battle; he who would not be tossed about should not go to sea; he who would not be heated should keep away from the fire. If men will get into the train which runs to the terminus of iniquity, they must expect to be carried to their journey's end. He who desires to keep awake should not go to bed. If I stand in the way of sinners I shall soon run with them. Oh to possess a godly fear, which shall lead me rather to go ten miles round about, than pass by the place of temptation! It is well to keep out of the smell of sin, for the very odour of it is baneful.

If we seek a temptation we shall soon find it; and within it, like a kernel in a nut, we shall meet with sin. Oh that our young people had the wit to see this, and were more firmly resolved not to stand in the broad road, or even near it, lest they should become regular travellers upon it! Lord, give them prudence. Yea, give *me* prudence, and, as I would not devour the carrion of sin, give me such a renewed nature that the most distant scent of it shall at once sicken me, and cause me to urge my steps as far from it as possible.

TONGS FOR HANDLING HOT IRON

Chrysostom hath the following comparison: 'A smith that taketh up his red-hot iron with his hands, and not with his tongs, what can he expect but to burn his fingers? So we destroy our souls when we judge of the mysteries of faith by the laws of common reason.'

Common enough is this error. Men must needs comprehend when their main business is to apprehend. That which God reveals to us is, to a large extent, beyond the reach of understanding, and, therefore, in refusing to believe until we can understand, we are doing ourselves and the truth a grievous wrong. Our wisdom lies as much in taking heed *how* we receive as in being careful *what* we receive. Spiritual truth must be received by a spiritual faculty; namely, by faith. As well hope to grasp a star by the hand, as divine truth by reason. Faith is well likened to the golden tongs, with which we may carry live coals; and carnal reason is the burned hand, which lets fall the glowing mass, which it is not capable of carrying.

Let it not, however, be thought that faith is contrary to reason. No: it is not unreasonable for a little child to believe its father's statements, though it be quite incapable of perceiving all their bearings. It is quite reasonable that a pupil should accept his master's principles at the beginning of his studies; he will get but little from his discipleship if he begins by disputing with his teacher. How are we to learn anything if we will not believe? In the gloriously sublime truths of Godhead, Incarnation, Atonement, Regeneration, and so forth, we must believe, or be forever ignorant: these masses of the molten metal of eternal truth must be handled by faith, or let alone.

All-gracious Lord, this one thing thou hast done for me—thou hast made me a willing believer. Let but thine authority be at the back of a statement, and it stands instead of reason: in fact, thy word is to me the surest evidence, and to believe it is my soundest common-sense. Lord, thy *logos* is my *logic*; thy *Testament* is my *argument*; thy *word* is my *warrant*. In the day which shall reveal all things it shall be seen that man's reasonings are but childish folly, and God's revelation is wisdom at its height.

GREEN WOOD

Green wood, which is wet and full of sap, cannot be kindled by a flash or a spark, but needeth much care and blowing ere it will burn.

When we are dealing with young and thoughtless minds, we must remember this, and be patient and persevering. Such will not readily take fire when we apply our match; we had better go down on our knees while we are trying to light the fire of attention in them, and if we use the warm breath of our anxious love we shall all the sooner do the work.

Lord, as I have seen my servant thus doing my work, help me as thy servant to copy her, and succeed in thy work.

GAMBLING

In gaming there is a secret witchery. A man will play a little, and only venture a small sum; but soon he is wormed in, and more and more entangled; and so men think it is no great matter to sin a little, and yet that little leadeth on to more.

The illustration is most forcible. Many persons have put down a piece of silver on the gaming-table when passing through the room, and from that moment their ruin has been sealed. They will be seen from day to day staking their hundreds, till the last fatal roll of the ball leaves them penniless. For the while gamblers live, and move, and have their being in the game: their eyes are quick, and their brains are sharp, to see each turn of the play: they are the willing, abject slaves of what is called amusement. Thus doth sin begin with littles, and glide into more serious faults; till the sinner is spellbound, and finds himself engrossed with folly, which he has no will to leave. Be it ours to give no place to the devil. Let him not have a spot whereon to set up his enchantment and work his diabolical arts. If we never venture a farthing upon Satan's table, we shall never be made beggars by his devices. If he is not allowed to spin a spider's web about us, he will never be able to hold us with the cords of iniquity. If we never wade into sin we shall never drown in it. Lord, keep us from the appearance of evil.

INWARD BLEEDING

Many die of inward bleeding as well as by outward wounds.

Every surgeon can give instances of such deaths. Not an abrasion of the skin was visible: the dying man had neither gash, nor cut, nor even a pin's prick, and yet his life oozed away in secret. Thus, without an open fault, a man's soul may perish. If wrath rage within, it is fatal, though no revengeful act has been perpetrated; if lust be burning in the heart, the man is lost, though he has never advanced to a lascivious deed; if unbelief proves an inward enmity against God, the man is condemned already, though no blasphemous word has crossed his lip. Sin is a bleeding at the heart. It is a disease which destroys the true life within, as well as the fruit of it without; therefore let every man beware of flattering himself that he is right with God because no glaring vice is manifest in his daily conversation. The worm none the less surely destroys the apple because its first operations are at the core, and quite out of sight. If fire be utterly hidden among combustible materials, it will not therefore be any the less sure and rapid in its devouring work.

'Sin, which dwelleth in me', is the enemy that I must fight against, as well as sin which goeth out of me. O Lord, help me to be healthy in the fountain of my being. Heal my heart, and so I shall be healed. Heart-disease baffles all physicians but thyself. This, however, is thy *specialité*, Lord, display thy sovereign power and skill in the centre of my being.

A CHILD ASKING AN APPLE

Prayers to God for spiritual things are the most acceptable, but prayers for temporals are not despised. A child pleaseth his father more when he desireth him to teach him his book than when he begs for an apple; yet this request is not refused when it will do him no ill to grant it.

A pretty, simple picture, rightly drawn upon divine authority; for the Lord himself teaches us to judge what our heavenly Father will do for us by that which we would do for our children. If I go to God, and ask for spiritual blessings, he will be pleased with my request, and most surely grant it, even as a father will readily give his boy a lesson in some useful work or book. But I may also beg for temporal mercies, as a child asks for its bread and butter. More than this, as a child may ask for an apple, or a sweet, so may I make request for that which I desire. Only in this latter case I am bound to remember that a child is not *bidden* to ask for the apple, though he is *allowed* to do so. 'Give me this day my daily bread', is a petition prescribed: if I ask for more it must be as a petition permitted. Moreover, the child's request is one which must be left entirely to the Father's own discretion: he is bound by promise to give his offspring necessaries, but he is under no bonds to grant them luxuries. Here is a difference ever to be noted between prayers commanded and prayers tolerated. As we are children of the great Father, we have a large liberty of request; if we delight ourselves in the Lord he will give us the desires of our hearts; but still when we are praying, it is well for us to press our suit just so far as it may be pressed, and no further. A child asking for necessary food may be vehement even unto tears; but if what he wishes for is only a sugar-stick, he will be a naughty child if he be passionately importunate. Mind this, ye babes in grace, when next ye pray. Ask, seek, knock, according as the promise invites; but in temporal matters consider the way of the Lord's house, and submit your will unto the will of the Father.

THE SHOWMAN'S JEST

Augustine speaketh of a jester who boasted that at the next fair he would undertake to show everyone what they did desire; and when there was a great concourse and expectation, he told them, 'Hoc omnes vultis, vili emere, et caro vendere',—You all desire to buy cheap and sell dear. Another showman, on like occasion, said, 'Ye all desire to be praised.' But Augustine saith rightly, these were but foolish answers, because many good men desire neither, the one being against justice, and the other against sincerity; but, saith he, 'Si dixisset, omnes beati esse vultis', If he had said,—Ye all desire to be happy, he had said right. Everyone may find this disposition in his own heart, every man desireth happiness.

No doubt this is true, and it is equally true that the notion of happiness is as varied as the wish for it is universal. What is my view of happiness? This is a question of the highest importance; for as I am sure to seek after that which I desire, and am sure to desire that which I conceive to be happiness, it is clear that my conception of happiness will largely regulate my whole course of life. Remember this, O my soul, and take good heed that thou seek not happiness apart from holiness, nor rest apart from Jesus, nor pleasure apart from pleasing God.

Lord, teach men that thou art their bliss, and then draw them to seek after thee with their whole hearts.

CONSCIENCE LIKE THE EYE OR THE STOMACH

The least dust, if it get into the eye, will pain it; so will conscience at first smite us for lesser failings and excesses; but afterward when you make bold with it, it is like the stomach of the ostrich, which digesteth iron; or like a part or member of the body which is seared with a hot iron, it hath no feeling (1 Tim. 4:2); or, like freezing water, which at first will not bear a pin, but afterward it freezeth, and freezeth, till it bear a cart-load. Some men lose their tender sense of sin by frequency of sinning.

If our offending against right did us no worse turn than this it would be bad enough, for to lose sensitiveness of conscience is to lose the excellence of our being. What is the eye worth when it can no longer feel pain, or the hand when its touch is gone, or the head when sensation has departed? As well take away from the goldsmith all his tests as from man his conscience. What is the use of a watchman who is in a dead sleep? How far any one of us may be proceeding in this direction it will be prudent for us to know at once, that by repentance we may arrest the process, and by faith may put ourselves into the hands of the Lord Jesus, that he may give back to us the heart of flesh. Let us entreat the Holy Spirit to continue his softening operations even to the end.

> Sin has been hammering my heart
> Unto a hardness void of love:
> Let suppling grace to cross its art
> Drop from above.

THE EAR-RING

Reproof is an ear-jewel; now an ear-jewel must not be too weighty and heavy, lest it tear and rend, rather than adorn the ear.

Rebuke requires delicacy. It is never wise to box a man on the ear to win his attention to a whisper. Too much zeal in this case is its own hindrance. It is only a dainty bit of pure gold, garnished with a rare jewel, that a lady will think fit for her ear: it would be idle to offer her a quoit, or even a curtain-ring. It was said of a good man that if he wished to brush off a fly from a friend's forehead he would look round for a beetle and wedges;[1] and of another that he washed off spots from a brother's face with scalding water. A man should note how reproofs affect himself, and he may from this observation discover that they need to be administered very tenderly. The rebukes of the righteous should always be as a precious ointment, sweet and gentle; never should they break the head. Whenever it is our reader's duty to attend to this painful business, let him remember Manton's figure of the ear-ring, and act accordingly. A friend who wished a lady to wear an ear-ring would go down to the jeweller's, and with dainty fingers examine various jewels, and select one of the best, suited for that exquisite piece of living coral which is such an adornment to a fair head. This he would not fling at the lady, nor force into her ear with violence, but he would proffer it with due courtesy, and leave her to fix it in its place herself. If a reproof be thus selected, and be really precious, it should be wisely presented to the person for whom it is intended; and much of the application must be adroitly left to the person's own conscience. Thus will the gem reach the ear, and the reproof reach the heart.

Lord, make us wise in this and all other things by thy Spirit. Let us not shun the duty of reproof, but help me to do it well, lest I do harm when I mean to do good, and thus myself need to be rebuked.

[1] A beetle is a heavy wooden mallet used for driving wedges or beating down paving stones.

THE YOKE LINED

The yoke of Christ will be more easy than we think of, especially when it is lined with grace.

We well remember an old man who carried pails with a yoke, and as he was infirm, and tender about the shoulders, his yoke was padded, and covered with white flannel where it touched him. But what a lining is 'love'! A cross of iron, lined with love, would never gall the neck, much less will Christ's wooden cross. Lined with Christ's love to us! Covered with our love to him! Truly the yoke is easy, and the burden is light.

Whenever the shoulder becomes sore let us look to the lining. Keep the lining right, and the yoke will be no more a burden to us than wings are to a bird, or her wedding-ring is to a bride. Love divine, line my whole life, my cares, my griefs, my pains; and what more can I ask?

PRESCRIPTIONS NOT TO BE ALTERED

The prescriptions of a physician must not be altered, either by the apothecary or the patient; so we, the preachers, must not alter God's prescriptions, neither must you, the hearers. We must not shun to declare, nor you to receive, 'the whole counsel of God'.

It is as much as a man's soul is worth to alter a word of the Lord's own writing: to take away from the book, or to add to it, is forbidden, and threatened with the heaviest penalties.

It is not ours to improve the gospel, but to repeat it when we preach, and obey it when we hear. The gospel, the whole gospel, and nothing but the gospel, must be our religion, or we are lost men. Imagine a dispenser altering the ingredients of a medicine to suit his own notions! We should soon have him on trial for manslaughter; and surely he would deserve to be tried on a still higher charge should a patient die through his folly. The gospel prescription is such that an omission or an addition may soon make that which was ordained to life to be unto death. We may not attempt to be wiser than God, for the idea involves constructive blasphemy. No, it is ours to follow our copy to the letter, come what may of it.

Lord, in my teaching I have ever kept to what thou hast said; and therefore men think me old-fashioned, and behind the age. Give me grace to continue so. Never may I aspire to practise a new pharmacy, but may I faithfully dispense thine own ancient and unvarying prescription of salvation by grace through faith.

TRUSTING AFTER FAILURE

As a prodigal, that hath once broken after he hath been set up, is not trusted with a like stock again; so God's children may not recover that largeness of spirit, and fulness of inward strength and comfort, which they had before. Many after a great disease do not regain that pitch of health which formerly they had, but they carry the fruits of their disease with them to their graves.

This is not always the case, for it may happen, as with Peter, that the bankrupt believer may so prosper in grace as to be richer than before his failure; but we fear that Manton here mentions the general rule. Men do not care to ride a bro-ken-kneed horse: if it has been down once, it may be down again. A wise father does not care to restore a son to a posi-tion for which he has proved himself to be unfit. Even so has the Lord dealt with many backsliding ones: like David, they have been restored, but never to their former peace, prosperity, and power. Into the army of our Lord the deserter is received with gladness; but he must begin in the ranks, and must prove his fidelity before he is again entrusted with a commission. A fallen one, when restored, may have gained in self-knowledge, but he must necessarily be a loser in many other respects.

A little boy, who had fallen into the habit of falsehood, was made by his father to drive a nail into a post every time he had exaggerated, or told a lie. At last the habit was conquered, and in several trials the boy had displayed complete truthfulness. Then his father allowed him to draw out some of the nails, and this was repeated till no nail was left in the post. The little fellow, so far from being proud when every nail was gone, exclaimed, 'Alas, father, the holes are there, where the nails used to be!' Just so does evil leave its marks. However fully restored, the fallen professor seldom loses the memory of impurity, and does not easily regain his injured influence. He is always weak in those points which led to his former fall, and, for the most part, weaker all round.

O Lord! if thou hast counted me faithful, putting me into thy service, I pray thee keep me from being either unfaithful to my charge, or negligent in my life. Let me be so upheld that I shall not have need to be picked out of the mire, and set on my feet again.

THE DEN OF THE COCKATRICE

If we play about the cockatrice's hole, no wonder we are bitten.

An old proverb advises us not to play with edged tools lest we cut our fingers. It is a sin to trifle with sin. If we must play, we had better find harmless toys: that evil which caused Christ a bloody sweat is no fit theme for any man's sport. Playing with wickedness is a hazardous game. Sooner or later, if we pluck the lion of sin by the beard, it will arouse itself, and we shall be torn in pieces. This is true of indulgence in strong drink: 'Look not thou upon the wine when it is red, when it giveth his colour in the cup, when it moveth itself aright. At the last it biteth like a serpent, and stingeth like an adder.' It is equally true of all other forms of evil, especially of the lusts of the flesh. Lewd words soon lead to foul deeds. Yet such is the folly of men that they run dreadful risks in sheer wantonness, as though asps and cobras were fine play-mates, and devils rare merry-makers.

'Lord, keep back thy servant from presumptuous sins; let them not have dominion over me; then shall I be upright, and I shall be innocent from the great transgression.'

SUNSHINE WITH RAIN

As many times the sun shineth when the rain falleth, so there may be in the soul a mixture of spiritual rejoicing and holy mourning; a deep sense of God's love, and yet a mourning because of the relics of corruption.

All spiritual persons understand this. The inexperienced ask how a man can be 'sorrowful, yet always rejoicing'. But this is no puzzle to a Christian. Our life is a paradox. Never in the world elsewhere is there such sunshine of delight as we enjoy, and never such rain as that which damps our joys. It seems at times as if heaven and hell met in our experience. Ours is a joy unspeakable, and yet an agony unutterable. We rise to the heavenlies in Christ, and sink to the abyss in ourselves. Those who have seen fire burning on the sea, trees living and flourishing upon a rock, feathers flying against the wind, and doves vanquishing eagles, have begun to see a list of marvels, all of which are to be found within the believer, and much more of equal or greater singularity.

Lord, when my own experience puzzles me, let me be comforted by the thought that it does not puzzle thee. What I know not now thou hast promised to make me know hereafter; and there I leave it.

THE SHIP AND ITS PASSENGERS

Look, as in a ship some sleep, and some walk contrary to the ship's motion, so in the world; some men are negligent, others keep bustling and stirring, and seek to resist the designs of God; but the ship goes on, and the world goes on.

Yes, a passenger may walk to the north along the deck, but the ship keeps on due south; he may sleep, but the vessel speeds over the waves; he may denounce its motion, but it holds on its way. So the heathen may rage, and the people imagine a vain thing, but the counsel of the Lord standeth fast forever. Men are free to will and to act, but omnipotent wisdom rules over them despite their free agency. Not as if they were logs and stones does God govern men, but as rational, intelligent, free agents he permits them to do their own will, and works his own purposes notwithstanding. This is a great marvel. Men are as free as if there were no predestination, and predestination is accomplished as surely as if there were no free agents in the universe. We are full of wonder at this, but it is true.

The figure before us is not perfect, but it has many merits; and, at any rate, it sets out the one idea that the rebellions and wilfulnesses of mankind do not thwart the eternal purposes of the Most High. The royal vessel pursues its way whether men delight in its glorious progress, or rail against it, 'The Lord reigneth; let the earth rejoice.'

THE INSULTED MERCHANT

A merchant that hath a precious commodity, and one biddeth a mean price, he foldeth up his wares with indignation.

We have seen the exhibitor turn away in utter disgust when some uninitiated spectator has offered pence where pounds would not have been accepted. The jeweller or artist has been as much offended as if he had been personally insulted by such a depreciation of his valuables. Do you wonder that the Lord God is grieved when men set a base price upon his priceless grace, and begin to bargain and chaffer as to what sins they will give up, and what duties they will perform? Do you wonder that he should take his gospel away from such a people, and turn to others who will set more store by his goodness? Not forever will Jesus cast his pearls before swine. Woe to that man who at last angers his God into turning from him, and taking the despised gospel elsewhere! He well deserves to perish who counts eternal life to be of less value than a passing pleasure, or reckons the righteousness of God to be no better than his own poor works.

PROVISIONED FOR A SIEGE

When a city is besieged, the prince who would defend it doth not leave it to its ordinary strength and the standing provisions which it had before, but sendeth in fresh supplies of soldiers, victuals, and ammunition, and such things as the present exigence calleth for. So doth God deal with his people; his Spirit cometh in with a new supply, that they may better repel sin, and stand out in the hour of trial.

What supplies of food, medicine, and ammunition are poured into a city which has to sustain a siege; and seldom do they prove to be more than are required! Even so, in our time of temptation, the Lord bestows vast stores of grace, strength, comfort, and wisdom; and yet there is need of them all ere the assault is over. It were well if we had a clearer idea of the needs of a beleaguered soul. We think far too lightly of the necessities which arise out of the attacks of Satan, and the blockade of the flesh. The City of Mansoul has no provision within itself, and if its commerce with heaven be cut off, black famine stares the inhabitants in the face. While the coast is clear it will be well to get in stores, and specially on those great market-days, the Sabbaths. None can fit us to stand a siege but that Universal Provider who daily feeds countless myriads of needy creatures.

Lord, thou knowest all things, thou knowest when next my nature shall be beleaguered by the adversary. Provision me, I pray thee, against the siege. Give me to rejoice because thou hast prayed for me that my faith fail not.

BLOWN INTO HARBOUR

Men in a tempest are sometimes cast upon a place of safety which they had not made for by intention and foresight.

Happy mariner, who is forced into port! Blessed is that wave which throws the drowning sailor upon the rock of safety! Such propitious forces are abroad at times, and especially in the spiritual world. We mean not to exclude the agency of the will when we speak of certain compulsions which have driven men into a happiness for which they had not looked. 'Had I not lost my eyes', said one, 'I had never seen my Saviour.' Another attributed his spiritual riches to the fact that he lost all his property, and so was driven to his God for consolation. The utmost faith in God has sometimes been created by the Holy Spirit by means of the utter and entire failure of all visible help. Many a wayward mind has been set free from the bonds of its own obstinate will by being yet more firmly bound by a sacred impulse which would not be denied.

When we reach the heights of glory we shall ascribe our felicity, not to our own will or merit, but to those sweet forces which drew us to heaven with cords of love and bands of a man; and perhaps not less to certain ruder agencies, which beat like hurricanes upon our pride, and sank our self-confidence in the floods, wrecking us into rest, destroying us into salvation.

A PEARL OF UNKNOWN VALUE

If a man find a pearl of great price, and knoweth not what it is, he maketh no more esteem of it than of a piece of glass or a common bead, and is ready to sell it for a few pence. But if upon the offer of it to a skilful lapidary, the jeweller at first sight biddeth two or three thousand crowns for it, doth he not change his mind, and think this jewel is of greater value than he took it to be? So here: a man knows not the value of his soul, and does not greatly set by it. Adam lost his own soul and the souls of all his posterity for an apple, and we sell our birthright for a mess of pottage. But when Christ, who made souls, and knoweth the value of them, came to recover lost souls, he gave himself for us; did he not hereby teach us to set a higher price upon them; for nothing but his precious blood could redeem them?

This is a suggestive simile, and may suggest the framework of a sermon on 'the estimate which men set upon their souls, and the hints which God has given them as to their real value by what he has done in reference thereto'. In the shop of a diamond-merchant at Amsterdam we saw great machinery and much power all brought to bear on what seemed to be a small piece of glass. One might be sure of the value of that transparent morsel if he would but look around and see what skill and labour were being expended upon it. God has laid out for the good of a soul the watchfulness of angels, the providence of this world, the glory of the next, the councils of eternity, himself and all that he hath, the Holy Spirit and all his divine influences—yea, he spared not his only Son. Say, soul, what must thou be worth thus to have all heaven's thought, and power, and love laid out for thee? 'What shall a man give in exchange for his soul?' Let not a man attempt to answer the question till he hath heard the Lord himself say, 'I gave Egypt for thy ransom, Ethiopia and Seba for thee.'

A POOR MAN ROBBED

If a poor man be robbed of twenty or thirty shillings, no wonder if he cry and take on, because he hath no more to help himself with; but now, if a rich man be robbed of such a sum, he is not much troubled, because he hath more at home. So a man that is justified by faith, and hath assurance of the favour of God, he can comfortably bear up against all the troubles and crosses he meets with in his way to heaven.

Remember the apostle's reckoning in Romans 8:18: 'For I reckon that the sufferings of this present time are not worthy to be compared with the glory which shall be revealed in us.' He was so rich in grace that all his losses were as nothing to him. One of old got his living by his losses, for he said, 'By these things men live, and in all these things is the life of my spirit': thus spiritual riches enable us to bear temporal losses with great patience. It is far otherwise with the worldling, whose goods are his god; for when these are taken he cries out like Micah, 'Ye have taken away my gods which I made, and what have I more?' He to whom God is all things cannot be robbed, for who can overcome and despoil the Almighty?

Lord, lead me to count nothing my treasure but thyself, and then I may defy the thief. If I have suffered loss, let me make a gain thereby by prizing thee the more.

A TANNED FACE

As a man that walks in the sun, unawares, before he thinks of it, his countenance is tanned; so our hearts are defiled by the slightest contact with sin.

We have seen men who were quite fair where their hats covered their foreheads, and thoroughly bronzed where the sun had looked upon them. A man's heart had need be covered with a veil of holy carefulness all over, or the world will get at it, and brown it with evil. Some trades and callings are like a tropical climate, and their blackening effect is soon visible: certain companies are still more so; they make their mark upon the best of men, and that mark is not to their improvement. With difficulty can a man prevent the world's influencing him for evil; evil communications will corrupt good manners unless a sacred remedy is heartily used. See the effect of evil upon professors in Jeremiah's day; he says: 'Her Nazarites were purer than snow, they were whiter than milk, they were more ruddy in body than rubies, their polishing was of sapphire: their visage is blacker than a coal; they are not known in the streets: their skin cleaveth to their bones; it is withered, it is become like a stick.'

Let us, as much as we can, keep ourselves to ourselves, and go quietly through life. A man of eminence, who outlived

the French Revolution, was asked how he escaped the guil-
lotine, and he replied, 'I made myself of no reputation, and
kept silence.' Let us, like him, stay within doors. If we must go
forth abroad, it is well to walk on the shady side of the street,
by keeping as much out of the world's influence as we can; and
it is also wise to carry with us such holy thoughts and feelings
as may act as a screen to ward off the excessive power of evil.
We have no wish to become as black as the inhabitants of this
sun-burnt clime, seeing we are not numbered with them, but
are here as strangers and foreigners.

Wash me, most blessed Jesus, in that sacred bath which
thou hast prepared; for it will make me fair forever. Black as
I now am, I shall then be whiter than snow. Renew me, and I
shall be without spot or wrinkle, or any such thing.

THE FOOT RACE

A true racer does not use to stand still, or look behind him, to see
how much of the way is already past, or to see how much the other
runners come short of him, but he sets to his business to get through
the remainder of the race.

The claim to perfection, which some have started, raises
a serious question as to whether they have ever entered that
race, of which the apostle Paul said, 'Brethren, I count not
myself to have apprehended: but this one thing I do, forgetting those things which are behind and reaching forth unto
those things which are before, I press toward the mark for the
prize of the high calling of God in Christ Jesus.' Surely these
men must be of another order to St Paul, or must be upon
another race-course. He saw much which he had not attained,
and they see nothing; he was all for pressing on, and they are at

the mark already. They speak fluently of their perfection, and he groaned over his imperfection. As for us, we have no belief in these pretenders, nor do we wish to think about them. We would have nothing to consider but the goal and the prize. We may not rest in what we are, we must hasten on to what we ought to be. Attainments and successes will breed no pride if we treat them as Paul did, when he regarded them as 'things which are behind', and therefore forgot them. 'Onward' be our watchword. Satisfaction, glorying, ease—these are not to be mentioned among us. Swift as arrows from the bow we would speed toward the mark of our high calling. The last thing that a man may utter is that fatal 'Rest and be thankful'; for it marks the end of a progress which ought to last through life.

Lord, if I am ever tempted to be satisfied, scourge me into a holy restlessness, and make the very ground beneath me burning to my feet. With my Lord before me, I am a traitor to him if I chink the pieces of silver in my hand, and accept a present satisfaction in barter for higher things.

THE WARRIOR'S THOUGHTS

A certain Grecian warrior, wherever he walked, was thinking of battles; he asked himself continually, if he should be assaulted on such a piece of ground how he would model and dispose his army for his defence. A Christian should be thinking of heaven, how he may get thither, and what he shall enjoy there.

To be engrossed in a pursuit is the readiest way to success in it. We are thoroughly alive unto God when we get so far as even to eat, and drink, and sleep eternal life. Where our treasure is there will our heart be also. The object which is supreme in our heart will continually make itself prominent in our life.

When Joshua saw the angel of the Lord, he gave him a military challenge, for his whole soul was in the war. The colour of our chosen occupation will tinge our whole existence. 'For to me to live is Christ', saith the apostle. The musician will be moving his fingers upon the table as if he were playing a tune; the sailor will roll about in his walk on shore as if he were still on board ship; and even so will the soul that communes with God rehearse its joys when it is busy with other matters. When God and heaven bear our thoughts away, it is good evidence that we are preparing for eternal felicity; for he must needs be soon in heaven who already hath heaven in him. When heavenly things take up our souls, our souls will soon be taken up to heaven.

Lord, let me think of thee and thy word all the while I am awake; and when I sleep, if I dream at all, let my imagination still tend thy way. Oh that I were fully and only filled with thee, till everywhere and at all times my every thought were thine! With all thy ransomed ones I would sing—

> In full and glad surrender
>   We give ourselves to Thee,
> Thine utterly, and only,
>   And evermore to be
>
> O Son of God, who lovest us,
>   We will be Thine alone,
> And all we are, and all we have,
>   Shall henceforth be Thine own!

NATURE TENDS TO ITS AUTHOR

Trees, that receive life from the earth and the sun, send forth their branches to receive the sun, and spread their roots into the earth, which brought them forth. Fishes will not live out of the water that breedeth them. Chickens are no sooner out of the shell but they shroud themselves under the feathers of the hen by whom they were at first hatched. The little lamb runneth to its dam, though there be a thousand sheep of the same wool and colour; as if it said, 'Here I received that which I have, and here will I seek that which I want.' By such a native inbred desire do the saints run to God to seek a supply of strength and nourishment.

This is an excellent lesson for every believer. All our instincts should lead us to our God. We ought not to need so much as directing, much less impelling, toward the great source of our spiritual life. We ought as naturally to seek after the Lord from day to day as the spark seeks the sun, or the river the ocean, or the sheep its pasture, or the bird its nest. 'O God, thou art my God; early will I seek thee', should be the perpetual cry of our heart. Onward and upward be still our movement, a secret ardour ever burning in us toward the Lord our God.

To whom else should we go? This question has never received an answer, and never will receive one. We are bound to dwell in God or perish. As we find all in God, so we find nothing out of him. What the fish would be without water, or the chick without the hen, or the tree without the earth—that we should be without our God. It is the height of folly for us to attempt a thought alone; there is but one greater absurdity, and that is to venture upon an act without him. 'Abide in me' is the voice of him in whom our life abides. Let us not be deaf to his tender warning.

SUNSHINE

A little sunshine enliveneth the poor creatures, the birds fall a-singing that were melancholy and sad before in cloudy weather; all things are cheered and comforted when the sun shines.

Just so. How often have we seen the change which is wrought by clear shining after rain! It has seemed as though heaven had come down in love to dry earth's tears and bedeck her with raiment of fair colours. Spiritually, the type is carried out in delightful fashion. The Lord's appearing sheds a glory upon our infirmities, and transforms our trials into triumphs. His presence removes the dulness which else hangs like a cloud on the best of our conditions, and in this way lightens all our glooms. His countenance is to his saints as a morning without clouds, it brings with it a surprise of joy. Till Jesus communed with me I did not know that I could be so happy. I heard more birds singing in my soul than I had ever dreamed could have dwelt within me. Never had my sad soul imagined that human life was half as capable of divine bliss, or earth within a thousand leagues so near to heaven. Truly it is worthwhile to have lived, if for nothing more than to have had an hour's fellowship with the Well-beloved. Earthly joy is no more to be compared with it than a lamp in a coal-mine can be likened to the sun in the heavens.

Oh, my God, I thank thee for having made me, because thou hast made me able to walk in the light of thy countenance. Now thou dost shine upon me, my summer-tide has come.

DOGS AND CATS WHERE THERE ARE NO CHILDREN
They that lack children take pleasure in little dogs and cats.

We have known houses turned into stables or menageries by those whose love, which should have gone out to human beings, went out to dogs and cats. People must have objects of affection, and if they have not the better they choose the worse. Those who disdain to live for God will live for their own bellies. Those who do not care for the great doctrines of revelation are usually disputatious over trifling opinions. Those who do not spend their time and strength in winning souls for Jesus often attach an inordinate importance to a national habit or a sanitary regulation. If we do not live in all seriousness for a noble object, the probability is that we shall industriously trifle our lives away in doing nothing. Are we prepared for this? Will we be numbered with cat-worshippers and dog-adorers?

My God, grant me grace to love thy children, and make much of them. Save me from petty and paltry objects. May the objects of my life's pursuit be worthy of an immortal spirit, worthy of an heir of heaven. Deliver me from whims and hobbies, and nerve me for the infinite possibilities which are opening up before me!

THE GARDENER AND THE ROOTS

A gardener knoweth what roots are in the ground long before they appear, and what flowers they will produce.

Look over the garden in winter, and you will not know that there is any preparation for spring; but the gardener sees in his mind's eye—here a circle of golden cups, as if set out for a royal banquet, and there a cluster of snow-white beauties, drooping with excess of modest purity. His eye knows where the daffodils and anemones lie asleep, waiting to rise in all their loveliness; and he has learned the secret of the primroses and the violets, who wait in ambush till the first warm breath of spring shall bid them reveal themselves. Even thus doth the Lord know his hidden ones long before the day of their manifestation with him. He sees his church before his ministers see it, and declares concerning heathen Corinth, 'I have much people in this city.'

The figure may be applied to the garden of the soul. What graces are planted in the renewed heart, waiting their season, the Creator of those graces knows right well! He sees our faith, and love, and hope, and patience, long before we can see them; yea, and he discerns them when we ourselves question their existence. He not only knows them that are his, but all that is his within them. Nothing of his implanting is hidden from his inspection. Bulbs and seeds of holiness are sown in the righteous, and therefore are out of their sight; but he that placed them where they are has marked the spot, and not one of them shall die. Expectantly he waits to see his people's lives become 'as beds of spices, as sweet flowers'.

Lord, it is because thou knowest all things that thou knowest that I love thee. Wert thou not omniscient, I fear thou hadst not discovered my sadly feeble love, buried as it is beneath so much sin and carnality. Lord, cause the sacred seed to grow, and then I too shall be assured of its existence, and my present questions and doubts shall flee away!

RESPONSIBILITY OF SERVANTS

If a rich farmer set a poor man to work to dig a ditch, or cast up a bank; if he be afterward troubled for it, his master is concerned to bear him harmless. David saith, 'O Lord, truly I am thy servant; I am thy servant, and the son of thine handmaid: thou hast loosed my bonds.' While we are engaged about our Master's business, and in his work, he is engaged to protect us, and bear us out in it.

If what we do is done under the command of God, the responsibility of its result does not lie with us. He who made the law will answer for those who keep it. If a man should, through obedience to the law of the Sabbath, lose his situation, his poverty would be no fault of his. If through strict honesty he should be despised of his employer, and forfeit his place, he need not blame himself for his dismission. These things are to be taken joyfully as a part of our living sacrifice to God. We need not fear that God will fail to justify us if we walk in the way of his commandments. Our quarrel is his quarrel if it be occasioned by our following his orders. Jesus asks of every persecutor, 'Why persecutest thou me?' When his servants are molested he is wounded. He will see us through with the business, and teach our opposers that in us they oppose him also.

When we go a way of our own choosing, we must bear our own hazard; but when our path is mapped out for us, we have the Lord engaged with us, and his name and honour would be compromised should we fail. Oh, happy condition! We are in the same boat with Jesus. He bade us trust, promising us salvation by faith, and, as we have trusted, he must and will save us. He bade us come out from the world, and, as we have come out, he must be a Father unto us. He bids us preach the gospel, and, as we do preach it, he must save men thereby. Let us more and more pledge the honour of his name, resting sure that he will never allow his orders to be discredited.

ASKING IN A PERSON'S NAME

If you send a child or servant to a friend for a thing in your name, the request is yours; and he that denieth the child or servant, denieth you. Jesus Christ hath bidden you ask in his name; so that in effect your request becomes Christ's request. God can no more deny your request in Christ's name than he can deny Christ himself.

This is the true meaning of asking in Christ's name. It is a higher plea than—for Jesus' sake. The one pleads the Saviour's merit as a penitent sinner; the other urges his authority as a favoured friend. Jesus permits his disciple to make request in his Master's stead, using the name and dignity of Christ as his warrant. Armed with this argument our prayers become akin to the intercession of the Lord himself. Herein lies at once the power of prayer and also its limit. For who will dare to use 'the name which is above every name' except with surest right to do so? I may beg for Christ's sake when my petition is somewhat doubtful; but the royal seal must only be set to requests which the most searching examination commends to our judgment as according to the divine promise, and needful for God's glory. We are trusted with the Prince's signet-ring, but gracious discretion must be used in its employment. When the Spirit of God prompts the desire, and faith sees how well Jesus deserves the blessing, and how surely he himself would have sought it of the Father, then prayer is power invincible, for it is the pierced hand held open before the Father's approving heart. Cannon have been called 'the last arguments of kings'; but the name of Jesus is the master-argument of the King's children.

Lord Jesus, cause me to know in my daily experience the glory and sweetness of thy name, and then teach me how to use it in my prayer, so that I may be even like Israel, a prince prevailing with God. Thy name is my passport, and secures me access; thy name is my plea, and secures me answer; thy name is my honour, and secures me glory. Blessed name, thou art honey in my mouth, music in my ear, heaven in my heart, and all in all to all my being!

A FATHER'S LOVE AND A CHILD'S LOVE

A father cannot forget how many children he hath. He that leadeth us by the hand wherever we go knoweth where and how we go.

This is a very simple statement, but exceedingly full of consolation. We, being evil, do not forget our children; we know our own, and do not omit even the last little one from our tender memory; how much more shall our heavenly Father think upon all his own, and have them under his watchful eye! It is a pleasure to us to think of our children, for they are parts of ourselves. We could almost as soon cease to be as cease to remember them. Our Father above is all a Father can be and more: we are poor and needy, yet the Lord thinketh upon us.

It were well if the converse of all this were true. We, alas! as children, too often forget our Father, and bear ourselves toward him otherwise than is meet. If we treated our God as good children do a loving father, our conduct toward him would lead us to a holy, happy life. We should long to be with him, and to be happy in his company; we should be jealous for the honour of his name, and feel pleased when we heard others extol him. He would be our rest, confidence, pattern, love, and delight. Miss Havergal, in her own sweet way, has worked out the ideal treatment of a father, and we can readily spiritualize it.

> How do you love your father?
>   Oh, in a thousand ways!
> I think there's no one like him
>   So worthy of my praise.
> I tell him all my troubles,
>   And ask him what to do;
> I know that he will give to me
>   His counsel kind and true.

Nor does the relationship merely lead us to expect from him, it helps us to yield to him anything which he desires from us.

Then every little service
　Of hand, or pen, or voice,
Becomes, if he has asked it,
　The service of my choice.
And from my own desires
　'Tis not so hard to part,
If once I know I follow so
　His wiser will and heart.

How it helps us in the hour of trial to find a father near in all the tenderness of his love! The same charming poetess tells us in a succeeding verse—

Once I was ill and suffering
　Upon a foreign shore,
And longed to see my father
　As I never longed before.
He came: his arm around me;
　I leaned upon his breast;
I did not long to feel more strong.
　So sweet that childlike rest.

Whatsoever a tender daughter would be to a kind, considerate father, that we should spiritually be unto our Lord. Let us muse over the model, and learn from it what our highest relationship deserves at our hand.

Lord, I would reflect thy love! Help me to remember thee, because thou dost without fail remember me.

LOOKERS-ON AND PLAYERS

They that stand upon the shore may easily say to those that are in the midst of the waves, and conflicting for life or death, Sail thus and sail thus! But what of that? When we are well we give counsel to the sick; but, if we were ill ourselves, how should we act?

Yes, we are usually ready with our good advice for others; but what are we willing to do ourselves? Men who never smelt powder know exactly how a commander should have acted in a battle; probably they would themselves have run away at the first shot. Safely on land, the wiseacre decides most positively how the pilot should steer—which sail should be hoisted, and which should be put away. If he were on board the labouring bark, he would be lying down below, forgotten as a dead man out of mind. This ought to render us a little more diffident in our advising. It is rather awkward when, after having prescribed for others, we fall sick ourselves, and then refuse our own remedies: yet many have done so. It is sad when the preacher of patience is himself petulant, and the advocate of faith is himself dubious. No: we must teach more by our example than by our advice, or else we shall be poor pleaders for the right.

Few things are more galling than to be at our wits' end in managing a difficult matter, and then to be charged and counselled by some intermeddling novice who could not even understand our difficulty, much less assist us out of it. When Balaam's ass spoke, it uttered sound sense, and we shall never welcome the speech of another such animal until it has as weighty a message to deliver. Alas! we do not always suffer fools *gladly*: though suffer them we do. We have wished ourselves deaf at times when the most idle nonsense has been proffered us in the moment of greatest suspense.

O Lord Jesus, we bless thee that thy counsel comes to us as that of experience! Thou art on the sea with us. Thou hast the tone and manner of one who is tied in us and with us. Our Counsellor art thou; and thus our surest helper, because thy counsel is infallible.

THE LUTE UNTUNED

As a lute that is not played upon, but hangs by the wall, soon grows out of order for want of use; so, if we do not constantly and diligently exercise ourselves in godliness, our hearts grow dead and vain.

It is the old story of the unused key. It would seem that there is no worse abuse of a good thing than to abstain from its use. While it lies idle it lies ill. Grace must be exercised toward God in devout contemplation, wrestling prayer, or adoring praise; and it must be exercised among men in patience, zeal, charity, and holy example; or, like an arm which has long been bound by a man's side, it will become withered. Some enemies were left in Canaan for the sole reason that the armies of Israel might not forget the art of war; and we, too, may expect troubles to exercise our graces in conflict, if we do not ourselves exercise them in happier service. The Lord will not allow the inner life of his people to degenerate because of inaction; nor ought we to allow it. Loud calls to energy are sounding forth on every hand. A curse will come upon us, like that invoked upon Meroz of old, if we come not to the help of the Lord, to the help of the Lord against the mighty.

To return to our author's figure. Are we like a lute upon the wall? Are the strings all out of order? Tune us, Lord, and then bring music out of us. Why should a single instrument in the whole concert be silent when the Lord is to be praised? 'Awake up, my glory; awake, psaltery and harp: I myself will awake early.'

> Be near me, Lord, and tune my notes,
>   And make them sweet and strong,
> To waft thy words to many a heart,
>   Upon the wings of song.

I know that men will listen,
  For my very heart shall sing.
And it shall be thy praise alone.
  My glorious Lord and King.

THE FISH IN A PAIL

We are now imperfect and straitened; like a fish in a pail, or small vessel of water, which cannot keep it alive: it would fain be in the ocean, or swimming in the broad and large rivers. So we are pent up, and cannot do what we would; but we long for a larger estate, namely, to be filled with all the fulness of God. That holiness which we have now, maketh us look and long for more; and, surely, this desire after holiness was never designed for our torment; there must be something to answer to the desire excited.

It is even so; we are now cribbed, cabined, and confined, and our renewed spirit feels itself in bondage. The fish cannot half so much desire the river as we desire a nobler sphere wherein the better life may have due scope and range. As a lion goeth to and fro in his den, impatient of restraint, so doth our spirit move restlessly after better things. We are not content with the measure of our liberty, the tether of our range. We are like the young chick which is pecking at the shell which shuts it in; we perceive that there is very much outside of our prison-wall, and we are anxious to break forth. Is not this the testimony of all saintly men? Are not the bonds felt? Are we not groaning under them?

The argument of our author is well drawn, and incontrovertible. God does not create desires without also providing corresponding objects: for thirst there is drink, for hunger there is food, for the eye there is light. So also for the soul which hungers and thirsts after righteousness there is a filling. The renewed heart shall yet see the perfection for which it pines, and the holy mind shall enjoy the communion with God for which it pants.

Be glad, O my heart, because of thine own pangs! If thou wert now content, there would be in thee no ensigns and evidences of better things yet to be revealed. Thy groanings and yearnings are prophecies of guaranteed perfection. If thou wert of the earth, thou wouldst be satisfied with earth; but because thou hast a higher nature, thou art not at home amid these lower things. There remaineth therefore a rest for thee, a home for thee, a heaven for thee.

THE SENTINEL

When a sentinel is set upon the watch, he must not come off without the commander's leave, and till he is discharged by authority. God hath set us in a watch, and we must not leave our ground till we have done all that is enjoined upon us, and receive a fair discharge.

The instance of the sentinel in Pompeii, whose skeleton was found erect at the city gate, when all but he had fled, need not be repeated in words; but it should be copied by each one of us in his life. If the earth should reel, it is ours to keep our place. If set to preach the gospel, let us maintain the truth, though philosophy should thin the number of our comrades till we remain alone. If commanded to teach a few little children, let us be as faithful to our trust as if we had been set to lead a legion of angels. Imagine what the universe would be if the stars forsook their marches, and the sun forbore to shine; yet this would only be among inanimate objects an imitation of the conduct of men who quit their posts, and leave their work undone. This is the spirit out of which fiends are made: first neglect, then omission, then treachery and rebellion. It is such an honour to bear his Majesty's commission that King Jesus should have around him the most joyously faithful band of servants. 'Whatsoever he saith unto you, do it' was Mary's advice in her day, and the spirit of it should abide with all Christians to the end of time. Where God's command has fixed us, there let us abide at all hazards. Our life, our honour, and our heaven lie, not in rising out of the place which our Master has allotted to us, but in fulfilling its duties to the uttermost. A sentinel must not leave his post even to gather pearls or diamonds; nor must we forsake our duty in order to acquire the highest honours. It matters nothing how well we have done other things if we neglect *the* thing. God bids us do *this*, and if we fail it will be no excuse to be able to say—we have done *that*. If the watcher forsakes his post it will not avail that he climbed a mountain, or swam a river: he was not where he was ordered to be.

MARTYRS IN BEARS' SKINS

It was a fashion, in the primitive persecutions, to invest Christians with bears' skins, and then to bait them as bears; and it is a usual practice of Satan and his instruments, first to blast the reputation of religious persons, and then to persecute them as offenders.

It is written of the worthies of old that 'they had trial of cruel mockings'. Tertullian says that in the primitive times the saints were called herds of asses, vile fellows, the disciples of a man crucified, Galileans, Nazarites, eaters of men's flesh, and drinkers of men's blood. The heathen painted the God of the Christians with the head of an ass, and with a book in his hand, to signify that, though Christians pretended to knowledge, they were a company of fools.

The like custom remains still. Good men are first slandered and then censured. They lay to our charge deeds which we never dreamed of, and then they pile on the adjectives of denunciation, and condemn us without mercy. Thanks be to God, a saint in a bear's skin is none the less a saint: the Lord knows the wolf in the sheep's skin, and the sheep in the bear's skin: he is not deceived by falsehood so as to judge his children unjustly. Not even for the present are the reputations of the godly injured in the sight of God, and as for the future, they shall suffer no tarnishing. Soon there shall be a resurrection of good names as well as of bodies: the Lord shall restore the honour and renown of each slandered believer.

Meanwhile, let us not be so easily led into harsh judgments as we have been. Let us refuse to regard our own brethren as wild beasts because wicked men thrust the bear's skin upon them. From us, at least, let them receive tokens of the charity which thinketh no evil. Persistently let each follower of the Lord Jesus say of reproach cast upon a brother, 'I will not believe it.' A believer in Christ should be an unbeliever in the world's many lies: this rule would rob slander of half its power. By holy confidence in our fellow-Christians we should snap the bowstring of malice, and burn its arrows in the fire.

As for ourselves, we are not made of such pliant stuff that we would alter our course to escape the calumny of men. We will not move a hair's-breadth because of

> the dread of tyrant custom, and the fear
> Lest fops should censure us, and fools should sneer.

PRIMING

A lower degree of faith maketh way for a higher, as the priming of the wood maketh it receptive of other colours.

Painters often use a paint at the first which is to be the preparation for quite another colour; red is commonly thus employed. So, in the work of grace, there may come first a dogmatical faith (as Manton calls it), which receives the doctrine of the word of God as truth. This does not save the soul, but it is a needful preparative for that receptive and trusting faith, by which salvation is actually received. Dogmatic faith is the priming upon which faith of a saving colour is laid by the Master-workman.

Much the same is true of those gracious influences by which a man is made a willing and attentive hearer, and a respecter of the Sabbath and of the worship of God. All this may exist and yet there may be no saving faith; still it is the 'priming' for the higher work. Faith cometh by hearing. Hence the value of all healthy moral influence, instruction, and example. None of these can save, but they may lead up to salvation. The paralyzed man was not cured by his friends, or by the bed, or by the ropes, but these brought him where Jesus was, and so he was healed. Make a man sober, and he is all the more likely to mind the preacher's admonitions: give him the power to read, and he may study the Scriptures. These things are not grace, but they may be stepping-stones to grace: they are not the permanent colour, but only the priming; yet it would never do to neglect them for that reason. He would be an unwise painter who put on the woodwork nothing but the priming; and he would be far more unwise who rested content with mere preparatory reforms. Yet in order to avoid this evil it is not necessary to forego the priming altogether, or to neglect anything by which a man is made even the least better.

Oh that I may be willing to do anything by which souls may be helped to a blessing! If I cannot actually heal the man's wounds, let me not refuse to wash them, or to set the wounded man upon my beast. He who will only do those works which are of the highest and utmost use is not so humble as he should be. Lord, make me willing to wash men's feet, if for the present I cannot win their souls. Incline me, my Lord, to teach a child his letters, or to reason with a drunkard, or to instruct a peasant in thrift, since any one of these may help to something better; for I know that everything which is pure and honest is on the side of Christ and his salvation.

MALICIOUS WASTE

He would be a cruel man who should cast his provisions and superfluities into the street, and deny them to the poor; or should allow his drink to run into the kennel, rather than that the thirsty should taste a drop of it. Such are we to God; we know not what to employ our thoughts upon, and yet we will not think of his name. We will go musing upon vanity all the day long, and thus grinding chaff rather than we will take good corn into the mill.

Well put! We meet with persons upon whose hands time hangs heavily; they have nothing to do, and are dying of *ennui*.[1] Why will they thus spend their time in waste? Yet all the while they give not God a thought, nor spend a little time in reading his word, or in conversing with him in prayer. Have they all their days on hand, and yet will they not afford their God an hour? Are they full of time even to a surfeit, and yet cannot

---

[1] A feeling of listlessness and dissatisfaction arising from a lack of occupation or excitement.

they give ten minutes' space to their Maker? Well does our author speak of *cruelty*. Was ever such cruelty on earth as this denial of an hour of our superfluous time to God? Will we rather waste it, or defile it, than give him a portion of it? Must we invent pastimes to pass time away, and yet refuse ten minutes for meditation?

Oh that this little parable might meet some careless eye, and through the eye pierce the heart! What, will you sooner kill time at cards, or with a novel, or in utter idleness, than do your greatest Benefactor the honour of thinking of him? Is he so distasteful to you that you count it a bore, a burden, a bug-bear even to hear his sacred name? Come, do thyself this favour—to give the next hour to God and to thine own soul. Your cruelty to your God will prove to be cruelty to yourself. Do not persevere in it, but yield to your heavenly Friend a portion of your weary time. Maybe you will thus find out a way of never being weary again in this fashion—find out, in fact, the way to make time pass like a river which flows over golden sands, with a paradise on either bank.

SQUABBLING WITH A SERVANT

Many a time a brabble[1] falleth out between a man and his lusts; but he delayeth, and all cometh to nothing. In a heat we bid a naughty servant begone; but he lingereth, and before the next morning all is cool and quiet, and he is again in favour.

Ungodly men have their quarrels with their favourite sins on various accounts; but these are like children's pets[2] with one another, soon over, because they come of passion, and not from principle. An unholy person will fall out with sin because it has

---

[1] A squabble.
[2] Petulant moods.

injured his health or his credit, or has brought him into difficulties with his neighbours; but when these temporary results
are ended he falls in love again with the same iniquity. Thus
we have seen the drunkard loathing his excess when his eyes
were red, and his head was aching; but ere the sun went down
the quarrel was ended, and he and Bacchus were rolling in the
gutter together. Our enmity to sin should be based upon sound
knowledge and solid reason, and be wrought in us by the Spirit
of God, and then it will lead us to join in solemn league with
the Lord who hath war with Amalek throughout all generations. We must have no peace with sin; nay, not with the least
sin. Our hate of evil must be as everlasting as the love of God.

Of old, converted Israelites cast their idols to the moles
and to the bats—away from sight with the moles, away from
light with the bats. Our detestation must lead us to put sin
among the dead and the forgotten. So far from ever entering
into amity with it, we must regard it as a dead and corrupted
thing, forever abandoned to silence and the worm. As heaven
and hell will never unite, so must it be plain that a saint and sin
will never come together on any terms whatever.

Lord, I pray thee keep me ever in desperate earnest in my war
with sin. Forbid that I should trifle in this conflict, or grow cold
in it. Let me be bound to never-ending warfare with my own sin,
and never may I be pacified till Christ has utterly crushed the
foe. Like thy servant David, I would hate every false way.

THE RIVER SWOLLEN BY BEING DAMMED

*Corruption, the more it is opposed the more it stormeth and groweth
outrageous; as a river swelleth by reason of dams and banks, which
are raised against it. Corruptions rage against restraints till the
floods break loose.*

This figure is a good one. Corrupt desires will often lie quiet till they are earnestly opposed, and then they swell and rage. The gracious man sets himself with resolution to overcome a habit, and, like a beast at bay, it fights tooth and nail as if for dear life. The more he prays, the more he mortifies himself; the more he avoids the sin, the more does it appear to force itself upon him. The water flows easily enough down the unimpeded bed of the river, and it will readily enough overflow and cover the meadows; but once put up an embankment, or attempt to stem the torrent, and it chafes and rages, and displays all its force. So sin may be quiet; but when grace enters the heart it revives, resists, and raises rebellion, setting the soul into a horrible tumult.

We must not think that the work of sanctification has ceased because impetuous passions are more clearly perceived, and the power of the flesh is more deeply deplored. It is possible that the energy of inbred sin may become all the more apparent because through divine grace it is more strenuously resisted. When the vital energy is great, it throws out upon the surface diseases which, with a feebler vitality, would have lain smouldering within: when spiritual life is forceful, it hunts to the surface evils which else would have festered in the heart.

There are times with the ungodly man when all goes smoothly, and the current of his life flows placidly; but, nevertheless, the whole stream is polluted from the fountain-head to the outfall, though he knows it not. With the godly man, life's inward stream is seldom thus deceitfully smooth. The Christian's old nature is opposed at every turn by his faith, repentance, prayers, and other dams and embankments of grace; and hence the dashing of the waves, and the roaring and the swelling of the evil torrent. Even the pure stream of the river of the water of life, which flows into him from the throne of God, for a while only creates a greater tumult. The waters will not blend, and hence they contend one with another till the man is placed in the position of Paul's ship when it fell into a place where two seas met. Truly, the entrance of Christ into the heart, though it ends in ultimate rest, yet for a while brings not peace, but a sword.

When a man dreams that he is perfect, and therefore ceases to fight against his secret sins, all seems well; but let him look into the depths of his heart, and behold the corruptions which slumber there, and let him seek to expel them; and a battle will begin, compared with which the strife of the warrior and the garments rolled in blood are as nothing. The heart is rent in pieces by the opposing parties, neither does it seem possible to live because of the conflict. Let us not despair while this fierce contest is going on: we are but suffering with the universe of which we form a part, for 'the whole creation groaneth and travaileth in pain together until now'. These groans and pangs are bringing on that glorious birth out of which shall come the new heavens and the new earth. Even so it is with us: our inward travail and sore conflict will work out an immortal perfection, which is the consummation of the work of the Spirit in the soul. When the waves rage terribly, let us remember that 'the Lord on high is mightier than the noise of many waters, yea, than the mighty waves of the sea'. He will quell the opposition, and in due time dry up the rivers of inbred sin, destroying the very fountains thereof, and giving to his people ineffable rest and unutterable delight.

O my Lord, give me grace to curb every evil tendency within myself, and the more I perceive that these evil affections chafe and rebel, the more determined may I be that I will dam them up, and that they shall not have their way. Only help thou me, and as the struggle grows more arduous, let thy grace become more plenteous. Surely in this conflict all power must come from thee, for thou alone canst impart the strength that I need. Hast thou not said, 'Behold, at my rebuke I dry up the sea, I make the rivers a wilderness'? Arise, Lord, let not sin prevail, but get to thyself the victory in me.

RABBI JOSEPH'S LOVE TO THE SYNAGOGUE

I have once and again read of one Rabbi Joseph, who, being allured by the hope of great gain, to teach Hebrew, at a place where there was no synagogue, is said to have brought forth this Scripture as his reason for refusing: 'The law of thy mouth is better unto me than thousands of gold and silver.'

Well done, Rabbi Joseph! We greatly fear that there are few of thy kindred who are of thy mind; for the heart of Israel seems to be set upon the precious metals. Nor can we blame Israel much, for the same is all too true concerning those who call themselves Christians. The clink of guineas is rare music even to them.

The greatest worldly advantages cannot compensate for the loss of spiritual privileges, and yet we know many who scarcely take this matter into consideration in the choice of their pursuits and positions in life.

A tradesman is earning a competence, and is able to attend the house of God, and to give part of his time and talents to the service of the church; and yet he thinks it to be advisable to cumber himself with extra worldly servitude, and thereby to render himself unable either to profit the church or to be profited himself by the services of the Lord's house. Is this the way of wisdom? Can this man say that God's words are more desired by him than gold, yea, than much fine gold?

A young man is in a fair position, where he has godly surroundings, and every opportunity for spiritual progress; and yet, for the sake of a few pounds more he puts himself into an un-Christian household, and loses every opportunity of uniting with his brethren in holy work and worship. Is this as it should be? Does not Rabbi Joseph greatly shame such a backsliding Ephraim?

If I were to choose a dwelling-house I would wish to be known as Justus was—for he was 'a man that worshipped God, whose house joined hard to the synagogue'. I would hope to reverse the proverb, and prove that the nearer the church the nearer to God. Of course one's calling, health, or circumstances might compel another choice; but I would ever give preference to a habitation near to a gospel ministry. If I were to choose a trade, I would select one which gave me leisure for the service of the Lord Jesus. If I had the option of my condition in life, I would rather have less earth and more heaven than more earth and less heaven. It argues a poor state of spiritual health when the mass of Christian professors estimate their position solely and entirely by the money which it yields them. Surely they know, unless they are hypocrites ingrain, that a man's life consists far more in the devotion which he enjoys than in the treasure which he accumulates.

My God, grant me grace ever to put the first first, and the last last. Let me use Paul's scales, which were the balances of the sanctuary, and reckon that gain to be loss which is gained by loss of communion with thee, and that profit to be unprofitable which renders me less profitable to thee.

A LEAN-TO SHED

Many men owe their religion, not to grace, but to the favour of the times; they follow it because it is in fashion, and they can profess it at a cheap rate, because none contradict it. They do not build upon the rock, but set up a shed leaning to another man's house, which costs them nothing.

The idea of a lean-to religion is somewhat rough, but eminently suggestive. Weak characters cannot stand alone, like mansions; but must needs lean on others, like the miserable shops which nestle under certain Continental cathedrals. Under the eaves of old customs many build their plaster nests, like swallows. Such are good, if good at all, because their patrons made virtue the price of their patronage. They love honesty because it proves to be the best policy, and piety because it serves as an introduction to trade with saints. Their religion is little more than courtesy to other men's opinions, civility to godliness.

Alas for an age when this sort of thing abounds! It is an injury to the architecture of godliness to be encumbered with these pitiful hovels. As parasites suck the life out of the goodly tree, so do these pretenders injure those to whom they cling with the servile homage of hireling-adulation. To themselves their vain profession and man-pleasing are a presage of destruction: for at the last day all must fall into eternal ruin which has not its own foundation on the rock. Our lives will be weighed one by one in personal judgment, and no other man can add an ounce to aid us if we are found wanting. The well-founded and well-compacted structure of the sincerely gracious will survive the time when once more the Lord shall shake not only earth but also heaven; but that frail fabric which leans on mortal aid will perish in that dread convulsion.

Lord, make me a self-contained man. Supported by thee, and by thee alone, may I be unmoved, though all other men should leave thee, and though the fashion of my company should be opposed to all godliness. Then shalt thou have glory through me.

RICHES OF CHILDREN AND MEN

The more abundance of truly valuable things a man hath, the more he hath of true riches; a child counteth himself rich when he hath a great many pins, and points, and cherry-stones, for these suit his childish age and fancy; a worldly man counteth himself rich when he hath a great store of gold and silver, or lands and heritages, or bills and bonds; but a child of God counteth himself rich when he hath God for his Portion, Christ to be his Redeemer, and the Spirit for his Guide, Sanctifier, and Comforter; which is as much above a carnal man's estate in the world, as a carnal man's estate is above a child's toys and trifles; yea, infinitely more.

It is above all things desirable that we adopt a correct scale of estimates. When we make our personal audit, we shall fall into grievous error if the principles of our reckoning are not thoroughly accurate. If we reckon brass as silver, and silver as gold, we shall dream that we are rich when we are in penury. In taking stock of our own condition, let us be sure only to reckon that for riches which is really riches to us. Wealth to the worldling is not wealth to the Christian. His currency is different, his valuables are of another sort.

Am I today poorer in money than I was ten years ago; and am I at the same time more humble, more patient, more earnest, more believing? Then set me down as a richer man. Have my worldly goods largely increased during the last few years? Am I some thousands of pounds in advance of my former position? but am I also more proud, more carnal-minded, more lukewarm, more petulant? Then I must write myself down as a poorer man, whatever men may think of my estate. A Christian's riches are within him. External belongings are by no means a sure gain to a man. A horse is none the better off for gilded trappings; and a man is, in very truth, none the richer for sumptuous surroundings. Paul was richer than Croesus, when he was able to say, 'I know both how to be abased, and I know how to abound: everywhere and in all things I am instructed both to be full and to be hungry, both to abound and to suffer need.' Such contentment surpasses riches. Outwardly Paul was 'poor',' but inasmuch as he was 'making many rich' he must have been rich himself; for nothing can come out of a man which is not in him. Solomon was a very Lazarus, when, after summing up all his possessions and delights, he was compelled to add, 'Vanity of vanities, all is vanity!'

If a man should labour to be rich after the African fashion, and should accumulate a large store of shells and beads; yet when he came home to England he would be a beggar, even though he had a shipload of such rubbish. So he who gives his heart and soul to the accumulation of gold and silver coin is a beggar when he comes into the spiritual realm, where such round medals are reckoned as mere forms of earth, non-current in heaven, and of less value than the least of spiritual blessings.

We have read that when Bernard visited a monastery of ascetic monks, they were shocked because the saddle on which he rode was most sumptuously adorned. They thought that this ill became his profession as a meek and lowly man. Judge of their surprise and satisfaction when he told them that he had never so much as noticed what it was whereon he sat. The fact was, that the horse and saddle were not his own, but had been lent to him by his uncle, and their nature had not been perceived by him during the whole of his journey. This is the way to use all earthly treasure, making small account whether we have it or not; even as Paul says, 'It remaineth, that both they that have wives be as though they had none; and they that weep, as though they wept not; and they that rejoice, as though they rejoiced not; and they that buy, as though they possessed not; and they that use this world, as not abusing it: for the fashion of this world passeth away.' Our goods are good if we do not account them our highest good. Even Jonah's gourd did him good until he quarrelled with God about it.

O, my Lord, let me not merely talk thus, and pretend to despise earthly treasure, when all the while I am hunting after it; but grant me grace to live above these things, never setting my heart upon them, nor caring whether I have them, or have them not; but exercising all my energy in pleasing thee, and in gaining those things which thou dost hold in esteem. Give me, I pray thee, the riches of thy grace that I may at last attain to the riches of thy glory, through Christ Jesus.

A PRINCELY CARVER

To be carved for at table by a great prince would be counted as great a favour as the meal itself. To take outward blessings out of God's hand, to see that he remembereth us, and sendeth in our provision at every turn; this endeareth the mercy, and increaseth our delight therein.

What, indeed, would most men give if they could say, 'The Queen herself carved for me, and was most anxious that I should be well supplied'? But each believer has the Lord himself for his Provider. He loads our table, and fills our cup.

Providence is no other than God providing. He measures out our joys, weighs our sorrows, appoints our labours, and selects our trials. There is no morsel on the saint's plate which is not of the Lord's carving, unless he has been so foolish as to put forth his hand unto iniquity.

Is it not delightful to know that our Father's hand broke for us the bread which we have eaten this day; that the Saviour's own fingers mingled our cup, and that every blessing has come direct from God's own table? Surely we are as dear to God as the little ewe lamb in Nathan's parable was to the poor man; for we are told that 'he had nourished it up, and it grew up together with him, and with his children; it did eat of his own meat, and drank of his own cup, and lay in his bosom'. Does not this make our meat, and drink, and lodging more than royal? Are we not more than content with such fare?

Yea, Lord, my portion tastes of love, for thy hand has sweetened it. A sacred perfume is on my raiment and in my chamber, for thou hast prepared both for me. And this would be true if I wore rags, and lay in a dungeon, in sore sickness. What a heritage is mine! One said, 'I am poor and needy, yet the Lord thinketh upon me.'

In this passage the second sentence underwrote the first, and undermined its meaning: how can he be poor and needy of whom it can be said that the Lord thinketh upon him? Lord, thou art my all, and my all in all: my all is more than all because it comes of thee, and is dealt out to me by thine own self.

SNOW SOFT, BUT SOAKING

Passionate outcries do only frighten easy and over-credulous souls, and that only for the present; proofs and arguments do a great deal more good. Snow that falleth soft soaketh deep. In the tempest, Christ slept; when passion is up, true zeal is usually asleep.

How gently fall the snowflakes, but how surely they penetrate into the ground; a driving rain hath not half such efficacy! The voice of the snowflakes is not heard, but their influence is felt. Proofs from Scripture, winsomely put, carry all before them, because Jesus loves to reach men's minds by such means, and not by wrath and fury.

This is a word to hasty disputants. Violent words appear to them to be forcible, but they are not. Hard arguments are best couched in soft language; the force of the lightning is not increased by the thunder. Wrath weakens reason, but gentleness gives double force to arguments. Alas, we too often forget this, and call in our evil passions to aid our holy principles. Then the Christ within us sleeps, and the devil is wide awake. It is to be feared that Protestantism has been rather hindered than furthered by the ferocity with which some have maintained it.

Our present controversies are some of them essential to fidelity; but it will be well if we all remember that to be faithful to truth we need not be wrathful toward opponents. Truth and charity are of the same heavenly family, and are loveliest when they walk hand in hand. It has happened that some have been so charitable that they would not lift a finger to save truth's life lest they should wound one of another opinion. This is a sad practical error. But we shall not mend matters if we fight truth's battles so savagely that we hurl shot and shell upon the abode of love.

Lord, teach us, for we are fearfully apt to err in this matter. Give us bold and clear words, taken from thine own word; and let us use these with the lowly confidence which comes of being filled with thy Spirit; but never allow our own spirit to get the upper hand, so that we breathe out threatenings and utter bitter expressions. Let our sword be always like that which cometh out of Christ's mouth; sharp but salutary; flaming, but only with the fire of love.

THE MALICIOUS GUEST

Sin is an ill guest, for it always sets its lodging on fire.

Entertained within the human breast, and cherished and fondled, it makes its host no return but an evil one. It places the burning coals of evil desire within the soul with evident intent to fire the whole man with fierce passions. Let these passions be suffered to rage, and the flame will burn even to the lowest hell.

Who would not shut his door on such a guest? Or if he be known to be lurking within, who would not drag him out? How foolish are those who find delight in such an enemy, and treat him with more care than their best friend!

KEEPING UP A SUIT

Keep up the suit, and it will come to a hearing-day ere it be long.

In a suit at law there are many and grievous delays, and yet the man who has been forced into the court does not dream of relinquishing his case. He urges on his solicitor, and entreats him to lose no opportunity of getting the business settled; but he does not in a pet[1] take the case out of his hands, for he expects that the judge will sooner or later decide the matter. It would be a pity not to continue steadfast in prayer, for it is certain that now is our salvation nearer than when we believed. Every hour of importunity brings us nearer to the time when the Judge shall avenge his own elect. To waste all the cost of former tears and entreaties, and to let months of praying go for nothing would be a sad waste of effort. Let us hope in the Lord, and wait patiently for him, abiding still at the mercy-seat. Has he not himself said, 'Though the vision tarry, wait for it; because it will surely come, it will not tarry'?

Sometimes, before we call, God hears us, and while we are yet speaking he answers us. This is to encourage us to a further trust in him; perhaps to prepare us for waiting times. Frequently the richest answers are not the speediest. Ships may return all the more quickly because they have a slender lading; and a prayer may be all the longer on its voyage because it is bringing us a heavier freight of blessing. Delayed answers are not only trials of faith, but they give us an opportunity of honouring God by our steadfast confidence in him under apparent repulses.

He that will only believe because he sees the answer to his prayer immediately hath but little faith. He is the man after God's own heart who can cry day and night unto the Lord by the month together, and yet never swerve from the full conviction that God is good to Israel, and that in waiting upon him there is great reward. David says, 'I waited patiently for the Lord, and he inclined unto me, and heard my cry.' This patience in waiting is the attribute of the full-grown saint, and perhaps it gives more

[1] That is, in a petulant mood.

glory to God than the songs of cherubim and seraphim. Jonah says, 'When my soul fainted within me I remembered the Lord: and my prayer came in unto thee, into thine holy temple.'

Desponding brother, keep up the suit. Perhaps this very day may be the hearing-day. Go again seven times. The little cloud, like a man's hand, may be visible on that last time of asking. Knock, and knock again, till the gate of heaven reverberates your blows. The door must open, and it will open all the wider because you have knocked so long. 'Wait on the Lord: be of good courage, and he shall strengthen thine heart. Wait, I say, on the Lord.'

CLOSE WRITING

When men have much to say in a letter, and perceive that they have little paper left, they write closely.

Looking at the shortness of life, and the much that has to be written upon its tablets, it becomes us also to do much in a short space, and so to write closely. 'No day without a line', is a good motto for a Christian. A thoroughly useful life is *multum in parvo:*[1] it is necessarily little, for it is but a span; but how much may be crowded into it for God, our souls, the church, our families, and our fellows! We cannot afford wide blanks of idleness; we should not only live by the day but by the twenty minutes, as Wesley did. He did not keep a diary, but an horary;[2] and each hour was divided into three parts. So scanty is our space that we must condense, and leave out superfluous matter; giving room only to that which is weighty, and of the first importance.

[1] Latin: Much in little; e.g., much information condensed into few words or into a small compass.

[2] That is, a record of his *hours*, rather than his *days*.

Lord, whether I live long or not, I leave to thee; but help me to live while I live, that I may live much. Thou canst give life more abundantly; let me receive it, and let my life be filled, yea, packed and crammed, with all manner of holy thoughts and words and deeds to thy glory.

THE MIRROR

Take a looking-glass and put it toward heaven; there you shall see the figure of heaven, the clouds and things above. Turn it downward toward the earth, you shall see the figure of the earth, trees, meadows, men. So doth the soul receive a figure from the things to which it is set. If the heart be set toward heaven, that puts thee into a heavenly frame; if thou appliest it to earthly objects, thou art a man of the earth.

Are our thoughts and our affections full of worldliness? Let us make good use of Manton's figure, and turn the looking-glass the other way. Our mind will readily enough reflect divine things if we turn it in that direction. Let us see if it be not so. Reach down the Bible, look at the biography of a holy man, or some lively book of devotion, and see if the heart be not straightway filled with holy and heavenly images. At any rate, if we spend our time on the newspaper, or sit hour after hour reading trashy novels, we have no reason to wonder that thought and heart go after vanity. This turning of the mind upward is half the battle. We cannot expect it to reflect that toward which it does not turn. Those who mind earthly things are earthly, those who set their affection upon things above are heavenly. Paul shows how practically useful it is to turn the mind God-ward when he says that 'denying ungodliness and worldly lusts, we should live soberly, righteously, and godly in this present world, looking for that blessed hope, and the glorious appearing of the great God and our Saviour Jesus Christ.'

We may well cry concerning this matter, 'Turn us, O Lord, and we shall be turned.' If we cannot see divine truth to our enjoyment, let us nevertheless look that way; for that eye is blessed which looks in the direction of the light. It is well to have our window open toward Jerusalem. He who would behold the sun at his rising must not look to the west. He that would see God to his delight must look God-ward. If the mirror of the soul be resolutely set toward the Lord, we shall all with open face behold, as in a glass, the glory of the Lord, and be changed into the same image from glory to glory, even as by the Spirit of the Lord.

O, my blessed Master, help me I pray thee to keep the mirror of my mind in the right position, that evermore I may see thee. True, it will be but as in a glass darkly, but even that will be a marvellous preparation for beholding thee face to face.

THE OLD HOUSE TAKEN DOWN TO BE REBUILT

If we lived in a house of our own, and the walls became decayed, and the roof ready to drop down upon our heads, we would desire to remove and depart for a while, but we should not therefore give up the ground, and the materials of the house. No, we would have it built up in a better manner.

Even thus the soul desires to leave the poor frail tenement of the body, but not that the body may be utterly destroyed: it quits it with the hope of having the house of clay rebuilt in more glorious form. 'Not that we would be unclothed', saith the apostle, 'but clothed upon with our house which is from heaven'; not that we would be turned out of house and home; but that we would enter upon our better and permanent abode, which the Lord will surely provide for us.

The Lord doth not despise this house of clay: he will rebuild it, and we shall inhabit it forever. Wherefore let us be comforted when the wind blows through the chinks, and the rain drips through the roof; it will all the sooner come down, and all the sooner will it be restored. The little while in which we shall be unhoused will cause us no inconvenience, for even then we shall be with the Lord; wherefore let us in all things be of good cheer.

O, my Lord, thou hast made me to know that this body will soon cease to be a body for me, therefore I will not pamper it. But thou promisest it a resurrection, therefore I will not defile it. Teach me how, in the body or out of the body, to dwell in thee, and honour thy holy name.

CHILDREN THANKING THE TAILOR FOR THEIR CLOTHES

As children will thank the tailor, and think they owe their new clothes to him rather than to their parent's bounty, so we look to the next hand, and set up that instead of God.

Second causes must never be made to stand before the first cause. Friends and helpers are all very well as servants of our Father, but our Father must have all our praise. There is a like evil in the matter of trouble. We are apt to be angry with the instrument of our affliction, instead of seeing the hand of God over all, and meekly bowing before it. It was a great help to David in bearing with railing Shimei, when he saw that God had appointed this provocation as a chastisement. He would not suffer his hasty captains to take the scoffer's head, but meekly said, 'Let him alone, and let him curse, for the Lord hath bidden him.' A dog when he is struck will bite the stick;

if he were wise, he would observe that the stick only moves as the hand directs it. When we discern God in our tribulations we are helped to be quiet and endure with patience.

Let us not act like silly children, but trace matters to their fountain-head, and act accordingly. May the Spirit of wisdom make us men in understanding.

PASSING SHIPS AT SEA

When we are on board ship, if another vessel passes us at sea, we think that it is sailing more swiftly than we are. Though both ships are passing along at the same rate, we do not so clearly discern our own motion. In like manner we see that others are mortal, but we do not number our own days.

This is an ordinary observation concerning that which is really an extraordinary piece of folly. What can it matter to us how other men's lives are going? Our main concern is our own conduct, and the spending of our own days. Come, friend, you too are getting old; snowflakes here and there upon those once raven locks are prophetic of coming winter. Those spectacles, too! 'First sight', you say. Just so; but you were not once dependent on them. Why, you will never see fifty again! Half a century have you lived, and more: surely it is time to be wise.

Friend Brown is getting quite the old man. No doubt; but you are moving onward, too. Brown does not get a year older in less time than you do. We are all sailing at the same rate. Is it not time that we took observations, and found out our longitude and latitude? At any rate, it were well to know what port we are bound for. Some have not even so much knowledge as this implies.

PLEASURE FORGETS LABOUR

*In hunting, fowling, and fishing, though there be as much labour
as in our ordinary employments, yet we count the toil nothing,
because of the delight we have in them.*

It is wonderful what fatigue men will bear to hunt a fox or
shoot a partridge, and yet they make nothing of it, but call it
sport. In like manner many a zealous worker for the Lord Jesus
will preach, and teach, and labour, and call it his recreation,
with which he fills up his leisure hours. We know many such,
and we hope we shall yet know more. Love makes labour light.
Men will do voluntarily that which they would never undertake for pay, and they will keep up freely under an amount of
pressure which would crush the hireling. There lies the grand
secret. Make holy service a delight, and you can do any amount
of it.

Lord, thy servant has no need to *reckon* thy service to be
this pleasure, for it is indeed so. Could he but serve thee perfectly, without hindrance and without mistake, it would be
heaven to him. No avocation is like our divine vocation for
pure delightfulness. It would be far more wearisome not to
serve thee, my God, than it ever can be to perform the most
arduous labour for thy love's sake.

IN TRAINING

*By running and breathing yourselves every day, you are the fitter
to run in a race; so the oftener you come into God's presence the
greater confidence, and freedom, and enlargement it will bring.*

No doubt by praying we learn to pray, and the more we
pray the oftener we can pray, and the better we can pray. He
who prays by fits and starts is never likely to attain to that

effectual, fervent prayer which availeth much. Prayer is good, the habit of prayer is better, but the spirit of prayer is the best of all. It is in the spirit of prayer that we pray without ceasing, and this can never be acquired by the man who ceases to pray.

It is wonderful what distances men can run who have long practised the art, and it is equally marvellous for what a length of time they can maintain a high speed after they have once acquired stamina, and skill in using their muscles. Great power in prayer is within our reach, but we must go to work to obtain it. Let us never imagine that Abraham could have interceded so successfully for Sodom if he had not been all his lifetime in the practice of communion with God. Jacob's all-night at Peniel was not the first occasion upon which he had met his God. We may even look upon our Lord's most choice and wonderful prayer with his disciples before his Passion as the flower and fruit of his many nights of devotion, and of his often rising up a great while before day to pray.

A man who becomes a great runner has to put himself in training, and to keep himself in it; and that training consists very much of the exercise of running. Those who have distinguished themselves for speed have not suddenly leaped into eminence, but have long been runners. If a man dreams that he can become mighty in prayer just when he pleases, he labours under a great mistake. The prayer of Elijah, which shut up heaven and afterward opened its floodgates, was one of a long series of mighty prevailings with God. Oh that Christian men would remember this! Perseverance in prayer is necessary to prevalence in prayer. Those great intercessors, who are not so often mentioned as they ought to be in connection with confessors and martyrs, were nevertheless the grandest benefactors of the church; but it was only by abiding at the mercy-seat that they attained to be such channels of mercy to men. We must pray to pray, and continue in prayer that our prayers may continue.

O thou, by whom we come to God, seeing thou hast thyself trodden the way of prayer, and didst never turn from it, teach me to remain a suppliant as long as I remain a sinner, and to wrestle in prayer so long as I have to wrestle with the powers of evil. Whatever else I may outgrow, may I never dream that I may relax my supplications; for well I know that—

> Long as they live should Christians pray,
> For only while they pray they live.

TASTERS, NOT BUYERS

The hearer's life is the preacher's best commendation. They that praise the man but do not practise the matter are like those that taste wines that they may commend them, not buy them.

What a worry such folk are to dealers who are in earnest to do business! Time is wasted, labour lost, hopes disappointed. Oh that these loafers and idlers would take themselves off from our market! We set forth the precious produce of heaven's own vintage, and hope that they will buy of us; but no, they lift the glass, and talk like thorough connoisseurs, and then go off without coming to a bargain. Sermons which we have studied with care, delivered with travail, prayed over, and wept over, are praised for such minor matters as taste, accuracy, and diction, and the truth they contain is not received. We cannot bring our hearers to a decided bargain, though our wares are the best that heaven can supply. Will it always be so? Reader, has it been so with you? Is it to be so still?

THE PLASTER

A plaster may be of sovereign efficacy, but when yon are still pulling it off and on it doth you no good.

Faith applies Christ to the soul; but what if unbelief tears him away? A promise is a great heal-all, but what if we believe and disbelieve, trust and distrust? How can the surest promise comfort us? Men turn to God in their fashion, and before any benefit can come of it they turn away from him. What do they expect from such folly? Instability in saving concerns is a deadly evil, a mockery of God, and a robbery of ourselves. Lord, thy Son's atonement is the blessed plaster which has healed my soul's sore. Thou hast applied it, and I will keep it on my heart forever, whatever may happen, and whoever may ridicule. This hope I have by thy grace, and none shall take it from me.

A MEETING-HOUSE FOR BEGGARS

If a charitable man should see a company of beggars wandering in the street during the time of worship, under pretence that there was no room for them, and he should build a chapel for them, they would then be without excuse. God hath been at so great a cost to provide a throne of grace, that we must not now neglect prayer.

The mercy-seat under the law was overlaid with pure gold to foreshadow the costliness of its antitype. It cost the death of Christ to erect a mercy-seat for men. To neglect it is a shameful ingratitude to God, and a wanton rejection of one of his costliest blessings. If there were no throne of grace, men might die of despair because they could not approach to God; but now that God has prepared a way of access for all who desire to approach him, the refusal to draw near must rank among the grossest and most wilful of rebellions. There is no conceivable excuse for the prayerless. A man who dies of starvation with bread before him, and perishes with disease when the remedy is in his hand, deserves no pity; and he who sinks down to hell beneath the burden of his sins because he will not pray, 'God be merciful to me a sinner', deserves all that damnation means. Pardon, life, salvation, heaven, are all to be had for the asking; and if he that asketh not receiveth not, who shall blame either the justice or the mercy of God?

Reader, has this day passed without a prayer from your heart? Tremble lest it should bring wrath upon you. One said, 'Perhaps the day in which the world shall perish will be the day unsanctified by a prayer.' What if the day of your death and final ruin should be a day in which you did not even turn a glance toward heaven?

A PIECE OF BARK, NOT THE TREE

A man that keeps the law only outwardly, can no more be said to keep the law, than he that hath undertaken to carry a tree, and only takes up a little piece of the bark.

The essence of the law lies in the things of the heart: external acts are as the outward bark. The Pharisees were great bark-mongers, but the solid timber was too heavy for their shoulders. David was the man to carry the whole of the blessed load. He said, 'I will delight myself in thy commandments, which I have loved. My hands also will I lift up unto thy commandments, which I have loved; and I will meditate in thy statutes.'

He who does not love the whole law is not holy. He who does not regard the law in his heart has no heart to the law. As he is not a Jew who is only one outwardly, so he is not a doer of the law who only attends to its externals. He would not have sacrificed a bullock unto the Lord, who should only have brought its horns and hoofs; and he has not yielded himself as a servant unto the Most High, who only brings his lips and hands.

O Lord, I would love all thy law, but especially those precepts of it which concern my inward parts. I beseech thee, therefore, to write thy law upon my heart, and engrave it upon my mind. Let its spiritual commands have full command of my spirit.

THE DOLE

Wisdom's dole is given at wisdom's gates.

Those who wish for it must go there for it. Go to the gate of hearing if you would obtain the gift of faith. Resort to the beautiful porch of the temple if you would obtain that healing which is given by the gospel. Search the Scriptures if you would find eternal life. Hasten humbly to the gate of prayer if you would obtain God's covenant blessings. Above all, wait at the cross-foot for the purchased boons of Jesus' love. The dole is free and large, but God hath his place appointed for its distribution: be often there.

Lord, I would not be out of the way when thine alms are being distributed, for I am as poor as poverty itself. See, I am even now waiting at the portal of thy grace. Give me, I pray thee, my daily bread from heaven, and send me on my way rejoicing.

READY FOR THE BREEZE

By tacking about men get the wind, not by lying still; many times a supply of grace cometh ere we are aware.

When we do not seem to have the favouring gale in our voyage toward heaven, let us not therefore cast anchor, and idly lie still, but let us use what wind we have, employing that measure of grace which is vouchsafed to us. Let us put up the sail to catch side winds, that we may be aided by indirect helps till we get where more propitious breezes blow. If I cannot pray, let me read a chapter. It may be that while I hear God speak to me I shall learn how to speak to him. If in my private reading I feel no unction upon the word, let me go forth and attend the meeting of the saints; perhaps God intends to bless me by the ear, or in company with others. If this fails, let me go and visit the sick, or perform some deed of charity. Perhaps in helping others I may find succour for my own soul: God has often saved a man from freezing by setting him to rub a brother into warmth and life. If all this shall not have succeeded, let me hold converse with some choice servant of God; and if this should fail me, let me get to my knees again, or begin to sing a psalm, or tell to others what I have experienced of God's love in times past.

How often it will happen that or ever I am aware my soul will make me like the chariots of Amminadib. 'While I was musing', said one, 'the fire burned.' 'The wind bloweth where it listeth', and a heavenly gale often comes upon a sudden; but it seldom or never comes to idle souls, or to those who are indifferent about it, listless, inactive, dead, careless whether it comes or not. Come then, brother, tack about. Complain not of the want of heavenly wind, rather complain of want of consecrated energy. Lord, grant that what I preach to others I may always practise myself.

MILK FOR BABES

As warm milk is fitter to nourish a babe than that which is cold, so the word of God delivered by a lively voice hath a greater congruity and suitableness to the work of grace.

Moreover, there is no milk for a babe like that which comes warm from the mother's breast. Reading the word, or hearing a borrowed sermon, is like a child's sucking from a bottle; but as that child grows best which takes its nutriment fresh from the mother, so hearing warm-hearted discourses, fresh from the preacher's heart, is the most nourishing to the child of God. There is no warmth like heart-warmth, and no testimony like that of experience.

This is the grand distinction between one preaching and another. One sermon is delivered with a cold propriety, as if the preacher had no concern in it, nor his hearers either, and as a rule it fails to satisfy the soul. Another discourse may have less food in it than the first, but as it comes from the preacher's inmost soul, and he speaks it with warmth of zeal and melting affection, it enters into the auditor, is assimilated by him, and makes him grow thereby. Surely there can be no greater farce than dull, lifeless preaching. As by taking the soul out of a man we cause him to become a loathsome and offensive corpse, so has the doctrine of the gospel, when it has been divorced from the affection of the minister, become a heartless creed, bringing more of bondage to men's intellects than of sustenance to their souls. If the shepherd is not alive, what will the sheep be? If men are compelled to feed upon ice, and to dwell among icebergs, they will be frozen; while those who are warmed by an ardent ministry are likely to become fervent Christians.

Lord, let me rather be dumb than so preach thy word as

to deprive it of that holy warmth which makes it nourishing food for thy children. Let me not set thy sick ones down to cold meats for which they will have no stomach. If I be not eloquent, yet let me be affectionate; if I cannot speak with the wisdom of a father, yet let me speak with the heart of a brother.

COMPLEXION

We do not judge of men's complexions by the colour they have when they sit before the fire. We cannot judge of a man by a holy fit which he hath when he is under the influence of a sermon, or in good company; but when at all times he labours to keep up a warmth of heart toward God.

If all were truly good who are occasionally good, good men would not be scarce. See how people weep under a moving sermon! Think not, therefore, that their hearts are changed, for even marble drips in certain weathers. A man fresh from a revival-meeting looks like a zealous Christian; but see him when he goes to market. As a face rendered red by the fire soon loses all its ruddiness, so do numbers lose all their godliness when they quit the society of the godly.

Lord, let me never be what I cannot be forever. Give me a complexion which I shall wear all my lifetime, and when time shall be no more.

THE MASTER'S EYE

As soldiers fight best in their general's presence, and scholars ply their books most attentively when under their master's eye, so, by living always in the sight of God, we are the more studious to please him. The oftener we consider the Lord, the more we see that no service can be holy enough or good enough for such a God as he is.

This needs no comment, but it needs to be realized. See, soldier of the cross, the eye of the Captain of our salvation is fixed upon thee! Jesus cries, 'I know thy works.' Will not this incite thee to valorous deeds, and make a hero of thee? If not, what will?

A BLIND EYE AS DANGEROUS AS A LAME FOOT

We should as carefully avoid errors as vices; a blind eye is even worse than a lame foot; yea a blind eye may cause a lame foot, for he that hath not light is apt to stumble.

Very few seem to think so, but there is solemn truth in this statement. Men fancy that their minds are their own, and that they may do what they will with them, thinking and believing just as their conceit suggests. But who gave them a release from the authority of God as to this part of their nature? True, they are not bound by the opinions of their fellow-men; but does this give them a dispensation from the supremacy of God? There are revealed truths: have we license to receive or reject them at our pleasure? If we set up our own conceptions as equal or superior to the teachings of the Holy Spirit, are we justified in so doing? One would fancy from the talk of the wiseacres of the period that God did not know his own mind when he wrote the Scriptures, or that, like an old almanac, divine revelation is out of date, and superseded by 'modern thought'.

Doctrinal laxity has led to moral license: professors now wander in ways which their sober forefathers would have shuddered at. They will soon be given over to return to the old idolatries of Rome, since they are growing weary of the grand truths of Protestantism. Falsehoods of belief are fitly followed by superstitions in ritual: those who slay the doctrines are not ashamed to mangle the ordinances. We wonder what next, and next!

O Lord, I am willing to be thought a simpleton for believing as reformers, confessors, and martyrs believed, and as thy word teaches. Do not allow me to be blind to thy truth, lest I stumble in my daily life, and become scandalous as well as heretical.

A LONG LEASE ENHANCES VALUE

If a man might have a cottage on a hundred years' lease, he would prize it much more than the possession of a palace for a day.

Of course he would; and this it is which adds so much preciousness to the joys of heaven, for they are eternal. The pleasures of this world, however bright they seem, are but for this one day of life, which is already half over. If they were all they profess to be, and a thousand times more, they would not be worthy to be mentioned in comparison with 'pleasures for evermore' at God's right hand.

O thou who fillest eternity, impress me with the solemn import of that word, and let me feel that all time's fleeting cares and caresses are as dreams; while the things of eternity alone have substance in them. Give me thy grace that I may 'lay hold on eternal life'.

INDEX OF SUBJECTS